PRESE

Some Uses of Tradition in

University Press of America, Inc.
Lanham • New York • Oxford

Copyright © 1997 by
University Press of America,® Inc.
4720 Boston Way
Lanham, Maryland 20706

12 Hid's Copse Rd.
Cummor Hill, Oxford OX2 9JJ

All rights reserved
Printed in the United States of America
British Library Cataloguing in Publication Information Available

Library of Congress Cataloging-in-Publication Data

Present is past : some uses of tradition in native societies / edited by
Marie Mauzé
p. cm.
Includes bibliographical references and index.
1. Indians of North America--Social life and customs. 2. Indian philosophy--North America. 3. Indians of North America--Ethnic identity. 4. Tradition (Philosophy)--North America. I. Mauzé, Marie.
E98.S7P4 1997 970'.00497--dc21 96-51052 CIP

ISBN 0-7618-0684-9 (cloth: alk. ppr.)
ISBN 0-7618-0685-7 (pbk: alk. ppr.)

∞™ The paper used in this publication meets the minimum requirements of American National Standard for information Sciences—Permanence of Paper for Printed Library Materials, ANSI Z39.48—1984

Contents

List of illustrations		v
Acknowlegments		vii
1.	On Concepts of Tradition: An Introduction *Marie Mauzé*	1
2.	The Ambiguity of Tradition: Begetting the Father *Jean Pouillon*	17
3.	Recurrence Without Transmission: The Intuitive Background of Religious Traditions *Pascal Boyer*	23
4.	History and Tradition *Gérard Lenclud*	43
5.	On Somes Uses of the Past in Native American Art and Art History *Christian F. Feest*	65
6.	Marketing Magic: Process, Identity and the Creation and Selling of Native Art *Jonathan C. H. King*	81

7.	A Tradition of Invention: Modern Ceremonialism on the Northwest Coast *Michael Harkin*	97
8.	The Berdache as Metahistorical Reference for the Urban Gay Indian Community *Massimiliano Carocci*	113
9.	The Reification of Aboriginal Culture in Canadian Prison Spirituality Programs *James B. Waldram*	131
10.	Avocational Medicine Men: Inventive "Traditions" and New Age Religiosity in a Western Great Lakes Algonquian Population *James A. Clifton*	145
11.	All the Old Spirits Have Come Back to Greet Him: Realizing the Sacred Pole of the Omaha Tribe *Robin Ridington*	159
12.	From Stone Tablets to Flying Saucers: Tradition and Invention in Hopi Prophecy *Armin W. Geertz*	175
13.	Empirical Anthropology, Postmodernism, and the Invention of Tradition *F. Allan Hanson*	195

References	215
Contributors	233
Index	237

Illustrations

6.1. Bill Holm's book open at the page illustrating the Northwest Coast horn bowl used in flattened form to create a brooch. Whole Earth factory, Seattle, 1980s (photo J.C.H. King).   87
6.2. The wood maquette and metal dye taken from the illustration of the horn bowl for the production of a brooch. Whole Earth factory, Seattle, 1980s (photo J.C.H. King).   87
6.3. A Nuu-Chah-Nulth design under discussion between the owner of the jewelry factory Whole Earth and Ron Hamilton, historian and artist from Port Alberni, B.C., 1980s (photo J.C.H. King).   88
6.4. Tourist at Cherokee photographing his partner with Chief Henry, 1990s (photo J.C.H. King).   90
6.5. Cherokee manufacture of drums, North Carolina, at The Cherokees business, 1990s (photo J.C.H. King).   91
6.6. Huron making commercial moccasins, Québec, 1986 (photo J.C.H. King).   93

Acknowledgments

The present work stems from a symposium I organized in Paris, at the Collège de France, in June 1993. The topic was "Tradition in North Amerindian Societies: Continuity and/or Invention." Some of the articles published here are revised versions of papers delivered during the conference. The other contributions, such as the essay on the invention of tradition among the Maoris, were solicited while the work was being conceived
 The organization of the book invites the reader to pass from efforts to define tradition to case studies that explore the use of the notion of tradition by both anthropologists and native people. Ultimately this leads to an examination of the role played by "tradition" in the dynamics of identity formation of Native Americans and other indigenous peoples with white society. Theory and method are not separated in these case studies; together they form a coherent whole representing contemporary comparative research. Some of the essays criticize approaches and interpretations exemplified in other papers in the volume, thus showing the complexity of the issues when dealing with the question of tradition.
 The 1993 symposium was organized as part of the 14th American Indian Workshop and as the annual workshop of the Association pour la recherche en anthropologie sociale (APRAS). The Centre national de la recherche scientifique, the Fondation Maison des sciences de l'Homme (Maison Suger), the Ministère de l'enseignement supérieur et de la recherche, and the APRAS took part in organizing the

symposium. I would like to thank all those who lent me their support, especially Maurice Aymard, Françoise Héritier, Michel Izard, Gérard Lenclud, Jean-Luc Lory, Claudine Mochel. Glenn Naumovitz translated the French articles (G. Lenclud, M. Mauzé and J. Pouillon) into English. I wish to express my appreciation to Marcel Skrobek for his help and patience. My thanks go to James Clifton for his wise counsel. I also thank Jacques Garnier for his expertise in word processing. Finally, I thank my colleague-contributors for their cooperation and patience.

1

On Concepts of Tradition: An Introduction

Marie Mauzé

Many anthropologists still think of culture—the culture of the Others—as something coherent and autonomous. Their foundations are seen as stable and therefore relatively immune from historical contingency. They are considered as immutable rather than changing (Clifford 1988). An opposition is set up between changeless so-called traditional societies and modern societies viewed as fundamentally dynamic. "Traditional" and "modern" societies are played against each other in how they relate to the past. On the one hand traditional societies represent the past as tradition, while on the other hand modern societies objectify the past through writing and *ad hoc* archival procedures constructing the past as historical knowledge. Later we will see, with Gérard Lenclud's essay (chapter 4), that the dichotomy between tradition and history raises more questions than it answers (see also Feest chapter 5). While the opposition between modalities of comprehending the past such as oral vs written, or myth vs history are pertinent to an analysis of tradition, this distinction does not coincide exactly with the opposition between traditional and modern societies. Indeed in modern societies oral tradition and myth are used extensively in certain contexts, and written history is also found in allegedly "traditional" societies.

A Novice Anthropologist

These presuppositions are still firmly entrenched in the practice of anthropology. This I know from personal experience, from my first encounter with the native peoples of the coast of British Columbia. Predictably, the facts disproved preconceived ideas about sharp contrasts between modern and traditional. It was not hard for me to discover that non-Western societies are contemporary with ours and therefore modern. In short that they are historical which means, among other things, that in one way or another they are aware of having a history. At the same period, there was within French anthropological circles in the 1970s a heightened awareness of the West's role in the destruction of "primitive" societies, which I shared. This sensibility caused pangs of guilt while at the same time I was driven by a lively curiosity about Native American societies. In the summer of 1978 I visited three Kwakwaka'wakw (Kwakiutl) communities in British Columbia. I arrived with a paradoxical background consisting of objective knowledge and a subjective view of Native American society that included a certain amount of romanticism and even primitivism. I had to reconcile the desire to establish my professional identity with the social identity I would be allowed to hold in this field context. I had the vague feeling that I was expecting this research experience to satisfy a certain yearning for adventure through experiencing a way of life that had been unknown to me.

What I started observing was of course quite different from the pictures Edward S. Curtis took in the second decade of this century. At the time I was unaware that Curtis's photographs were a theatrical reconstruction of Indian clothing and activities. The subjects it happened were made to dress up and act in ways that mimicked the past. What novice (European) anthropologist nurtured on such images would not be disappointed on his/her first visit to a reserve? None of the inhabitants' current expressed attitudes or interests matched long established anthropological images of Native American society and culture. The disappointment is productive. A long stay is an eye-opener for the naive fieldworker who soon realizes that each native community, even neighboring ones, lives out its own economic, social and cultural destiny.

When I arrived in one of the three British Columbia villages in which I would spend fifteen months in 1980-1981, I was quite surprised to find a community of approximately 300 inhabitants who at least at first glance, was no different from any other small town on the city's outskirts. The people live in suburban houses and mobile homes. Dwarfs, pink flamingos and other typical ornaments were on the carefully tended lawns. The houses were lined up in two parallel rows across from the ocean. The village stood out because of two or three small wooden dwellings, several smoke-houses and a few run-down homes. The two main streets were deserted except for a few children, some dogs and one anthropologist. From time to time, especially on the eve of the fishing season, the streets did come alive with the movement of brand new pick-up trucks. Fancy cars such as Cadillacs or vehicles of similar prestige were necessary for important outings. Automobiles indicated their owner's economic and social status. Immediately, the most striking thing about such a small community was the residents' differing social and economic status. Some of them owned ultra-modern fishing boats equipped with state-of-the-art electronics and houses where comfort was measured in terms of how thick the carpet was or how big the television and freezer were. They were the ones who spent their vacations in Hawaii and Reno or took part in meetings of native peoples from all over the world in places like New Zealand and Japan. Others were either eking out a living from fishing, not as skippers but as crew members, or on welfare. Some women sported "Afro" hairdos. A red-headed little girl playing with other children said to me: "See, with a feather in my hair I look like a real Indian." The sports fans watched hockey and basketball games on television. Yet the appeal of Euro-Canadian style and comfort did not entirely turn them away from Indian life: it is certainly quite appropriate to dine occasionally in trendy white restaurants while continuing to enjoy traditional meals of smoked or dried salmon, eulachon grease and dried seaweed.

Surprise modified the disappointment. I wondered whether I actually was among "real" Indians. Influenced by theories of acculturation and the assumption of white civilization's harmful effects on indigenous societies, I had internalized the claim that the economic conditions of native peoples could be nothing other than poverty, an inevitable consequence of the confrontation with the white world.

Surprise can go hand in hand with a sense of frustration. Anthropologists are tempted to forget the current condition of the society under examination and to overlook contemporary issues. Instead they follow the tradition of salvage ethnology and attempt to reconstruct the past. Baffled by the complexity of contemporary life—the inability to understand it without knowing its history or being able to distinguish more recent from older concerns—many novice anthropologists retreat into a study of the past, which is often conceived as a search for origins. This familiar methodological turn—which does not exclude setbacks in data collection, for the ethnographer does not necessarily ask the right questions—provokes the consideration that contemporary Natives sometimes know little about their tribal past or, more generally about their traditional culture. That information is contained in the ethnographic literature, which the researcher has assimilated. "Absent" from today's society, the ethnographer, more or less reluctantly, sets out in search of a society that no longer exists and that often no longer existed even at the time the earlier ethnographic data were gathered. Ironically, I found myself in a similar position for different reasons.

Although I never did find the "primitive" society I was looking for, I did have the opportunity to assemble data on their culture and history, with their agreement (Mauzé 1992). The Lekwiltoq community was especially responsive to my offer to contribute to this project since they had recently succeeded in repatriating a collection of ceremonial objects. The Canadian government had confiscated the artifacts in 1922 after a potlatch that violated its potlatch law banning all ritual practices. The Kwagiulth Museum's inauguration in June 1979 set the stage for a renewed interest in history. The attempt to reconstruct knowledge of the past for the community and for a broader public made clear to me that having knowledge entails having a point of view. The past is definitly seen from the perspective of the present (Mauzé 1993, 1995). To be honest, I must add, it quickly became evident that research on the past was less politically fraught than research on present-day life. Without being aware of what was happening, I found myself in a liminal position of part outsider, part insider.

Double language

The word "tradition" is one of those apparently consensual, catch-all terms used without giving much thought to what they really mean. However, right from the start the word does not seem to refer to the same thing, depending on whether one is speaking of tradition in general or *a* specific tradition. Lenclud (1994, 27) points out that the word "tradition" "refers at the same time to a fact and an attribute, to a given and a value, to what is experienced and thought." The expression "invention of tradition," which combines two words with opposite meanings, is even more problematic. It creates confusion because we sense that this term goes beyond usual anthropological discourse to entail political and ethical positions.

Tradition is commonly thought of as the perfect transmission of beliefs and statements handed down unchanged from one generation to the next:

> Tradition is usually taken to be something handed down unchanged from the past that remains relatively invariant from generation to generation. Thus, to call something a "tradition" is to assert continuity with the past. The whole concept invokes a sense of history. (Dominguez 1986, 594)[1]

Tradition is viewed as the expression of conservatism which is the touchstone of traditional societies. Through it these societies are thought to maintain a primordial order which constitutes the foundations of social organization. Tradition implies antiquity, continuity and heritability.

These assertions raise several challenging questions. How can anyone be sure a tradition is really old? As Eric Hobsbawm writes: "Traditions which appear or claim to be old are often quite recent in origin and sometimes invented" (1983, 1). Sometimes it only takes a few years for an event to be considered traditional (Pouillon chapter 2). How can anyone be sure a tradition is more or less a carbon copy of the original version? Can the expression "pristine tradition" be used? Is it possible to develop a sort of coefficient of *traditionality* (Lenclud 1994, 30)? Generally speaking, any statement whose transmission under the supervision of a recognized authority is assigned a truth value is considered a tradition. Repetition validates the statement. Some authors (e.g. Boyer 1990) suggest a new way of analyzing tradition. It does not consist of assessing a tradition's "purity" or what we have called a coefficient of traditionality, but of looking at the conditions which a discourse and actions must fulfill to be considered traditional. A statement's authority and traditionality are inseparable from the conditions of its enunciation, taking into account the speaker's status, the social context of the speech act and the interlocutors' reception.

In addition to questions of age and continuity there are questions about the content of traditional discourse and the nature of the information conveyed. Should tradition be limited to the narrative of past events or should the concept be broadened to include observed practices framed by an anthropologist? For example, should the description of a ritual be considered tradition? Today most anthropologists agree that a tradition reproduces conceptions, representations and value systems; in sum, a world view. From this point of view tradition appears to be the form of cultural transmission *par excellence.*

Pascal Boyer (chapter 3) puts forward an alternative hypothesis. For him, cultural representations which are recurrent (and therefore labelled "traditional") are not constrained by cultural transmission. Their salience and stability over time is an effect of the psychological mechanisms underpinning acquisition. The locus of this acquisition process is the individual mind. Some cultural representations are likely to become "traditional" because they violate ordinary, intuitive expectations. These constitute a universal, intuitive ontology. For instance intuitive physics provides us with definite expectations about the visibility or embodiment of intentional agents. But intuitive physics has nothing to say about the processes that would result in such agents. This type of violation, for Boyer, is what makes certain cultural representations salient. It explains why they are memorized and communicated. In this framework, recurrence and transmission are not explained by studying the particular world view of a culture or the social mechanisms that favour stability. Instead, it can be described within a psychological theory that is concerned with universal dispositions of the human mind. The mechanism that turns representations into a tradition resides, not in social interaction, but in functional properties of the mind.

Let us return to the relationship between tradition and invention.[2] At times tradition has been imagined as an old, gradually declining heritage. Today many anthropologists consider tradition as something that is continually being produced and nurtured by new ideas. In other words, the notion that the present is descended from a traditional past has given way to the opposite notion. The past is reached through inductive reasoning that takes place in the present. In an essay appearing in chapter 2, Jean Pouillon clearly shows that tradition flows from the present to the past. "Tradition," he writes "is often a 'retroprojection' and a 'reverse filiation'." In other words, "We want to appear as if we were the successors of those whom we have made our fore-fathers."

For fifteen years or so anthropologists have been engaged in a critical debate over static models of culture. Today most consider that tradition is not a collection of archaic customs but something alive and fully a part of the present (Hanson [chapter 13]; Harkin [chapter 7]; Geertz [chapter 12].) Armin Geertz, for example, claims that invented traditions that anthropologists happen to witness have no different origin or essence than any other traditions. Tradition encompasses both continuity and change as any other cultural product. This view under-scores tradition's dynamism, which stands in sharp contrast with ossified traditionalism. Indeed, traditionalism as aptly observed by Jonathan Friedman "attempts to reinstate the values of cultural fixity of a supposedly lost world" (1992, 847). By striking out in search of a lost world traditionalism runs counter to tradition itself, which is not concerned with making value judgements on the past or the present.

A tradition," writes Lenclud, "is invented and recreated... traditionally" (1994, 33). It is an attempt "to read the present in terms of the past by writing the past in terms of the present" (Lindstrom 1982, 317). Tradition is used to justify the present through remembering the past. It interprets the past according to the needs of the present. Thus the past is continually reassessed and reconstructed depending on the course of events (Eisenstadt 1973, 23; Linnekin 1983, 242). From this point of view, tradition does not appear as a corpus of statements handed down unchanged from one generation to the next. It is a succession of answers to questions about the present, and consequently it takes on the status of an always correct answer to the questions asked. The questions are those the society is asking itself at the present time. "Invented traditions," writes Hobsbawm, "are responses to novel situations which take the form of reference to old situations, or which establish their own past by quasi-obligatory repetition" (1983, 2).

A tradition can be no more "false" than "true" (Harkin chapter 7; Geertz chapter 12). Describing a tradition as false implies going back to the currently outmoded concept of tradition as a body of statements about beliefs and practices handed down unchanged from time immemorial. This hypothesis is untenable because it is impossible to verify whether a tradition is the same as its original version, if an original version ever really existed. Might the "true" tradition refer to a period before the native peoples came into contact with the Europeans? Those who support the term's common definition, especially the Canadian courts, and a few anthropologists share this point of view.[3] They express the somewhat romanticized, relativist opinion that the culture's essence is based on timeless beliefs and values. Perhaps it is still difficult to admit that native peoples, like everyone else, adapt their cultural repertories to the present.

The concept of "invented tradition" has spurred new research on how ethnic minorities construct their identities. At the same time, however, the notion has been challenged as the idea of invented tradition has gained a wider audience. There has been a lot of resistance by non-academic advocates for indigenous groups. The use of "invention of tradition" elicits strong reactions from various political activists who advocate Fourth World nationalism (Hanson 1991; chapter 13)[4] As Jocelyn Linnekin has rightly argued:

> The concern, at time phrased as an accusation, is that writing about the contemporary construction or "invention" of culture undercuts the cultural authority of indigenous people by calling into question their authenticity. Implicitly, authenticity is thus equated with the transmission through time of a tradition, that is, an objectively definable essence or core of customs and beliefs. (1991, 446)

What is at stake is the instrumentalization of tradition as a conscious model in the construction of identity. This very issue analyzed by anthropologists either defending a positivist approach or interested in how a tradition comes into being often leads to a dead-lock situation. As Jonathan Hill remarks:

> ... invocations of a uniquely valid, objectivist concept of the past can in many instances be interpreted as a supremely political act of "disauthentificating" or preempting the validity of alternative ways of defining the past by reducing the latter to falsehoods, ideologies, or political agendas. (1992, 809)

Emphasizing the constructed quality of culture and cultural representations denies the possibility that tradition can foster ethnic identity and therefore makes apparent the mystifying nature of tradition and ethnic consciousness.

We have just discussed the construction of identity. It is commonly assumed that tradition and identity are associated and, more specifically that identity draws its legitimacy from tradition; therefore tradition must be more than a mere "construction." However, there are cases where reference to tradition seems to be counter-productive. Instead of drawing the group together, re-traditionalization can be a source of division. The sacred pole of the Omaha, at one point a unifying symbol, later came to represent the lost world of historic Omaha culture. Some of the present community's members wished to restore the sacred pole's former meaning as part of an effort to revive tribal history and culture. The re-inauguration of the pole was conceived as a way of wiping away the passage of time. This attempted reappropriation split the Omaha tribe into two groups, one for, the other against. The neo-traditionalists seemed to suggest that the pole's proximity, if not its actual presence would bring about the perceived peace and harmony of a previous age and set up a new order dressed up in the old one's trappings. The others thought the traditionalists' proposal could only bring misfortune and increase the potential for division with the community (Ridington chapter 11).

Perhaps we should avoid adopting too radical a position on an idea like the invention of tradition, considering the confusion it causes. Friedman points out, "The 'invention of tradition' is a double-edged sword that criticizes the assumptions of cultural continuity while implicitly reprimanding those who would identify with such cultural fantasies today" (1992, 846). Consequently, this approach brings to the fore the mystifying character of the tradition and thus of the conciousness of the identity that originates from it. From some perspectives, this approach amounts to little more than playing an intellectual game with the identities of people anthropologists are supposed to defend. Nevertheless the question of authenticity does not call for an all or nothing approach (Clifton chapter 10; Hanson 1989, chapter 13). The use of the term itself automatically leads to the question, "Authentic in relation to what?" Indeed as James Clifford (1988, 12) argued, "If authenticity is relational, there can be no essence except as a political, cultural invention, a local tactic" This leads to another question: "Who does the inventing?"

A play of mirrors

Inventing is a complex process because cultural representations—observers and the observed, dominators and the dominated—are interdependant. It is like a play of mirrors. Western societies invented traditional societies.[5] In doing so, they attributed a cultural identity to objects (Stocking 1985, 4-5), facts and representations, which amounted to ascribing these cultural products a role defined only in relation to Western society and to ethnological gaze.

Whenever the problem of the continuity of tradition is raised, it is always a question of textuality. Cultural facts reified in ethnographic monographs and objects gathered in museums not only refer to the past; they also become the foundations for present as well as future identities. Native American groups are turning to the past for affirming their identity and are in some sense drawing from past conceptions of cultural essence. Indeed traditions have been perpetuated to the present day despite profound changes within. From the Western perspective, the preservation of artifacts and descriptions of rituals have been thought equivalent to preserving tribal cultures, which have been metonymically represented especially by material culture (Keesing 1989, 33-34). Anthropologists have described cultures they have not seen "alive." In this sense, what they have written is fiction. Ethnographic representation is contingent upon the vagaries of fieldwork. Observers always base their descriptions of local culture on their knowledge and experience. Thus, they generally set up a distinction between "traditional" and "non-traditional" cultural facts based on criteria such as common sense," simple bias and informants' status and authority, from which they construct comparative studies and develop models of social organization; in a word, they speculate on the philosophical themes of the diversity and the universality of human nature.

Basically the concept of a "true" tradition refers to a supposed state of cultural purity that is thought to have existed before contact with Europeans. Between the mid-nineteenth century and the 1930s, American anthropologists in particular set about reconstructing the traditions of societies viewed as in danger of disappearing. It was as if they believed it was possible to create an immense "freezer" for the preservation of customs and beliefs imbued with authenticity and assigned a timeless value. By preserving tradition anthropologists have made "preservability" its main attribute. The driving force behind this approach was the implicit idea that there was an urgent need to save and record institutions not as they were at the time of the field research but as they were assumed to have been before undergoing change. Consequently, change came to be seen as inherently bad because it resulted in the loss and corruption of tradition. At the time, the position was based on a double assumption. First, Native American societies by their very nature can neither change nor evolve; second, if these societies were transformed through selective assimilation of elements of colonial culture—which they could not fail to do—then they are no longer authentically Indian.

Anthropologists set out in search of supposedly lost worlds. Might they be more traditionalist than Indians? The question seems more relevant than ever. We have seen that anthropologists often adopt a maximalist concept of tradition wherever a minimalist concept is in order, reducing tradition to the enshrinement of few core elements which produce an illusion of continuity and even permanence. We must not think that this antiquarian attitude, which reifies tradition, serves the interests of native peoples. By referring to an ahistoric past, court judges have rejected claims on the grounds that tradition's non-evolutionary character is as valid for the present and future as it is for the past. Setting up an opposition between traditional and modern societies confines the former to a space where change is not allowed to take place, which obviously cuts them off from the possibility of acceding to modernity. Native societies and their authorized representatives, including anthropologists, have also played this hand and found themselves trapped by the unintended effects of the relationships they have set up between identity and tradition. Establishing a relative identity may at the same time establish an absolute otherness and result in straying outside the context within which land claims, for example, make sense.

Facets of tradition

Native tradition has always managed to adapt to specific socio-political situations, especially colonization. Some cultural facts have been perpetuated, others transformed, still others dropped. In North America, indigenous peoples have abandoned practices such as slavery, cannibalism and infanticide. Other practices have survived transformed or are undergoing a renewal. Examples include the potlatch on the Northwest Coast and the Sun Dance of the Plains Indians. Some late rituals that grew out of the specific context of the conflict with Euro-American domination are prevalent in native communities (Price 1990, 257-58). Even more the interest Euro-Americans show in these rituals validates the Indians' own cultural practices. New artistic traditions have developed under the influence of collectors, archeologists, anthropologists, merchants and museums.[6] The relationship to the past takes on many shapes. Artists and craftspeople base their work on a blend of personal sensibility and references to a constructed historical past (Feest chapter 5).

For over a century tourism has played an important role in preserving tradition. Tradition has taken on its most ossified form in this context. Tourism is necessarily a cooperative venture which requires the participation of both worlds. Some communities deliberately foster an archaic image of themselves by staging folk shows and creating a "traditional" environment that lives up to tourists' expectations. The Indian culture they consume must conform to their preconceptions of it. By the same token, tourist art features supposedly "symbolic" stereotypical motifs that draw from an impoverished repertoire of native designs. It comes out of what might be called neo-traditionalism, which respects neither the form nor the spirit of historic artistic expression. At most, in some cases an item looks so little like a genuine artifact that the *Indian-made* label is all that attests to the object's authenticity (King chapter 6).

As already argued, reference to tradition is a metaphor for identity. This means it encompasses and illustrates a past, a present and a future. It is not only the memory of the past frozen in time that reemerges; it is also a reference necessary for elaborating a version of the contemporary world, which is the "space" where traditional and modern social life occur side by side. Tradition is primarily a political instrument for regulating both internal and external relations.

One example illustrates this point. In 1987 a heraldic pole was erected in the Tsimshian village of Kitsumkalum. This event made some aspects of the community's social life visible and, consequently, more or less clearly redefined the members' status and the situation of the Tsimshian in relation to the Euro-Canadian world. This occasion explicitly aimed at creating the conditions necessary for developing a new political arena where negotiations concerning land claims, economic development and local political autonomy could be conducted (McDonald 1990). In the same vein, the reactualized potlatch among the Heiltsuq has come to represent and validate assertions of individual and group identity. The resurgence of the canoe—a powerful symbol—in ceremonial contexts allows Northwest Coast Nations to negotiate their identity among themselves and vis-à-vis the white world (Harkin chapter 7).

In the construction of tribal identity a cultural heritage is not only subjected to a selective reappropriation of certain of the elements which are perceived as emblematic, precisely through the lens of tradition. What is striking is that cultural invention finds its material in what anthropologists called "grand institutions of expressive culture," such as the potlatch for the Northwest Coast, and religion for almost all of North America. Frequently these phenomena are influenced by pan-Indian beliefs and practices which arose in the post-colonial Plains. Myth and ritual practice seem to be the royal road to invented traditions regardless of the complexity of social conditions (Leach 1954). Ritual and myth are among those cultural phenomena that are easily assimilated into new traditions. They are supposedly the foundation for cultural norms and values.

It is assumed that non-Western people employ rituals against a hostile nature to gain an imagined control over uncontrolable forces and ensure the fulfilment of material needs. The "primitive" is thus a *homo religiosus* rather than a *homo politicus*. Because of this assumption, which reigned in Americanist anthropology at the turn of the century, references to political life were frequently omitted while religious activities were emphasized. The signifiers *par excellence* of tribal culture were found primarily in the ritual realm.

Hopi prophecy is an idiom for political intrigue and social strategy (Geertz 1992). In chapter 12, Geertz's critical analysis of three texts produced between the 1930's and 1970's by Dan Qötshongva, the leader of the Traditionalist Movement, allows to distinguish what constitutes invention and what constitutes continuity in the Hopi religious context. It also documents the rise and the fall of Qötshongva's career linked to a difference in nature of the prophecy which inevitably lead to changes in the role played by the prophet. Instead of remaining a symbol of Hopi resistance, Qötshongva became a charismatic symbol for Euro-Americans in want of some kind of ecological mysticism.

A case analyzed by James Waldram (chapter 9) refers to religion as a cultural tradition on which an explicit definition of collective and individual Indian identity can be based. In Manitoba and Saskatchewan prisons, inmates from the Cree, Dene and other ethnic groups turn to specialists in hopes of acquiring spiritual knowledge and learning ritual practices. These beliefs and practices are centered upon visible symbols of pan-Indian religion such as the sacred pipe, the sacred circle and the sweetgrass.

American Indian homosexuals living in cities borrow ways to build both an ethnic and a sexual identity from pan-Indian ideology and from berdachism. Pan-Indianism brings together intertribal customs and institutions to help develop a pan-tribal Indian culture. In a similar way, berdachism helps cross ethnic boundaries when it comes to sex and gender relationships. Only the berdache's role as mediator remains. This construction of identity makes the abrupt transition from berdache to homosexual possible. It gives rise to a new identity: that of the "two-spirits." This new figure is inextricably bound up with a spiritual dimension and expresses the disjunction between the categories of sex and gender within an individual (Carocci chapter 8).[7]

Here we come to a more radical formulation of the possible relation between tradition and identity, to the point where one is tempted to posit as James Clifton does it in his essay (chapter 10), that the more specific an assumed identity is the vaguer and more composite the tradition called on to give its legitimacy.

A self-styled medicine man,[8] assisted by members of an Algonquian group claiming nationhood status, reinstated the Green Corn ritual with the aim of distinguishing themselves from Euro-Americans within the same social sphere. The ritual is no longer part of a tradition—if ever it had been—-but stems from the medicine man's person-al experience as a boy scout, when he was a member of the Order of the Arrow. This New Age-inspired ceremony never caught on for various reasons. The historian Paul Veyne once wrote, that "there is no tradition on command" (quoted by Lenclud 1994, 35). Indeed the manufacturing of a new tradition must follow certain rules that have been long anchored in a reference system. In this case, none of the people who took part in the updated Green Corn ritual shared that frame of reference, perhaps explaining the ritual's failure. Yet other similar attempts have been made to fill what Clifton calls an "identity vacuum," which is no more typical of the indigenous than of the white world.

Urban neo-berdachism and the attempt to construct a neo-Indian identity in stratified North American society show how problematic this volume's theme is. This collection of essays begins as an anthropological study of Native American traditions with an examination of issues affecting American society as a whole in the age of political correctness. One cannot leave out the epistemological question of the anthropologist's position vis-à-vis an object of research he/she defined at the outset, but which escapes his/her grasp, carried out on the tide of political ideology. Anthropologists find themselves in paradoxical positions in relation with Native American or other indigenous communities. On the one hand, they are committed to pursuing their academic task of collecting and analyzing data according to the rules of the discipline. On the other, personal conviction as well as a response to requests from the native community to use their knowledge as a political tool in the service of a cause places them in a position which is clearly beyond the scope of their original intentions.[9] This carries them from their initial orientation, as they no longer report or analyze what *is* but have a hand in changing what is into what *should be*. In this case, not all researchers make the same choice, and the multiplicity of individual situations leads to a comparable multiplicity of individual attitudes. In the case of the Algonquian middle class, James Clifton, called upon to legitimize the Green Corn ceremony, sets out to present his approach as that of a traditional scholar working on an object of research. When discussing the Omaha tribe's attempt to provide the sacred pole with new symbolic meaning, Robin Ridington adopts a position which is not the direct opposite of the former, but stakes out an alternative territory for an anthropologist involved in these issues. Ridington choses to ally himself with the Omaha traditionalists, who are bent on finding a remedy to the problems afflicting their society. Ridington's position is admirable but raises further problems because when a society is split between traditionalists and modernists, support-ing either side involves making not only an ethical but also political choice. What do we choose? In a more or less confused manner, today it seems that the quest for identity is a symptom of a possibly irremediable loss of meaning in a rather frightening world. The real question for us in this context is whether anthropological research remains a meaningful undertaking in its search for knowledge independant of local influence.

Notes

1. Among many references see for example Hobsbawm (1983, 1-2); Pouillon (1991, 710); Lenclud (1994, 28-29).
2. For recent work on the notion of "invention of tradition" and "invention of culture", see Handler and Linnekin 1984; Hobsbawn and Ranger 1983; Hanson 1989; Linnekin 1983; Wagner 1981.
3. The Gitksan-Wet'suwet'en case illustrates this point. See for example B. Miller (1992, 55-65). See also McEachern 1991; Mills 1994.
4. Hanson's article (1989) has been the object of many comments. See "Commentaries" by R. Langdon, H.B. Levine and J. Linnekin in the *American Anthropologist* (1991, 440-449). See also Friedman (1992, 851-853).
5. Western societies have done more than that. When it comes to Indians, they have also manufactured myths and traditions for themselves (see for example Bieder 1986; Berkhofer 1978; Clifton, ed. 1990; Feest ed. 1990; Pearce 1988.
6. See King (1986) and essays by Jonaitis, Fane, Cahodas in *The Early Years of Native American Art History* edited by Berlo (1992).
7. See also Sue-Ellen Jacobs and Wesley Thomas, "Native American Two-Spirits"(1994).
8. For the origins and connotation of the term "medicine man", see Clifton (1994, 192, 201-204).
9. Harvey Feit (1982) supports the hypothesis that on some theoretical and methodological points, anthropology has everything to gain from its commitment to native peoples.

2

The Ambiguity of Tradition: Begetting the Father

Jean Pouillon

When Chomsky entitled one of his books *Cartesian Linguistics*, he was probably right in trying to fit in with a certain tradition. But can we really assume his theories were based on the *Grammaire de Port-Royal*? A more likely source may be the critique of contemporary linguists with whom he disagreed. Chomsky thought he could bolster and legitimize his opposition to them by rooting it in ancestral tradition. Of course, others have taken the same approach. Tradition is often "retroprojection." We pick and choose those by whom we say were are guided, if not determined, from a reconstructed past. We want to appear as if we were the successors of those whom we have made our fore-fathers. Tradition, then, works backwards from biological heredity while basing itself on its model. It is actually a reverse filiation. The son begets the father, and he may claim to have several of them!

Individual, voluntarist traditions aimed at giving a certain representation of the self are not the only ones under discussion here. The same can be said about many conflicts between groups. For example, when battling over an issue political parties often invoke traditions they have more or less turned into myths in order to demonize or idealize them. Similarly, groups within a society as well as various societies as a whole, in general neighboring ones, perceive themselves and each other through stereotypes. These caricatures sum up the self-ascribed traditions they invoke in order to distinguish themselves from each other. Just look at the image the French and the English have of one another. We always look the same in the eyes of the foreigner, but this stems from being attributed a traditional identity we would most often rather disavow.

In other words, traditions are discriminating. That is their basic function. They work like totems. If various traditions could be put into a system—at least within a given cultural area—a totemic system in Lévi-Strauss's sense of the term would surely be the result. The references in this structured series would matter less because of the similarities they encourage people to imagine between ancestors and descendants than because of the differences they express between contemporaries.

This does not mean that all traditions are more or less well-constructed illusions and that our present has neither a past nor a future. Beliefs, representations, and behaviors are passed down from one generation to the next, which does not contradict the preceding statements. When a group maintains beliefs and behaviors, the purpose is precisely to characterize itself for others. These traditions always have a diacritical function. Tradition is defined as the part of the past that persists in the present to which it has been transmitted and where it remains active for those who have received and accepted it and, in turn, pass it down through speech, education or writing.

What is transmitted? Everything believed to be worth knowing and doing within a population and that confers an enduring identity. Identity does not become reality unless it lasts. The most important thing is not so much to rationally justify tradition as to correctly conform with it, or at least to believe it is being conformed with. This involves retelling myths the way they were heard, identifying with a history the way it was learned and making passed-down ideas one's own, turning them into generally accepted notions. This more or less coherent group of factors is what we call a culture. Every culture is therefore traditional or, in the case of an emerging one, destined to become so. But then what is the point of frequently making a distinction between traditional societies and those that claim not to be or are called non-traditional because they are historical and changing—as if the others were not as well— and therefore always characterized by their successive modernities?

They are actually no less traditional than the others. Similarly, they also "belong to history." How they view their historicity is what sets them apart, but that is another story. Furthermore, Hocart argues that the most traditionalist societies are not necessarily the ones we think they are. In an article entitled "Are savages custom-bound?" he wrote, "If there is one thing that a long residence in the Pacific and daily intercourse with the people, especially the children, has impressed upon me, it is the thinness of their customary life as compared with the extraordinary complexity and pervasiveness of ours" (1979, 205). The reason is that Western children are steeped in custom from the earliest age—so early that they forget their learning and end up believing that reason or the order of things is what determines their behavior. The Melanesians Hocart wrote about learn later, so they internalize traditional precepts to a lesser degree. Sometimes this makes them capable of taking more liberties with their traditions than we do with ours. Hocart concludes that Europeans are the ones who bear the "tremendous burden of custom," more often without realizing it (1979, 207). However, there would be no point in measuring the influence of tradition in each society. The lesson to be drawn from Hocart is simpler. Tradition is never as strong nor as dominant as when it is unknown as such and, as it were, subconscious. In other words, there is something arbitrary about any tradition because it is social, and something contingent because it is historical. However, tradition's effectiveness and reality stem from the feeling that it is natural and self-evident for those on whom it is exerted.

Might a tradition's age explain this feature? "Because this is the way our grandfathers did it" is the common, sometimes exasperated answer given to anthropologits when they ask about a certain behavior. Isn't a tradition natural because it is how things have always been done? Yet in my view the feeling that a behavior is "natural" does not seem to depend on how long the tradition has been in practice, even if age is often mentioned in its favor and used as an argument to encourage those who do not follow it to fall into step. The tradition seems timeless to those who observe it. The proof is given *a contrario*: a tradition that seems so natural is barely perceived as such; it is so basic that no one has ever bothered to date it, and sometimes it turns out to be of recent origin.

Here is a personal example. In September 1958, a referendum on membership in the community of former colonies set up by the new constitution was held in all the new nations that had recently won their independence from France. I was living in a village in Chad at the time and had agreed to be in charge of a polling station. All three campaigning parties had come out in favor of a "yes" vote, so there was no risk of my being caught in a political crossfire. I had to explain the balloting procedure to the villagers, all of whom considered the voting booth absurd. Why not publicly announce one's vote? Why not vote by lineage or by clan and send the office a single ballot? I did my best, but they made me understand that to them there was nothing *natural* about this *imposed* procedure. It could only be a white man's tradition! But since when? I did not know the answer but the year "1848" came to mind. Back in France I asked several friends about this. All of them gave me a different answer, none of which was the right one. Much later I found out by chance that a law passed in 1913 made the voting booth mandatory (after a debate that did not break down along the traditional lines of left and right). The law was observed for the first time during the legislative elections in the spring of 1914. This was not long before I was born. However my father, who had become a major in 1906, may have voted at least once without going into a polling booth, but he never mentioned it to me. True, I never thought of asking him about it. The reason is that to me, and probably to him as well, this procedure did not seem like an imposed rule we felt a conscious duty to obey. We complied without giving it a second thought. The secret ballot was natural, therefore repeatable, and in this sense only, traditional.

So far I have discussed tradition as totem and argued that a tradition is effective because it is not perceived as such. But tradition may also be revived or, more accurately, consciously claimed. This is tradition that formerly colonized peoples seek to update in order to reassert themselves and find their place in a world that has changed. They are searching for themselves in a past they have rearranged or even, at least in part, reinvented, or that they believe has been distorted by foreign observers. But this is less a matter of recovering the past or rediscovering a lost or forgotten identity than of drawing from it the means to guarantee the future and build or at least detect continuity.

Tradition, continuity, invention are three terms that come together to form a single reality. Invention and continuity shape tradition because every society wants to change while staying the same. Change, then, must not merely invent something new, and inventing something new must not change everything. This raises an important point. Perhaps a forgotten past can actually be unwittingly found in innovation. Perhaps we are never more the same as when we believe we are making a clean break with the past. Conversely, perhaps it is when we claim to be preserving or recovering our heritage that a reconstructed past is invented.

It does not matter. In an article on Amazonian societies published in *L'Homme,* Claude Lévi-Strauss (1992, 10) notices a positive claim emerging "... in both Americas, where Indian societies rebelled against the fate imposed upon them by the colonizers, they are becoming aware of their common interests, joining forces in self-defense and, sometimes successfully, claiming their lost land and freedom." Conversely, at the same time a negative claim is emerging in Western societies:

> A renascent attachment to heritage... would give our societies, responsible for or the victims of horrible tragedies, terrified by the effects of uncontrolled population growth, unemployment, wars and other scourges, the illusion... that they can—obviously in a purely symbolic way—move against the flow of history and suspend its course. (1992, 10)

Shouldn't we wonder whether the resurgent interest in heritage signifies the death of what it seeks to preserve and elegantly embalm? Wouldn't we be better off as subconscious traditionalists? After all, are we ever modern?

3

Recurrence Without Transmission: The Intuitive Background of Religious Tradition

Pascal Boyer

Our common understanding of tradition implies that social transmission accounts for all the theoretically relevant aspects of cultural representations. But this proposition is vague; and when it is made more precise, it is empirically false. Here I will examine some problems created by this kind of assumption and show that there is an alternative understanding of tradition that is grounded in a psychologically plausible account of cultural acquisition (Boyer 1990, 1994). In particular, cognitive processes make it possible to understand how the recurrence of some "traditional" aspects of cultural representations requires (virtually) no social transmission.

It may be of help to begin with some conceptual tidying up as concerns the diverse, not altogether consistent senses of the term "tradition." Anthropological usage is based on four kinds of signs or symptoms that identify cultural representations and practices as "traditional." First, we generally call traditional those cultural elements which are justified by members of a particular groups in terms of putative precedents ("we've always done things this way," "our ancestors decided it should always be so," etc.). Whether the precedents are genuine or invented as one goes along is immaterial here. Second, we use "tradition" to denote those elements that are recurrent across generations, whether or not the people concerned attach any value to this transmission or are even aware of it. Third, we also call "traditional" all sorts of cultural ways that simply go without saying in a particular environment. Here tradition is a kind of "habitus" which often disguises particular historical conditions as natural or inevitable. Fourth, anthropologists and many other people call traditional those cultural elements that are explicitly used by social groups as markers of identity, the scope of which is of course highly contextual (see e.g. the plastic notion of *kastom* in Melanesia and Polynesia). There is no good reason to think that those four partly overlapping senses converge on one set of phenomena; it makes there fore little sense to seek the "proper" definition of tradition.

I am interested here in the psychological processes underlying "tradition" in the first and second senses mentioned above. People have a certain representation of past ideas and practices stored in memory, that serves as a charter for present action. Because of this dependence on memories, the actual recurrence or persistence of certain forms of social interaction is caused by (among other things) cognitive processes that are rarely if ever accessible to conscious examination. For this reason, too, the processes whereby particular themes and notions are represented and memorized cannot be studied only on the sole basis of anthropological data. One needs a precise description of the cognitive processes involved, therefore some experimental and theoretical input from psychology. Moreover, from a cognitive standpoint, there is no reason to think that all types of cultural representations are acquired and transmitted in similar ways. So general accounts of "tradition" and "transmission" may be replaced with domain-specific accounts of the acquisition of particular domains of representations.

Here I will examine one such domain, that of the premises or assumptions underpinning religious representations in a variety of cultural environments. In particular, I want to focus on three different sets of representations likely to be found in any system of religious representations, to do with (i) ontology, (ii) social categories and (iii) the evaluation of truth. A set of religious representations always implies some *ontological* and *causal* assumptions, to do with the existence and the particular qualities of a set of putative entities, particularly agencies: gods, spirits, ancestors, zombies, mythical animals, etc. As we will see, these representations are based on a rather small number of recurrent underlying principles. In religious representations, one also finds a number of assumptions about the special qualities of particular human agents (priests, shamans, mediums, etc.), particularly in terms of their special connections with non-human agencies. Again, a variety of specific representations are based on a few underlying premises, the recurrence of which should be explained. Finally, in any cultural environment, some contexts or persons are singled out as offering guarantees of truth. For instance, divination techniques may be used to produce guaranteed statements, which provide (among other things) a true description of what the ancestors want. In many cases, the fact that some utterances are produced by particular people provides the guarantee in question. The question then is what particular features are represented as criteria of truth, and whether some more general way of evaluating truth underpins their cultural variation.

The recurrence of certain underlying assumptions can be explained economically in terms of universal cognitive dispositions which constrain the acquisition of cultural representations. Religious categories constitute a limiting-case here, in the sense that they seem to be among the most variable domains of cultural representations, and therefore one of the domains where cognitive constraints would not seem immediately relevant. Religious representations, because they seem culturally specific, also appear to be entirely constrained by cultural input. This view, however, is not really plausible, and a psychologically realistic alternative can be put forward.

Intuitive Ontologies and their Consequences

Our common-sense notion of cognitive development is generally characterized by a strong *empiricist* bias. That is to say, we tend to think that the processes whereby children gradually acquire adult competence, in most cognitive domains, is mainly driven by experience, both individual experience and social interaction. In this view, subjects store observational data, and use recurrent features in those data as the starting point in the elaboration of abstract hypotheses, which are then modified on the basis of further experiential data. No cognitive system, however, could achieve this without being equipped with cognitive capacities that make it possible (i) to isolate that series of stimuli as, precisely, a series, and (ii) to narrow down the number of possible interpretations that can be given, for any recurrent feature. The variety of situations experienced supports indefinitely many possible inferences, of which only a very small subset are ever entertained by the organism. This of course applies to humans, as organisms that can acquire vast amounts of complex information. One should expect to find their cognitive development constrained by rich prior structures.

Developmental research provides experimental evidence for a variety of such structures. I will mention only those aspects that are relevant to our anthropological problem. An important result of research in this domain is that early conceptual structures are dependent on *domain-specific principles* rather than general heuristics. Some of these principles may be seen to correspond to broad ontological categories, e.g. EVENT, PHYSICAL OBJECT, LIVING THING, ANIMATE BEING, PERSON, etc. These domains are informed by principles or presumptions which develop early and seem relatively independent from the structuring principles of other domains. These principles constitute the skeletons of what are often called "intuitive" or "naive" theories (as opposed to scientific ones). They are generally implicit, and seem to play a crucial role in the development of later, partly explicit representations of the domains concerned. Early cognitive development relies on the construction of a naive theory of physical objects (Spelke 1990), a naive biology (Keil 1986, 1989) and a naive theory of mental processes (Astington, Harris and Orson 1988; Wellmann 1990; Perner 1991; Whiten 1991), to mention a few domains explored so far (see the essays collected in Hirschfeld and Gelman 1994 for a general survey).

Intuitive "theoretical" principles are *under-determined* by tuition or experiential input. That is to say, the form and organization of the principles, as well as their developmental schedule, cannot be explained solely as a consequence of social interaction or experience. Take for example the domain of the intuitive principles that direct our common-sense understanding of people's behaviour in terms of beliefs and desire, our intuitive psychology. These partly tacit principles stipulate that people's behaviour is caused by immaterial entities, such as beliefs and intentions. They also assume that definite causal links can be routinely postulated from actual situations to perceptions, from perceptions to beliefs, from beliefs to desires, whilst causal links in the other direction are non-standard. Also, intuitive psychology allows us to make specific inferences about people's mental states; we can for example predict that someone who wants X and believes that X cannot be achieved unless Y, will (all else being equal) be led to desire Y. These principles generally remain tacit; they are constantly used and entirely "transparent" to the user. The content of those principles cannot be easily traced to experiential input. It is almost impossible to describe how one could "learn" the basic principles of intuitive psychology from encounters with people. Indeed, interaction with other subjects has cognitive effects only insofar as it is conceived through the filter of intuitive psychological principles. Moreover, intuitive psychology has a particular developmental schedule. Three year olds for instance (and autistic children at any stage) seem to have difficulty in predicting how an agent will behave, when the agent considered has beliefs which the child knows to be false (see a discussion in Perner 1991; Wellmann 1990). Normal four or five year olds on the other hand have no such difficulty. Given that there is no clear change in the child's experience at this stage, it is difficult not to interpret this shift as the consequence of a maturational programme.

To take another, related domain, our intuitive understanding of biological kinds seems to be based on a set of prior principles, which organize the domain of LIVING THINGS and inform our gradual acquisition of biological concepts. Here, too, the structure of such intuitive principles is best revealed by a study of their early development. It is now clear that even young children display a sensitivity to the categorical distinction between animate and non-animate objects in their environment. There is considerable evidence that the distinction is present even in infants (R. Gelman, Spelke and Meck 1983; Bullock 1985; Richards and Siegler 1986) and may be grounded in an early sensitivity to the difference between self- and non-self-generated movement in physical objects (Massey and R. Gelman 1988). This distinction is then enriched with a variety of specific intuitive principles which describe biological aspects of live beings. The identification of living kinds also activates an "essentialist principle" following which an undefined internal principle, which is exclusive to the species, causes the external features of living objects as well as certain aspects of their behaviour.[1]

If intuitive principles are not derived from experience, then they cannot vary as a function of the cultural environment. Indeed, there is a range of evidence to show that important variations in cultural settings do not affect the content of intuitive presumptions or their developmental schedule in a significant way. As regards biological knowledge, the universality of its basic taxonomic and essentialist principles is demonstrated by the study of folk classifications (Atran 1990). Other aspects of conceptual development appear to be similar, even in domains which could give rise to strong cultural influences. For instance, Walker-Jeyifous observed that standard developmental shifts in particular domains (e.g. ARTEFACTS as opposed to LIVING KINDS) described on the basis of US children's performance, occured in the same form as the same age in Yoruba subjects. If anything, more variation could be found within Yoruba subjects, between rural and urban subjects, than between the Yoruba average and the American results (Walker [Jeyifous] 1985, 1990). Similar results can be found in the study of intuitive psychological principles. Take for instance the shift described above, between the ages of 3 and 4, in terms of understanding other people's false beliefs. As Avis and Harris have shown (1990), this particular developmental shift can be observed in Cameroon Pygmy children at exactly the same age as in US subjects. Given the enormous differences in socio-cultural settings, it would require some quasi-miraculous coincidence for such shifts to occur at the same age in the same way in the cultures compared.

To sum up, conceptual development is made possible by a set of complex domain-specific structures, which result in stable specific *expectations* about the behaviour, aspect, internal structures and processes of such things as artefacts, plants, persons or animals. Obviously, such presumptions are not taught, and are certainly under-determined by experience. Far from being inferred from experience, "the initial principles of a domain establish the boundary conditions for the stimuli that are candidates for feeding coherent development in that domain" (R. Gelman 1990, 83). Domain-specific principles constitute the necessary background for the acquisition of complex information from experience and tuition. The tacit principles orient and constrain inferences about the information received. They therefore have important consequences, as concerns cultural input, as it consists of interaction and utterances and events from which nothing could be extracted without prior ontological assumptions.

Counter-intuitive Assumptions and their Background

I am concerned here with recurrent ontological assumptions that can be found in a variety of cultural environments. The starting point of this account is that the most religious systems, in otherwise diverse environments, generally center on a limited number of claims that constitute direct violations of the intuitive expectations described above. For instance, one of the most widespread ontological assumptions in religious categories postulates the existence of agencies (spirits, gods, ancestors) whose physical properties are counter-intuitive. They are invisible or immaterial, they can move instantaneously, and in some cases can be at different locations at the same time. Or, to take another example, religious systems the world over include assumptions about particular artefacts, statues for instance, which are counter-intuitive in that they are endowed with intentional psychological processes. They can perceive states of affairs, form beliefs, have intentions, etc.

The notion of religious claims as counter-intuitive and culturally recurrent because of that feature conflicts with common anthropological assumptions. In particular, it is often taken for granted that religious categories are completely plausible and "intuitive" to the people concerned. This must be discussed, if only because a misunderstanding of this point gives rise to much theoretical confusion in cultural anthropology.

What is claimed here is that religious categories very often include assumptions that are counter-intuitive *relative to intuitive ontological expectations*, and nothing more than that. Whether some phenomenon is counter-intuitive or not in this specific sense does not depend on people's explicit, culturally transmitted theories about such things as "nature" or "reality" (if they hold any such explicit conceptions). This is because intuitive ontology delivers expectations, not theoretical justifications for their existence. For instance, we intuitively expect the internal structure of living things to be stable within a species, or the trajectories of physical objects to be predictably affected by collisions. In some cultural environments, there is a body of reflective, speculative representations on these expectations and on their correspondence to real properties of the world. There is little evidence, however, that such explicit, culturally transmitted notions have much effect on the expectations themselves; in this domain there does not seem to be much cultural variation or "top-down" influence from explicit conceptions. By the same token, one should not confuse what is intuitively counter-intuitive from a cognitive viewpoint, with what is perceived as *unfamiliar*. Some religious assumptions can become part of a cultural "routine," this is orthogonal, to the question whether they violate tacit, intuitive ontological principles.[2] Finally, one should not confuse the counter-intuitive and the *unreal*. People may be convinced of the actuality of some counter-intuitive phenomenon; this does not make it less counter-intuitive in the precise sense used here. If I show people that I can make objects move by just looking at them, some will be convinced that I really have extraordinary powers; the fact that "psychokinesis" is thought to be real does not make it less counter-intuitive. This point is particularly important; that religious assumptions are counter-intuitive *and* construed as actually true is probably what makes them of particular interest and triggers significant cognitive investment on the part of the people concerned. Counter-intuitive assumptions are indeed counter-intuitive to the people who hold them, and this is probably the main explanation for their *attention-grabbing* potential.

A second hypothesis is that such counter-intuitive assumptions are not the only element found in religious representations. Indeed, representations consisting only of such counter-intuitive assumptions are unlikely to "survive" cycles of transmission. What is necessary then is a *back-

ground of additional assumptions, which are not counter-intuitive and in fact are directly provided by intuitive ontological expectations. Take for instance spirits and other such agencies. These are construed in terms that make them clearly counter-intuitive: their physi-cal properties in particular make them a particular class of agents, whose features mark them off from other, non-counter-intuitive agents. At the same time, these assumptions are clearly insufficient to be the starting point for any inferences about spirits. In order to understand or explain or predict the spirits' behaviour, one needs to use a number of tacit assumptions, about their psychological processes. These assumptions are neither simple nor obvious; they direct people's inferences in understanding stories or statements about the ancestors, but also in making various predictions about their behaviour. These tacit assumptions are not "given" by cultural transmission, however vaguely one wants to construe cultural transmission. They appear at certain stages of conceptual development, without much influence from experiential variables, including cultural ones.

Religious concepts, then, are constrained by intuitive ontologies in two different ways. First, religious representations would not be attention-grabbing if they did not include some counter-intuitive assumptions; but these are counter-intuitive only against a background of intuitive expectations. The idea of spirits being in several places at once would not be counter-intuitive, if there was not a stable expectation that agents are solid objects and that solid objects occupy a unique point in space. Second, religious representations invariably include a host of assumptions directly provided by intuitive ontologies, and these assumptions direct the inferences made about putative religious entities.

This double constraint from intuitive ontology may be necessary to the "survival" of religious representations in cycles of transmission. Religious representations would probably not be acquired at all, if their counter-intuitive aspects did not make them sufficiently salient to be an object of attention and cognitive investment. Conversely, they would probably not be acquired and transmitted, if their intuitive part did not give them sufficient inferential potential.

There is now some experimental evidence that this is precisely what takes place in the representation of some religious categories. In a series of ingenious experiments, Justin Barett and Frank Keil examined the assumptions underlying concepts of "God" and other non-natural agents in both believers and non-believers (Barett and Keil 1996). The subjects' explicit notions of God are a catalogue of counter-intuitive claims for extraordinary cognitive powers; God can perceive everything at once, focus his attention on multiple events simultaneously, and so on. The subjects were then tested on their recall of simple stories that involve God in various scenarios where such capacities are involved. In general, subjects tend to distort or add to the stories in ways that are directly influenced by their tacit, intuitive principles of psychology. For instance, they recall that God attended to some problem *and then* turned his attention to another, or that God *could not perceive* some event because of some obstacle, all details that were not in the original stories. Notice that this application of intuitive principles which specify limitations on cognitive powers (e.g. perceptions are hindered by obstacles between the object and the perceiving subject) is in direct contradiction to the subjects' explicit beliefs about God. There can be such contradictions because, as predicted in the original model, the two types of representations are distinct and contribute to different aspects of the representation of religious categories: attention-grabbing salience for counter-intuitive assumptions and inferential potential for tacit intuitive assumptions.

A consequence of the constraints describe here is that the number of such combinations should be limited. Intuitive ontologies produce specific expectations that apply to a limited number of broad ontological categories, so that the number of assumptions that directly violate them should be limited too. Moreover, not all violations are compatible with maintaining an intuitive background that supports inferences about the agencies postulated. In the case described here, the counter-intuitive assumptions focus on the physical properties of some agents, whilst the intuitive background consists mainly of expectations concerning their psychological processes. This is certainly a very common combination, and a central one of we want to understand "anthropomorphism," but it is certainly not the only one. Counter-intuitive assumptions typically focus on the biological aspects of putative agents (e.g. gods feeding on smells or ancestors being immortal), or even on thought-processes (e.g. zombies who are unaware and deprived of volition). This allows us to predict a number of salient combinations. One should expect recurrent cultural assumptions to include such constructions as:
• persons with counter-intuitive physical properties (e.g. spirits, etc.);
• persons with counter-intuitive biological properties (e.g. immortal, or with particular reproduction, etc.);
• persons with counter-intuitive psychological properties (e.g. zombies or possessed people);
• animals with counter-intuitive biological properties (e.g. metamorphosed into other animals);
• artefacts with intentional properties (e.g. thinking statues).

The list may include other, less frequent combinations as well.

However elementary, this "catalogue" accounts for most of the assumptions actually found in religious categories. That is to say, most recurrent assumptions, in otherwise very different cultural environments, turn out to be based on one or several of these combinations. This, obviously, applies to the fundamental principles underlying religious representations, not to the specific set of "surface" features that accompany them. For instance, the principle of intentional agents with counter-intuitive physical properties is widespread the world over; but in each cultural environment it is accompanied with detailed, and highly variable explicit notions about the characteristics and behaviour of those agents. As concerns underlying principles, however, the actual distribution of cultural representations seems to confirm the prediction that, all else being equal, representations that combine counter-intuitive principles and intuitive background in the way described here are more likely than others to be acquired, stored and transmitted, thereby giving rise to those roughly stable sets commonly described as "traditional."

Charismatic Proclivity and Essentialism

Most religious activities imply a principled distribution of activities on particular people, according to the social categories they belong to. This may apply to broad categories, the characterization of which is found outside religious representations; in some situations for instance, only adults or men or women can participate. In other cases, the categories are mainly represented in connection to religious ontological assumptions, and this is the situation I will examine here. I will start with a familiar, though far from trivial generalization from the anthropology of religious roles, and show how it can be interpreted to some extent as a function of cognitive constraints.

Ever since Weber, notions of charisma and charismatic authority have been central to our descriptions of religious roles; but they have proved as problematic as they are apparently inevitable. Take for instance Beidelmann's comments on Evans-Pritchard's description of Nuer religion. Evans-Pritchard (1940) makes a strong distinction between two types of religious officers. On the one hand, "leopard-skin chiefs" are specialized "priests of the earth," whose intervention is necessary to perform sacrifices. The role of sacrificial specialists is an aspect of the structure of Nuer kinship and politics; it implies no personal power, beyond that which is granted by the structure itself. On the other hand, "spirit-owners" are self-styled prophets, whose possession by one or several spirits gives them particular capacities, such as divination or healing; prophets generally exert considerable influence through their followers. As Beidelman points out (1971 *passim*), the situation is far more complex than this tradition-charisma opposition would suggest. "Leopard skin chiefs," whatever the institutional nature of their position, invariably try to infuse charismatic elements in their practice, and to build rudimentary cults around their persons. Prophets on the other hand, far from being isolated healers, constitute a strong political response to colonial pressure.

Such difficulties are very common, and particularly salient in the description of large-scale religious institutions. The "official," or theologically oriented description of religious roles centers on the external, role-based criteria. Priests are characterized as ordained people, specialized Brahmins as caste members who have undergone the initiation rituals and observe ritual prohibitions, 'ulema as specially trained scholars, etc. On the other hand, however, all descriptions of such religions "on the ground" invariably highlight the fact that such characterizations are incomplete. Local congregations or groups either ignore them, or complete them with representations which are much closer to the charismatic mode. Charismatic features may be ascribed to the very personnel that is characterized in non-charismatic ways by the institution. This is the case for Catholic priests, often taken by congregations to be endowed with special personal qualities, although the Church would certainly oppose, and has repeatedly tried to curb such cultic tendencies. In other cases, the groups simply add extra positions to the official religious personnel, as in the Muslim case.

These discrepancies point to a familiar *charismatic proclivity*, a tendency to interpret social positions as based on undefined or underlying personal attributes. People tend to "misconstrue" religious social positions as person-based, even in cases where an institution provides clear role-based criteria for the categories, and even when such criteria are made explicit and publicly available by literate institutions. This does not just mean that subjects misinterpret social dynamics; it means they tend to misinterpret them in a very specific way.[3] The problem, then, is to understand what makes this person-based interpretation so salient and pervasive.

The recurrence of such representations may be easier to understand if we remember that intuitive ontologies include a number of strong presumptions about the internal structure of living things, and about the causal processes that account for their appearance and behaviour. To return to points briefly mentioned above, knowledge of the biological domain is constrained, from an early age, by strong essentialist presumptions. Intuitive biology accounts for the observable features of each species in terms of an unobservable, causally stable essence. One of the main assumptions underlying intuitive biology is that there is an explanatory connection between undefined "essence" and observable causal powers. Possession of a special essence "causes" the characteristics of a species; conversely, salient differences (e.g. in terms of diet or reproduction) between otherwise similar animals tend to suggest that they belong to different essence-based categories. To sum up, essentialist assumptions are among the most salient resources available, for the explanation of overt differences in causal propensities.

Religious social categories are often characterized in terms of particular causal propensities. Priests are special because particular rituals are efficacious when performed by them, shamans are special because only they can be affected in particular ways by spirits, and so on. The "charismatic" interpretation of such categories, then, seems to be based on a straightforward transfer of essentialist principles to the social domain, as a salient "explanation" for the particular causal powers of people belonging to these categories. Indeed, there is empirical evidence that similar quasi-essential principles are involved in the representation of other social categories; see for instance Hirschfeld's studies on categories of "race", which display similar processes (1986, 1988). This transfer of biological assumptions is of course partly counter-intuitive, since it violates another intuitive biological principle, following which internal structure is similar for all exemplars of a species, e.g. for all human beings. The salience of such representations may well depend on this combination of initial counter-intuitive quality and background inferential power, as I mentioned in the above section.

Evidential Accounts and Truth in Tradition

Let me now turn to the question of the evaluation of true statements in religious contexts. Here I am considering the straightforward and explicit distinction between ordinary contexts or forms of discourse on the one hand and those which result in guaranteed truths. In order to describe certain "truth-making" inferential processes in detail, I must begin with a rough description of the evaluation of truth in general.

There are certainly many different ways in which listeners can represent what makes a particular utterance true, its *evidential account*. This consists of a set of (partly) tacit assumptions which, if true, make it the case that the utterance is true. Evidential accounts generally include at least a rough description of the process whereby the true information has been acquired by the speaker. This account can be called a *causal-representational* story, and runs as follows. The speaker has intended to communicate some aspect of some state of affairs, e.g. "there is a direct train from O'Hare airport to downtown Chicago." I presume her utterance expresses a true fact about the Chicago transit system. The speaker's utterance is (taken as) true because it conveys a mental representation, which happens to correspond to the way that system is organized. Now what makes this representation true is that, in some more or less direct way, the features of the system led the speaker to produce it. For instance, being at O'Hare she experienced taking a direct train to downtown. The actual state of affairs triggered the mental representation (this is what makes the story a *causal* one) and her utterance conveyed that mental representation (this is the *representational* aspect of the story).

The causal-representational (or "C-R") account is a very general, and spontaneous way of providing an evidential account for an utterance. When they hear people making straightforward statements, intended to convey some information about some state of affairs, listeners spontaneously activate a C-R account as a default value. From the earliest stages of cognitive development, children tend to take for granted this aspect of communicative behaviour. Inasmuch as listeners take an utterance as conveying some information, they activate some minimal representation of an evidential account, which has a causal aspect (from state of affairs to representations) and a representational one (between the representation and the communicative act). A consequence is that we tend to suspend or at least re-consider our assumption that the utter-ances heard are true when we are led to believe, either that the causal link is not obvious, or that the representational aspect of the utterance is muddled.[4] The more we know about the directness of the causal connection, and the less we consider the representational complexities, the more we are led to take the utterance as true.[5] It is important to remember that in many or most cases the evidential account assumed to obtain is left largely *under-specified*. The evidential account for an utterance can even be reduced to a bare existential generalization, to the effect that "there is a account E, such that E makes it the case that utter-ance U is true." Indeed, this is the way most utterances are evaluated in ordinary circumstances, by postulating the existence of some undefined but appropriate evidential context.

In many situations of religious interaction, one can find utterances that constitute a direct challenge to this causal-representational account. The utterances and the situations in which they are produced have properties which should, in principle, make it particularly difficult to build a coherent representation of the evidential account along the story described above. Consider for instance the following features:

1. *Obscure contents.* This is a very common, and often misunderstood characteristic. The utterances which many listeners consider to be the expression of important truths about religious agencies or events, are couched in particularly vague or obscure terms, obscure even to the speakers themselves. In some cases the utterances in question are expressed in formalized "special tongues," that is, artificial languages deliberately devised to make understanding difficult or impossible. In other cases, the supposedly true statements consists in gnomic formulae.

2. *Non-intentional production.* This corresponds, roughly, to the domain of divination. Supposedly true statements are produced by using particular techniques, which determine the content of the utter-ances. A consequence of these techniques is that the content of the utterances, as far as the listeners can judge, is not determined by the speaker's intentions. This provides a salient contrast with ordinary utterances. In divination situations, although a person is actually making a statement, the content is clearly determined by a process which is not controlled by the speaker him- or herself.

3. *Non-obvious experiential basis.* In many cultural environments, the capacity to make true statements about crucial religious matters is reserved to particular categories of speakers. This is one central aspect of the creation of religious social categories. Typically, a particular experience is among the features activated in the identification of such categories; priests are priests because they have been ordained. In many cases, it is interesting to note that the experience in question, which is supposed to provide a guarantee of truth, has little to do with the transmission of information.

These features make it difficult to build a coherent version of the *representational* part of the evidential account. If a speaker makes statements in formulae that are not entirely interpreted, it becomes more difficult for the listeners to construe what mental representations are involved in the production of the utterance. This difficulty is used systematically in the case of divination, where it is clearly stated that the speaker's mental representations, whatever they are, do not take part in the production of the utterance. The representational part of evidential accounts is also hampered by appeals to experience, for instance in cases of initiation. In such situations, the speaker is presented or construed as truthful by virtue of his participation in particular episodes. The nature of these episodes, however, makes it impossible to imagine in what way they could have contributed to the speaker's representations. It is for instance a salient feature of initiation rites, that they are consistently presented as contexts in which knowledge is acquired; at the same time, however, the nature of the episodes demonstrates clearly that no specific information is being transmitted.[6] Having gone through initiation does not contribute to a speaker's subsequent utterances in a way that can be represented by the listeners.

A consequence of these particular properties of some religious utter-ances, then, is that the evidential accounts constructed by listeners will be fragmentary; in particular, their representational part is likely to be either empty or else filled with the assumption that the speaker's mental representations *cannot* be involved in the utterance. Yet these utter-ances are taken as true. More often than not, they are taken as true not *despite* these particular properties, but *because* of them. This deserves some special explanation.

Since the representational part of the evidential account is either missing or known to be absent, the assumptions activated in such contexts are likely to focus on the causal part of the account. In other words, the listeners are likely to represent the various causal factors which link the utterance to the state of affairs it purports to describe. Indeed, this is not only what listeners actually do, but also what certain aspects of the utterances and the situations suggest to them very clearly.[7] Listeners are led to conjecture that the specific form of the utter-ances, which was not a result of the speaker's representations, was on the other hand a direct consequence of the state of affairs described. As I said above, assuming that there is *some* causal link does not necessarily imply representing what that link consists of. Indeed, in many cases the listeners who assume that there is a direct causal connection between a state of affairs, on the one hand, and the utterances about it on the other, would be unable to specify what the connection consists of.[8] Assuming some causal connection, however unspecified, is enough to create an evidential account for the utterance, an account which marks it off from ordinary statements.

The various situations briefly described here make it possible to represent and in many cases clearly suggest a causal connection between the state of affairs described in the utterances and the utterances themselves. How does this constitute a criterion of truth? The postulation of a direct causal link is likely to contribute to the evaluation of an utterance as true, because of the listeners' intuitive assumptions about mental processes, on the one hand, and typical causal connections on the other. The assumption that mental entities are immaterial, and can *mis*-represent a perceived situation, is available very early in cognitive development. Even very young (normal) children can grasp the notion of mis-representation, its possibility and its consequences. On the other hand, prototypical causal connections consist, again very early in cognitive development, in mechanical cause-effect sequences in which it would be surprising to observe the effect if the cause was not present.

In the kind of situation described above, the utterances are represented as directly caused by the states or events they describe, not by the speaker's mental representations of those states and events. In other words, the aspects of utterances which are intuitively represented as a potential source of misrepresentation are excluded from the evidential account, which on the other hand is the aspects which suggest a stable, potentially general pattern are salient. In slightly metaphorical terms, one could say that the utterances are supposed to be true because they are construed as the stable symptoms or indices of the situations they describe.

Tradition without Transmission: Cues and Inferences

To explain the "persistence" or "stability" of a "tradition," as well as the various changes that affect those cultural phenomena, we should go beyond the common assumption, that all important aspects of cultural representations can be explained in terms of social transmission. It is clear to most anthropologists that very little cultural material is transmitted through "explicit tuition." Even in modern Western societies, a substantial part of what is acquired is not transmitted in such situations. This is why anthropological models of socialization assume that most of the ideas are transmitted in an *implicit* manner. To take the case of religious ideas, where such processes are particularly clear, people are seldom given "lessons" on ghosts and spirits, but they gradually form some representation of these entities, from the material that is given indirectly in social interaction. Subjects do not need to be told that witchcraft is something against which one should get some protection. From the variety of situations in which witchcraft is mentioned they can easily derive that inference by a simple generalization based on numerous confirming instances.

This type of account gives the notion of "implicit transmission" its apparent plausibility, and may explain why it is so popular among anthropologists. That is to say, it seems to explain why certain cultural representations seem stable from one generation to another, whilst it is difficult to describe in what situations they were transmitted. This is the technical version of the popular notion that people find their culture "in the air they breathe," that it pervades every action and utterance. The idea may seem reasonable, but it is theoretically unclear, and in fact the plausibility of the account vanishes if we try to apply it to any particular type of representations.

Take for instance the "background" assumptions that give inferential potential to religious categories. Spirits are the object of precise representations and expectations because one can make complex inferences as regards their perceptions, beliefs and intentions. As I argued at the beginning of this paper, it is difficult to acquire anything as concerns the spirits or other such notions, unless one activates a complex set of quasi-theoretical principles of intuitive psychology. It is not a trivial or unimportant fact, that ghosts and spirits and gods are represented as agents whose thought-processes are constrained by those principles. Now one could say that the assumption, "the ghosts have thoughts constrained by belief-desire psychology" is transmitted "implicitly." However, we must be more specific about what this means. In this case, to say that some information is "implicit" in the cultural material, simply means that it *can be inferred* from that material. However, *this* information can be inferred by people on the basis of *that* input only if people's inferences are constrained by a rich set of prior principles. From people's statements about ghosts (e.g. that they are "angry"), one cannot *deduce* the principles and mechanisms of intentional psychology. One may infer that they apply, but only if one has a set of prior hypotheses, about the contents and mechanisms of mental states (e.g. that anger is a mental state, that it is caused by beliefs, which are caused by perceptions, etc.). Inferences that reconstitute the "implicit" messages about the ghosts' psychology can be produced only by cognitive systems which take intentional psychology to consist of precisely those assumptions. But the specific principles of mentalistic psychology are not given by the cultural input.

More generally, whatever the domain of cultural representations, the notion of "implicit transmission" is incoherent simply because the notion of "explicit" transmission is vacuous. Acquiring cultural representations does not and in fact cannot consist in "downloading" the conceptual scheme of cultural peers and elders. There is no known mechanism that would provide human minds with direct access to other minds' representations. There are, on the other hand, complex mechanisms that allow subjects to produce an optimally plausible description of other people's representations or intentions. All such processes, like all processes whereby cultural representations are built on the basis of cultural input, consist in *inferential* processes. Inferences are not a straightforward deductive consequence of their input. In other words, you cannot produce inferences unless some prior structures lead you along particular inferential paths.

This is what I tried to show here, in the limited if crucial domain of religious representations. I showed how recurrent assumptions about religious agents can be explained in a simple way, once we take into account the particular combinations of intuitive violations and intuitive background that they include. This also applies, although in a rather different way, to the representations about actual people as endowed with particular causal powers, relying on a transfer of particular assumptions of intuitive biology. Finally, the evaluation of certain utterances in religious situations seems to be based on a salient distortion of the intuitive processes whereby utterances are routinely (and tacitly) evaluated. Our anthropological notion of "religious" representations obviously includes many other types of representations, for which a cognitive account is required. The domains examined here, however, are central enough to show that a single, domain-general account is misleading.

These particular arguments demonstrate, in a more general way, how cultural representations are generally *under-determined* by cultural input. People have prior intuitive ontological assumptions, by contrast to which particular cultural representations are salient and attention-demanding. The contents and organization of cultural representations, what we would sometimes call "cultural competence" in the adult, are not strongly determined by the cultural input. All that can be found in the cultural input are specific *cues*, which trigger inferences in the subject. Because intuitive ontologies are roughly similar in all human subjects, such cues normally result in roughly similar inferences in all the subjects exposed to them. In other words, one does not need to "transmit" a religious system even "implicitly" in order to have it reproduced from generation to generation. All one has to do is provide salient cues as to which aspects of intuitive ontology are violated. People's inferential capacities are powerful enough to do the rest of the job, as it were, and produce roughly consistent versions of the "tradition." Some theoretically important aspects of cultural representations and "traditions," even if they are recurrent from generation to generation, need not be transmitted at all.

Notes

1. For instance, even pre-schoolers assume that membership of a kind is more important than observable features, in predicting the typical behaviour of an unknown animal (S. Gelman and Markman 1986; Massey and Gelman 1988; Becker and Ward 1991). Also, they assume that such kind-based inductive generalizations are more plausible if the properties projected are "inherent" properties of the exemplars, e.g. ways of breathing and feeding, rather than weight or speed (S. Gelman and Markman 1987 *passim*, see also S. Gelman 1988). These theoretical assumptions are also manifest in children's reactions to putative scenarios of artificial transformation from one kind to another. Such changes are judged more plausible between types of artefacts than from one living kind to another, even in cases where an animal is described as having gradually acquired the other's outside appearance or behaviour (Keil 1986).
2. No-one in the West would find it terribly surprising if they were told that ghosts can walk through walls. However banal the assumption that ghosts can walk through walls, it still violates some principles concerning the behaviour of solid objects and the fact that agents are solid physical objects.
3. Note, however, that the "proclivity" described here should be understood, precisely, as nothing more than a proclivity. Obviously, both institutional and person-based interpretations of a single social category can be concurrently held in a given human group, and in fact even in one single mind. My point here is not that religious positions are never interpreted in institutional terms; it is only that the person-based interpretation tends to be chosen even in contexts in which the alternative, institutional understanding is available.
4. If the speaker who tells me that "there is a direct train..." has never set foot in the US, I may be led to have initial doubts about her description of Chicago trains, because the *causal* connection between trains in Chicago and her ideas about them becomes much more complex. If I know her to be a pathological liar or an aphasic patient, I will have doubts too, in this case as regards the *representational* link between her utterances and her sincere beliefs.
5. If on my arrival at Chicago airport, I see a poster explaining the different ways of reaching downtown, I do not bother to imagine by what experience or process the authors of the poster acquired their knowledge of the city. I take the information as true, on the assumption that there is *some* evidential context, such that it provided the authors with true information, although I know little about that context.
6. The initiation "lessons" are often obscure or reduce to re-acquiring skills that were already mastered. Also, the rites often center on paradoxical ordeals which by their very nature preclude the transmission of any coherent content. When information is indeed transmitted, its acquisition is not considered a sufficient or even necessary condition for successful

initiation. As Gardner puts it, in his description of a New Guinea initiation, "rituals are considered efficient regardless of what can be called the cognitive change brought about in the candidates" (Gardner 1983, 352).

7. To return to the properties mentioned above, a recurrent theme in divination techniques for instance is that the diagnosis is directly caused by the situation it describes. A similar kind of direct causal link is often suggested in the case of obscure or formulaic statements, presented as directly inspired or indeed produced by super-natural agencies; a recurrent characteristic of these utterances is that they are supposed to contain true statements about the very agencies that caused them. The causal link is also suggested, although in a less direct form, in the case of statements supposedly guaranteed by previous experience of initiation episodes. To return to Gardner's New Guinea example, the candidates are not required to memorize or even hear the ancestors' secret songs, communicated during initiation. What makes initiates different from non-initiates, for the group, is that they have been "exposed" to the ancestors' power. In other words, what makes them, in subsequent situations, authoritative on matters relating to the ancestors, is a causal link between the ancestors themselves and the utterances about them.

8. It is perfectly possible to assume that "the cards would not have turned up this way if I was not being threatened by So-and-so," without representing by what process a situation, the alleged threat in this instance, could have brought about the particular display of the cards. In other cultural environments, some explanations are available, and listeners make use of them to a variable extent.

4

History and Tradition

Gérard Lenclud

Since the late eighteenth century if not earlier, Western thinkers have gone to great lengths to sort out the various ways humans make use of the past in the present and fit themselves into history. Much effort went into distinguishing different modes of historicity through the plurality of cultural experiences. Historians retrace those of yesterday, while anthropologists describe those of today. Hegel put forth the most radical idea. He simply divided societies into two distinct groups, those that have a history and those that do not.

Nowadays of course no one would dream of arguing that some societies have a history and others do not, or that some have more or less than others. Strictly speaking, the hypothesis that there are "objective" differences in historicity is unintelligible. This supposition assumes that societies undergo the passage of time in a myriad of ways. Furthermore, the comparison implies that societies and cultures can be ascribed an identity in time,[1] a date of birth and, consequently, an age. Claude Lévi-Strauss has been unfairly accused of reintroducing this hypothesis when he draws a line, for purely heuristic purposes, between "cold" and "hot" societies.

Some people would fully agree that "subjective" differences in historicity exist, that human societies can be divided along an ideal scale based on their propensity to recognize themselves in a historical dimension. Some of these societies would draw the consequences for interpreting the present and building the future. Others would "choose" to ignore this dimension and, therefore, claim to be planning their future with their eyes set on the past (Lévi-Strauss 1983). All societies are historical and as such they are "so many individual cases of a general law" (Karl Jaspers 1976).[2] But apparently they are not historical in the same way. Although they follow the general law, they would live and, consequently, make their history—and bear its marks—, each of them in its own way.

This is where the discussion takes a noteworthy turn. Of course no anthropologist or historian—in my opinion, at least—would set out on a quest for a single criterion distributing the semantic experience of time and of history on either side of a continuous line. The great divide is no longer conceivable, especially between an *us* whose homogeneity is quite problematic and a *them*, all of whom are tossed together into a single category. Today no one would defend the argument that there are only two ways of living in history, relating the present to the past or conceiving the actions that will shape the future. We know that contrasting attitudes towards the historical future may manifest themselves in the same culture—at least when it comes to *us*; anthropologists are more cautious when it comes to *them*.[3]

However, the idea that human societies fall on either side of a dividing line depending on how they are historical crops up with alarming regularity. The fault lies with the notions used in the comparison, which are never discussed singly but in twos. As conceptual language, each one leads to its supposed opposite. Together they form an inseparable pair that can be applied in all ages and on every continent: written versus oral transmission, history versus myth, history versus memory, event versus structure, and so on. The idea of conceptual opposites inevitably leads back to the wrong-headed view that a fault line runs through the cultural crust.

When the word *history* is applied to the knowledge that man can acquire of it rather than to a historical reality (History with a capital H), the term plays a crucial role in this language. *History*, either directly or through the back door, becomes part of all the classic opposites. The word is always accompanied by a—so-called—antonym, triggering an almost automatic succession of thoughts. Let's take a few examples. The only kind of history is written. Therefore it must be admitted that societies without writing have no history, only a tradition whose memory they preserve. However tradition tells the observer more about the present of the people who collect, transform and invent it than about their past. Therefore cultures with oral traditions are probably incapable of grasping the strictly historical dimension of their past. Now what about historical memory? Some people will immediately raise the objection that genuine history is built as a safeguard against flawed memories. Societies without historians and archives would be forced to rely on the randomness of memory and word-of-mouth. As soon as the term myth enters the picture, the contrast machine starts up again. Myth competes with history to make the past intelligible. Wherever myth is the predominant mode of transmission, the ways of thinking spontaneously associated with it will nip historical consciousness in the bud. Living in close contact with a society's origins probably prevents its members from grasping them as historical. The notion of event fulfills the same function. The classic argument goes like this: discovering historiography assumes that a society's collective mind contains the "principle of event" (Lefort 1952) by having the ability to convert it into a "moment of experience." The logical outcome is that the meaning attached to facts stored in the memory of a society without history is independent of their context. Each fact is important for its intrinsic value rather than for the place it fills on the overall time scale. The history of societies without historiography would then be full of edifying examples. Anthropologists go to great lengths to write down the past of these societies without archives or historians in the same terms these cultures would use to conceptualize their past, for lack of being able to commit it to paper. They fall victim to the discourse of the great divide, labelling their endeavor *ethnohistory*. Our history is history, written in the *etic* form. The history of others is ethnohistory, a product of the mind created in the *emic* mode. This is yielding to the variant of ethnocentrism called historiocentrism.

The argument's premises and conclusions have been criticized. Ethnographic and historiographic research has demonstrated that this language fails to express the reality of cultural experiences of the past. Despite the efforts of historians, these societies do not fit into the model - yet one always comes back to it. At first this leads to the tendency to define other forms of historicity in negative terms. Later awareness that this approach is ethnocentric led to relativism. "Different cultural orders have their own modes of historical action, consciousness and determination—their own historical practice" (Sahlins 1984, 34).

Why return to the idea that there are "subjective" differences in historicity under the pretext of a conceptual opposition between tradition and history? This essay's title suggests that there are two ways of communicating with the past and relating it to the present. One consists of receiving[4] it and establishing it as tradition, the other of promoting it to the rank of history, in other words to an object of knowledge. Now no one can deny that an endless variety of societies have written or are writing their history, and that other, equally diverse cultures have not or do not possess the means to carry out such a project. This puts societies that do not write their history on the side of tradition, leading to the conclusion that they have no historical consciousness. Adopting the conceptual opposition between tradition and history presupposes a rift between modes of consciousness of the past simply by vitue of the absence of historiography in some cultures. Yet this remains to be proven by patient investigation, comparison and, above all perhaps, logical argument.

I am fully aware of the risk involved in reviving the idea of the great divide. I am all the more eager to venture that gamble since, despite the customary half-hearted disavowals, in my view, it seems impossible to avoid it. Following and examining the logical argument inherent in the great divide concept will be an interesting adventure.

For a moment let us think about why is it impossible to avoid the risk. The long-term formation of historical knowledge and the feeling of its self-evidence have fueled and continue to fuel Western societies' conviction that they are the guardians of an absolutely singular historical consciousness. In this and in many other fields they believe they are unique, which makes them similar to all the others. The West invented history writing or, more exactly, a model of historiography that serves as a model today—and which leads anthropologists to use the term ethnohistory when discussing non-Western peoples. This invention is thought to stem from a revolution in historical consciousness, and therefore in self-awareness. It engendered an attitude towards historicity that probably has no equivalent in the cultures where this invention did not take place[5] as well as in societies where historiography took different forms. This discourse is too familiar to be rejected out of hand. However, the Western experience of promoting the past to the rank of historical object is necessarily the comparison's point of departure, at least for the Western observer. All the other semantic experiences of the past are analyzed and assessed in relation to this one and in the language that gives it shape. If we want to compare all systems to each other, it is impossible to avoid comparisons between our mode, or rather modes, of historicity and those that are different from them. This is true even if we want to go out of our way not to give the Western system preeminence. It is hard to see how things could be otherwise. We can place ourselves among other modes only after comparing them with our own.

Hence, studying the historiocentric discourse on the great divide between tradition and history is more interesting than rejecting the conclusions straight away. Like it or not, the split is the starting point for any comparisons between modes of historicity. Making use of this discourse and of this structure of argumentation helps verify whether they are really relevant for societies placed on the side of tradition. It also enables us to see whether they reflect a singular illusion regarding our own societies, which invented and fixed the historiographic genre and consequently believe they are living and thinking closer to History with a capital H.

History and historical consciousness

Western societies claim a certain form of historical consciousness as their exclusive property. How can it be defined? In my view it is conceived as the historical and painfully acquired product of a string of intellectual discoveries,[6] each of which apparently led to all the subsequent ones. These would include the formation of the concept of tradition, the invention of history, the establishment of bygone times as a historical past cut off from the present, the critique of the content of tradition, the discovery of the time process and the operative link between historical knowledge of the past, the independence of human action and, consequently, the availability of the future. Raymond Aron (1961). summed up the deep and unitary meaning given to this succession of discoveries in one sentence when he wrote that: "Man does not really have a past unless he is aware of having one, because only this awareness ushers in the possibility of dialogue and choice."

The argumentation starts with the idea that the various forms of history were invented in a culture where the concept of tradition was forged as early as Antiquity. Now, having the concept of tradition means applying it to one's own tradition and, according to the reasoning developed by Eric Weil (1991), consequently recognizing one's tradition as *a* tradition. The latter becomes discernible for what it is—convention rather than nature—, to anyone who applies this concept to his own tradition. The tradition is relativized regardless of how many virtues it has. It becomes one among other existing or possible competing traditions in whose light it can be evaluated. As a result, a society with a concept of tradition has stopped living completely in tradition and is no longer unwittingly nurtured, as naturally as breathing, by those beliefs and practices. Tradition no longer belongs to the realm of fact but turns into an object of knowledge and, therefore, a basis of judgment. Individuals in such a society have the power to replace "blind obedience," which according to Weil is a hallmark of cultures that are unaware of their tradition (and where there is no cause for traditionalism because following the age-old ways would be self-evident) with conscious "justification" or "critique." As soon as individuals start judging their tradition, the latter becomes an open question, a subject of debate and a matter of choice. Tradition is either the road to take for the sake of its exemplary nature vaunted by the traditionalist or, as the Moderns who regard it as a burden declare, the road to abandon. And the Moderns (almost) always win out because a tradition which has been duly recognized, itemized and established as an open question turns out to be a tradition that is soon left behind (Pouillon 1975).

The argumentation continues with the establishment of a sort of equivalence between examining tradition and returning to the past. This is when judging tradition, in a way, is tantamount to separating from the past by reviewing it in front of one's eyes. The past no longer acts upon those who return to it in the same way that it does upon those who evaluate their tradition and are no longer players in it. The latter step back and take on the stance of the spectator. They leave tradition behind or rise above it. They adopt a "perspective from outside the memorial tradition" (Detienne 1981). The individual who judges tradition and contemplates the past becomes aware of the break between that past and the present. The past is, if not history, re-imagined in a history, in a tale that unfolds before oneself. Recapturing the past requires formally recognizing that it has vanished and cannot be brought back to life in any way other than through memory or celebration.

That is why Hannah Arendt (1972) pinpoints the birth of history, poetically if not historically, as the moment when Ulysses hears the bard Demodocus tell the story of his own Trojan War adventures at the court of the king of the Phaeacians.[7] The story of Odysseus's life, writes Arendt, is presented to him like an external thing, an object for everyone to see and hear. The actor of History is turned into someone listening to a story. In other words, he is transformed into a suddenly overwhelmed spectator. Odysseus is his own witness.

Yet Odysseus's feelings are not historical if the tale about himself told by a third person is already a forerunner of historical narration. He receives his history, whereas the historian conquers facts. Conquest is possible when there is an enemy and a territory to invade. The historian's foes are false versions of the past, which writing alone can rectify by comparing and, consequently, challenging them with other versions (Goody 1979). For example, at the dawn of the fifth century Hecataeus of Miletus is credited with the critical act that founded history. He wrote, "I write these accounts as they seem true to me, for the tales of the Greeks are many and ludicrous as they appear to me" (quoted by Detienne 1981).

The logical reasoning now takes us to the eighteenth century, the age of criticism. According to the Enlightenment philosophers, everything must be subjected to criticism, which is the art of judging. John Locke raised this art to the dignified level of philosophical Law, which is enshrined beside moral and civil Law. Critical activity which stems from the faculty of reason consists of taking nothing for granted, especially in the name of the immemorial. It means questioning any "given" fact to determine its accuracy and, therefore, making a judgment. Lived History is turned into a "judicial arena" (Koselleck 1979). Written History is transformed into an "enormous critical trial." Pierre Bayle, whose 1720 *Dictionnaire* combines the words *historique* and *critique* in the title, argued that the historian's task is to hunt down mistakes and blanks, shed light on dark corners and reveal the contradictions in narratives of the past. The historian's work is primarily and necessarily negative (Cassirer 1966). *Critic* and *censor* mean the same thing.[8] "Human reason," writes Bayle,"... is a principle of destruction rather than of construction. Instilling doubt is the only thing for which it is suited" (quoted by Koselleck 1979). The historian's primary task, then, is to bring together a collection of "mistakes." Once written down, history can be asked to take the stand and testify against tradition, which is the enemy to be vanquished. Tradition is what passes down (edifying) "facts" whose "truthfulness" is based on the authority of a word fraudulently shielded from any kind of critical scrutiny.

According to Weil (1991), the Enlightenment philosophers defined tradition in the West as that absolutely singular tradition which "endlessly calls its own validity into question" and "is not satisfied with tradition." Tradition has freed itself from tradition. History plays an important role in this emancipation because it is written *against* what is held to be true in tradition. Receiving tradition and writing history are diametrically opposed.

The eighteenth-century emergence of the modern concept of history put the finishing touches on an already completed process and gave full meaning to the conquest of the historic world. This concept resulted in the merging of two ideas that had been sketched out in the European mind (Koselleck 1985). The first is that man's reason enables him to know history "in itself" rather than merely as different, individual stories combining facts in specialized accounts. "Beyond histories",

Droysen famously declared," there is History." The singular and the absence of an article are significant. They point to the understanding of history as a unitary *process*. The idea follows that a man guided by judgment alone is able to make his history or at least to change its course. The discovered process is the result of human endeavors. In other words, the conception of history as the realm of independent, unified and accessible facts is now inseparable from the representation of History as a feasible reality. The future is open and no longer an imposed fate. It is to be created rather than fulfilled. As Koselleck sums it up, history is available for knowledge as well as for realization.

The idea of progress dominated the theory of history traced out towards the end of the Age of Enlightenment. Historical consciousness was "at the time largely identical to the concept of *Geschichte*-history" (Koselleck 1985). Three parts of this discourse on historical consciousness should be emphasized, since they will constantly be used to widen the gap between *us*, who possess this consciousness, and *them*. The first notion concerns promoting the course of history as process. This implies that all of man's achievements and everything that happens to him cannot be fully understood unless they are placed within an evolutionary context. The individual event's splendor, singularity and unforgettable nature no longer have any intrinsic value. The event is meaningful only as a milestone in the course of history. It has a before and an after. Second, the content of tradition, whose mode of transmission has already been under attack, is undergoing an equally spirited assault as message from the past. In a way the past itself is devalued. For those who nurture the idea of progress, this key concept presupposes respect for the past but only insofar as one phase of the past represents the future of a previous phase. In other words, it is a forerunner. The bearer of the new historical consciousness spontaneously rushes into the future. The past is over and done with; it is a served sentence. The same will happen to the present, a momentary stop on the way to tomorrow, as soon as it, too, has been judged. "Everything is changed and must change," Raynal wrote in his *Histoire philosophique* (quoted in Cassirer 1951). According to Koselleck's semantic analysis, what is "new" takes on the character of the "unprecedented." Consequently it is not integrated into the old and interpreted by appealing to tradition.[9] This is why people talk about a "crisis of tradition." Tocqueville wrote, "Since the past no longer enlightens the future, the mind is walking through darkness" (quoted in Arendt 1972). The past and its messages (tradition) may teach something about the present and shed light on the future, but tomorrow is what provides information about today and, to an even greater extent, yesterday. The future reveals the limitations and the shortcomings of the past, which is merely a waystation and proof that the future still lies ahead. This is exactly the point. If the future must be achieved, action is the way to meet that goal. In the new historical consciousness, knowledge of the past and thoughts of action are closely connected. Tradition, the instrument of submission, is replaced by history, the tool of liberation. *Political action* comes on the scene at the crossroads between past and future (Arendt 1972). History leads to action. François Hartog (1989) recalls that Thucydides and Polybus, who were politicians until they went into exile, conceived of and presented history as similar to politics.

Let us take a look at a singular fact. This discourse has become partly foreign to us. The form of historical consciousness it describes has itself been transformed into an object of historic knowledge. This is equivalent to saying it belongs to a past from which we have gradually become estranged. We ourselves admit that *we* no longer have this attitude towards the future. Yet we continue to use this discourse to exclude *them* from this form of consciousness and, *therefore*, from any historical consciousness. Everything suggests that we are using the difference between historical consciousness and its absence whose content we refuse for *us* but that we still accept when it comes to *them*.

It is commonly agreed that we no longer regard history the same way as it was viewed during the Enlightenment. Philosophies of history are on the wane. The "great narratives" written when the idea and the proof of progress dominated historical discourse have been replaced by a science of history that spiritedly repudiates the need for the future and the representation of a compulsory destination. The enemy is teleology! Just think of the extent to which social and cultural evolutionism has been discredited in the field of anthropology. The values underpinning historical knowledge are disinterested curiosity and a certain skepticism towards human deeds. More generally, the future no longer enlightens the present and, consequently, the past itself has been thrust into a kind of darkness that must still be dispelled, but without too many illusions. Granted, history is available but everyone agrees that it is fulfilled according to its own plans, which are multifarious, contradictory, and impossible to totalize. The impression that things happen differently from the way they were predicted and planned has been overwhelmingly proven. Marx himself wrote that "history has more imagination than we do." The gap between historic knowledge and experience has grown even wider (Nipperdey 1992).

The kind of historicity with which we credit societies that do not write their history (which we write in their place) is usually based on the Enlightenment model. *They* have not formed the concept of tradition. For them, tradition is self-evident rather than a subject of discussion. *They* would never be spectators watching themselves. *They* receive their past instead of mastering it with critical judgement. Their ways of talking about the past, unlike ours, is intended to teach moral lessons. Since *they* do not realize history is a knowable process, the thought would not occur to them that it is available, that the past is over, that tradition is incapable of solving the riddles of the present and that the future is open and can be created through action.

To Westerners it is self-evident that the subject of history—or of commemoration—is the past. They are like the curious visitor who asks a Huron, a Persian, or anyone else from a society that does not seem to have historical consciousness, "You don't know your own history? How strange! How can you live without history?"

From one Huron to another

There are many ways of turning the great divide around and dispelling a few of the misconceptions upon which forms of historicity and their distribution around the world are based. Methodologically speaking, the primary one consists of questioning the very nature of the historical consciousness we claim as exclusively ours. What if it were all make-believe, like a novel we have written about ourselves?

Historic consciousness, historical consciousness and common consciousness

Arnaldo Momigliano wrote a refreshingly ironic article about how pointless it is for historiography specialists to search for clear-cut time concepts that are radically opposed to each other "Many students of historiography," he said "appear to assume that there are neat and mutually exclusive views about time" (1966: 39).[10] He goes on to point out that "there is no reason to consider Plato's thoughts about time as typical of the ordinary Greek man." Momigliano simply recommends that philosophers should be compared to philosophers.

But what happens when we compare supposedly Western historical consciousness to the ways in which Amerindian peoples are historical? First, and almost unwittingly, we attribute all of the people in our culture with representations stemming from a philosophy of history or from a discourse with a scholarly purpose. Were late eighteenth-century

Germans aware of the history process? Did they form an image of the future as the "book of the human soul in time and in the nations?" Do non-historians in France today, or even historians in everyday life, base their conceptions of the *longue durée* on *Annales* school precepts? In the West, the semantic experience or experiences of history are collected and organized into comparable data and written down by one or several historians with the aim of expanding on them point by point. In contrast, the Amerindians' "semantic experience of history" is painstakingly but quite randomly drawn from a hodgepodge of materials gathered together in the ethnographical laboratory. In other words, it is collective thought reconstructed by one observer. No one would think of arguing that Michelet's preface to *L'histoire du XIXème siècle* or Daniel Halévy's *Essai sur l'accélération de l'histoire* could be put on the same plane as Evans-Pritchard's proposition about Nuer that "time passes quickly or slowly depending on the age" on the pretext that both involve a plurality of time rhythms (the rhythms of history). That would be a little like trying to compare the cosmogonical system explained to the French anthropologist Marcel Griaule by the Dogon Ogotommelli and the spontaneous ontology gathered piecemeal by a collection of European informants, including you and I. Coherence would not be on our side.

Are we in possession of the historical consciousness that the scholarly West attributes to itself? Are we in possession of *our* historic past — therefore *theirs* is myth? Would history have had the power to free us from the imaginative transformations wrought by tradition? In his opening lecture at Cambridge, *The Ancestral Constitution* (1971), Moses Finley offhandedly mentioned several situations where references to "the good old days" and "the golden age" obscure the arguments made available by historical knowledge. In late fifth-century Athens for example, the representative of the oligarchy suggested going back to the laws of the forefathers and the mythical ancestral constitution in order to abolish democracy. Half a century later Isocrates urged his fellow citizens to choose between "the good democracy of yesteryear" and corrupt democracy. The orator did not provide a single piece of historical information but let loose a flow of "sententious rhetoric about a mythical past," and for good reason. During the English seventeenth-century constitutional crisis that pitted the king and parliament against each other, common law legal experts invoked the laws of Edward the Confessor, "rooted by Heaven itself in the hearts of Englishmen," and the authority of the ancient Saxons, which is hardly grounded in his-torical reality. Lastly, during the 1900 American presidential elections both candidates "practiced the cult of ancestors like the Chinese." During the New Deal, Thomas Jefferson was touted as the spiritual father of an administration seeking to cope with an industrial crisis in a highly urbanized society. This should come as a surprise, at least to historians, since Jefferson once wrote that he considered the laboring classes as the henchmen of revolutions that would overturn freedom. It need not be stressed that examples like these abound.

In the West, the "sublime and powerful non-historicity of tradition" (Finley 1971) is bravely holding out against the concept of tradition and its application to our ancestral ways, against the critical process at work in the mastering of historical facts, against our ability to think of the event as unique but no longer exemplary and against attempts to cut us off from our past by taking for granted whatever no longer sheds light on the future. This leads Finley to question whether historians actually play a significant role. Does the science of history have a decisive impact on how the past is used? Is ordinary historical consciousness "historian?"

Western societies pride themselves on their historical consciousness as well as on the idea that it allows them to outdistance the past. Because the past is reconstituted in a historical past, it thrusts the present into a space that embraces action and fosters creation of the future. Almost everyone agrees with the latest "philosophy of history" which argues that looking back is not necessary for taking action. History has apparently taught that the future is realizable. Once that message is transmitted, history is gradually confined to the historian's workshop, becoming the object of intellectual, scholarly and disinterested work. The idea of consulting the past to obtain a blueprint or to predict the future would no longer occur to anyone. It is often said that this too sets us apart from traditional societies, which are bound by the past's ever-present lessons.[11] However, the case of the former USSR easily demonstrates that the relationship between past and future is far more complex. The past does not only exist in the present in the form of objective data shaping circumstances. What happens when a European society "loses" its past because the present radically invalidates historical knowledge that had been firmly established as the truth for a long time?

The events that rocked Eastern Europe in 1989 were unpredictable, or least not predicted. One of the many consequences was that first the recent, then the distant past were returned to opacity and, in a way, to "unpredictability," as it has been said. The past "objectively" closed off by the event, was called into question, as if it were expropriated.

History had to be rewritten.[12] An entire society was "liberated" from its past in one fell swoop! Was this situation conducive to creating the future? *Pravda* did not mince words when it answered that question in an editorial: "From blank pages... to the black hole" (quoted by Garros 1992). It is impossible to predict, much less to implement, a future freed from any connections to a past that has been thoroughly abolished and yet which it is not possible to leave behind. The past was not over and done with. Is there any connection between the expropriation of the past and the unpredictability of the future? A Russian historian asserts, "The future is not a continuation of the present. We have a right to speak about the future as long as the past exists. We should even base both of these ideas on a single one: the past future" (Mikhail Gifter quoted in Garros 1992). But historians are not the only ones who think this way. Letters to the editor poured into newspaper and magazine offices, demonstrating a close correlation between a past that has been erased ("Why did I work hard all my life?", "Why did I fight in the war?") and a future that is unclear ("For whom did I help build this society?", "Does the Soviet people exist?" The former Soviet Union established the philosophy of history stemming from the Enlightenment as official doctrine. People there have come to the realization that thinking about the future requires reconquering the past, just as reconquering the past—rewriting history— requires the feeling that there will be a future.

Are we the way we think we are and, consequently, are others the way we do not think they are?

Writing versus recording

There is another way to relativize the contrast between societies that write their history and those that transmit the past through tradition. This involves taking a closer look at the variety of ways history is written and questioning the results of the transition to writing in those societies that are just beginning to commit their histories to paper (Detienne 1994). From this point of view, the modern Western way of writing history is just one possibility among others, and not at all the model to which any knowledge of the past *must* aspire. Some of the thought processes described are entirely arbitrary and culture-bound.

Writing may be a necessary condition for recording history, but it does not necessarily lead a society to preserve the past. For example, in ancient Greece the Syro-Phoenician alphabet reappeared three centuries before Herodotus wrote the *Histories* (Hartog 1987). The most startling example of a society that did not use writing to record its history is India. On the one hand, the practice of writing over the centuries did not lead to the formation of a historical discourse. On the other hand, the use made of sacred texts and the role played by learning them by heart stripped the scriptures of any historical dimension in their users' collective awareness. Until recently, Westerners alone used these texts to piece together the puzzle of a history.

For us it goes without saying that recording facts every day and, even more so, writing about the past inevitably leads to the formation of a "historical past," a time that slips away, filled with nothing but human achievements. The abundant historical sources of Mesopotamia include inscriptions, royal letters, lists of names of years, kings and oracles, appointments, historical accounts and annals, pseudo-autobiographies and prophecies (Glassner 1993). The few observable facts are unsettling in light of our semantic experience of time and of history. First, the Akkadians used a word meaning *forward* to signify time gone by. Like the Sumerians, they used a word meaning *backward* to signify the future. In short, Glassner writes, they moved into the future backwards while keeping a close eye on the past. Like Gilgamesh, the hero of the Akkadian epic poem "When he was *ahead...* by seven double-lengths, darkness was total. He was not allowed to see what was *behind* him." In Mesopotamia the flow of time was conceived as both linear and cyclical. Oracles projected past chains of events into the future. In collective Mesopotamian thought, it seems that man had a hold on his future, which is exactly why it was necessary to know and draw omens from the past. While "life was steeped in theology at every level" (Glassner 1993). Mesopotamian historiography dealt with history the way men made it. The gods ruled the world but history was the realm of people. In a society where predicting the future played a vital role and the past provided precedents, rulers could have their scribes glorify them for achieving what no previous king ever had.

Before the early twentieth century, Chinese historians under State supervision recorded everything that happened as it took place over very long periods of time. They took painstaking care to be factually accurate and wrote summaries on a regular basis. The mind of a "historian" in the modern, Western sense of the word is clearly necessary for such an endeavor. Yet Chinese historiography was not aimed at reconstructing the past in any way (Vandermeersch 1989). The goal of historical discourse was to explain "the meaning of historiographically reported events." Classical Chinese historiography was divided either thematically,— for example, everything relating to foreign peoples,or horizontally in time—everything that happened at the same time, or finally verti-cally—the unfolding of "individual events treated one after the other". Chinese historians attempted to recognize what Vandermeersch calls the "pattern of great lines of change." A mountain of information was processed to verify whether human nature was part of universal nature. The future made sense only in relation to changes in the cosmos. The scribe duly recorded human activity, writing down the ruler's most mundane business. In this historiographical model, human activity is not worthy of the least bit of attention. Many would be tempted to conclude that for centuries, history writing in China was subjugated to tradition. This, however, would not make sense.

Finally, contrary to Jack Goody's argument (1977), when a society starts using the written word to process the past, the "historians'" versions do not necessarily win out over the others. Goody maintains that in the oral mode, whether or not a version of the past is valid apparently depends on the social authority invested in whoever transmits it and, consequently, establishes it as tradition. With writing, comparisons between different accounts would become possible and critical discussion would gradually, spontaneously become the norm. A historical proposition's truthfulness could be assessed independently of the context and writing would ensure history's triumph over tradition. However, the situation Maurice Bloch (1989) describes in Madagascar contradicts these assumptions. The elders are socially authorized to possess knowledge and to speak, and writing is basically used to put down on paper what they have to say. The traditional, oral mode of recording the past made the transition to writing without an accompanying change in the style of discourse. Tradition is passed down by both the spoken and the written word.

In an article that focuses more narrowly on the Zafimaniry people Bloch (1993) emphasized the plurality of narrative forms in Madagascar. First there is what might be called the edifying narrative (*tantara*), in which the events are related for no reason other than to impart a moral lesson. The past is a teacher of life. Second, in the legendary narrative (*anganon*) there is no claim that the reported facts have any historical value whatsoever. They are about the mythical past. Lastly, Bloch stresses, there is one kind of narrative that does not come under the scope of any particular term. These accounts aim for truthfulness and tell what actually happened. The summary of price fluctuations on local markets falls into this category of narrative, which is similar in spirit to Western history. Writing has been steadily spreading since being introduced to Madagascar in the early nineteenth century.

For a long time it was used only to record *tantara* narratives. According to our criteria, this is an odd situation. To the observer, the written "historical" account has all the signs of an ahistorical conception of the future. The oral narration of past events is what reveals that a genuinely historical time takes root in the collective mind.

On the side of tradition

Associating history writing with a single model of historical consciousness is clearly, at the very least, a risky endeavor. The relationship between the written word and the past, which can be understood through a historiographical system, is not necessarily foremost in the collective mind at a given moment. As Finley (1971) recalls, it would be wrong to equate this relationship to the past with a cultural conception of history in the singular. The historian is not the people's spokesman, nor have they elected him/her to manage their historical memory. Furthermore, societies that write their own history, however they do it, have very different ways of "experiencing" and "living in" it.

Western society claims that each of its members is in exclusive possession of a particular model of historical consciousness, even though it has been developed in highly specialized universities and research institutes. Based on this model, and with the help of contrasts, we claim the ability to describe cultural conceptions of history in societies without historiography. In short, we react in the following way. Since these societies do not write their history, they probably do not have our self-attributed capacities, which are closely connected to the existence of history-as-science. These skills include the ability to tell the difference between myth and historical reality, to analyze events and to establish the past as the past, that is, as something separate from the present. Since judging the past is the same as judging oneself, these societies are viewed as incapable of separating from their origins and, as Thomas Mann put it, "working on themselves." In short, societies that do not write their history are regarded as lacking historical consciousness. They turn their past into tradition.

In the early twentieth century Robert Lowie (1917) vigorously defended this position when he strongly denied that primitive man is endowed with historical sense or perspective. Lowie based his argument on the fact that the oral tradition does not reveal the kind of data required by history writing. He takes as an example the introduction of the horse among the Assiniboine. The event was recent, since it occurred in the early years of the nineteenth century. Yet the Assiniboine's tradition sets the episode in an indeterminate, mythical past. Amerindians certainly retain facts from the past, but not as bearers of historical meaning. Therefore they do not have a historian's (historical) consciousness. Their "history" is no more history than their astronomy represents a contribution to the Western study of heavenly bodies.

Surely no anthropologist would be satisfied with the grounds and the conclusion of the logical argument developed by Lowie. Many books have since been written on how the oral tradition is used for the purposes of historical knowledge. However, the nature of historical consciousness in societies that do not write their history is a question that has been answered in many different and often equivocal ways. The notion of ethnohistory offers a perfect example of this ambiguity because it refers to history written by anthropologists but from the standpoint of the people being studied, according to their categories and within the framework of their historical "epistemology." The point is obviously to determine to what extent the ethnohistorian might misinterpret a radically different usage of the past and turn it into history. Of course I do not claim to be fully examining the question of whether or not societies that do not write their history have a historical consciousness. An entire book on the subject would not be enough. I would simply like to stress that the problems that arise when dealing with this issue probab-ly stem from how they are put and from the concepts that are used, especially that of historical consciousness. These questions in fact already include their answer.

First of all, it must be recalled that all human societies possess a sense of the past precisely because they are human. The semantic experience of time varies from one culture to another, but the lived experience of time certainly does not.[13] For example, people living in a society where the past is not referred to with a specific term do not mix up yesterday and today or confuse the meal they had last night and the one they are looking forward to this evening. Yet having a sense of the past does not mean possessing a historical consciousness and showing evidence of a cultural conception of *history*. In other words, spotting temporal markers in a society's cultural repertory (narratives and rites) is not enough to conclude that they "write" history their own (traditional) way. Completing a ritual act or summing up a cosmogony could be regarded as historical practices only at the risk of making a conceptual generalization. Not all accounts of the past are an exercise in history.

That said, it would be just as wrong to infer the lack of a historical consciousness from a society's mythical discourse. The divide between myth and history is not exclusively found in societies that write their past.[14] Anthropologists specializing in the study of West African States emphasize that the distinction between myth and history is just as essential for us, although we grant a truth value to the latter that we do not recognize in the former (Adler 1987). Michel Izard wrote of his own research, where history plays a large part, "I came to history because every social institution which I planned to study was weighed down not only with historicity, of course, but also with a historiality produced by the historicizing consciousness of people. *They* are the ones who led me to history in the first place" (Izard 1992a).

In these societies oral traditions, that is narratives, spoken genealogies and lists of dynasties, connect the past to the present, but to Western minds they do not guarantee enough objectivity. Their past does not acquire the degree of reality we ascribe to our own, which is based on a system of written accounts and documents that are the undeniable proof of its existence. Their past is murky to *us*, according to our criteria, but not to *them*, according to theirs. This is where our tendency to reject their history as legend comes from.

Their past is clear to them. Izard shows that the traditional discourse on the past is rooted in a space "conceived as an interweaving network of fixed milestones, monuments and sites. All of them are places where memory has accumulated and where messages are sent and received, to the point where one could speak of an 'oral' literature and an 'oral' epigraphy" (Izard 1992b). Renato Rosaldo made a similar observation about the Ilongot people in the Philippines when he wrote, "Whether about the shared or the unseen past, Ilongot recollections are located intelligibly through what could be called the spatialization of time" (1980: 55). Reading space is thus a method of historical enunciation. The places that speak of the past—and that make the past speak—and relate it to the present are not set once and for all. They are landmarks and clues, established as such and processed by an active memory. They are the answer to questions and the results of a historical survey. Space used in such a way is both an archive and a continually created "narrative." But just try and present a place to a panel of historians!

The excess of meaning in our notion of historical consciousness gives the discussion another twist here. A concept of such far-reaching scope naturally raises a problem. Scholars will agree that a society which does not write its history has the ability to tell the difference between myth and reality. It can target the real past, and not just receive it, by organizing its memory and creating media on which the products of knowledge are inscribed. But is this reason to talk about a historical past? Is the past detached enough from the present and left behind like an "outside object," or is it commented upon from within the tradition of memory? Tradition processing history is one thing. Tradition processing history as history is quite another.

To make this issue clear, let us turn to the work of a native North American author. The book is significantly entitled *For an Amerindian Autohistory* (Sioui 1992). In Sioui's view, choosing the term *autohistory* implies that the form of thought guiding Western historical discourse (which he calls heterohistory) has nothing to do with native North American historical consciousness. Sioui dedicates his book to "All our ancestors who speak through us." No Western historian would ever offer such a dedication because one aim of the historian's discourse is, in a way, to break with the ancestors' spoken word and to demonstrate the otherness of the past. Sioui does not assert, as others do, that historical consciousness is foreign to the traditional pattern of Amerindian thought. But he writes that Amerindians do not consider history as a meaning that humans can confer on life. This sentence expresses the difference between our history—heterohistory to Amerindians, according to Sioui—, and their history—ethnohistory to us. Ours puts distance between the past and present. Theirs sets the past in the present by interpreting the course of history with the help of a perennial cultural code. We would consider this to be anachronism, a major sin for a historian. Sioui believes that our historical discourse on non-Western cultures conveys the myth of evolution and of history-as-process. For us, "the past is not definitively set until it no longer has a future" (Aron 1961). According to Sioui, the Amerindians' past always lies *before* them. Following his argument leads to recognizing that "each society has its own historicity," especially when the conflict between tradition *(them)* and history *(us)* comes to the fore again.

Let us follow the logical argument on these grounds. Suppose the past is never over—at least in the official version provided by the culture—for "historians" of societies that do not write their history. It logically follows that the past could never be the subject of critical discussion or debate because it is never left behind. Strangely, anthropologists who most strongly endorse the position that non-Western "historiographical" thought exists provide their opponents with ammunition. For example, Richard Price (1983) attributes to the Saramaka of Surinam the same historical consciousness as ours. They apparently have the concepts of event and historical causality, select facts and critique oral sources. Price asserts that they want to tell, as Ranke puts it," what actually was." However, the Saramaka's awareness of the past is a secret knowledge reserved for just a small handful of men. It was acquired alone at certain special moments and, most importantly, is carefully kept within the circle of initiates because it is considered highly active and dangerous.[15] Therefore each Saramaka historian has his own version of the past. He would never think of comparing it to the others' versions, or of sharing and making it available to everyone so that they can judge it for themselves. In the same way, the Ilongot people described by Rosaldo (1980) who are the individual possessors of a historical consciousness, do not attempt to fit knowledge into a standardized collective history. The order of history apparently rules out dialogue, which is the only way to achieve perspective outside traditional memory.

A comparison between *us* and *them* conducted in these terms leads to one conclusion. If societies that do not write their history produce narratives about the past that are exempt from critical scrutiny, then these narratives cannot assume the function of reflexivity that we associate with historical consciousness. In this sense, their history is tradition not because it is oral or undeveloped, but because it is shut off inside a lived relationship to the past and consequently to itself. The logical argument runs more or less as follows. Since Hegel we have known that there is a close relationship between the "structure of historicity" and the "structure of self-knowledge." So discussing the past means discussing one's own self-determination, one's roots and, therefore, oneself. Not discussing it means not being able to separate from oneself. Our history is a liberating form of communication with the past. Through it we are able to analyze our own experience. Their history is nothing more than a dialogue with the self. Tradition is not subjected to critical judgement.

By way of a conclusion

Admittedly, anthropological research on societies that do not write their history has not contributed much to invalidating the conclusion to which the logical argument we have expounded leads. Very few anthropologists have demonstrated the existence of a critical space within these cultures. Everything suggests that when dealing with them we are celebrating an "art" we thought was lost: inheriting without benefit of an inventory.

The great divide discourse has been criticized scores of times. The rift will continue cropping up—sometimes without its proponents being aware of it—until we know more about it. Kant said that cutting a conglomeration of heterogeneous things in half does not lead to any specific concept. Our historical consciousness is a conglomeration of parts that can be linked together only by discourse. By setting up a total opposition between it and that of other cultures, we probably not only come to wrong conclusions about them, but deceive ourselves as well. One is the consequence of the other.

Notes

1. Writing the long-term history of a society amounts to considering that, despite centuries of transformation, this society has preserved something changeless, an essence, of which little may remain beyond the proper noun that it has been given. France is and always will be France. Notice, by the way, that this postulated essence can be grasped only through a description of how it changes, which then becomes the "realization or actualization of its hidden potentials" (Popper 1957). Everyone unhesitatingly agrees that France is several centuries old but in that case the conclusion that medieval society carried the germ of modern industrial society must follow. Ethnologists are saying the same thing when they establish an essence of identity between a people before they were colonized, for example, and the same people today. Yet is it the *same* society and the *same* culture?
2. Almost all quotations from French and German authors have been translated into English. Therefore only quotations from English and American authors are fully referenced.
3. Renaissance thinkers dealt with the lessons to be drawn from the past in two opposite ways. Montaigne argued that history could teach us nothing because it could not be generalized, while Jean Bodin maintained that the past must act as a guide for action (Koselleck 1985). Ancients and Moderns in late seventeenth-century Paris belonged to the same culture but did not go to the same salons.
4. Hans R. Jauss (1982) usefully emphasizes the distinction between a literary work's effect, which remains determined by the work and is experienced by the person coming into contact with it, and how it is received by an active and free reader. In this sense the establishment of a tradition has to do with an attitude of reception.
5. For a lively critique of this idea see the work by Paul Veyne (1971). Veyne argues that the question of the genesis of history is a "false problem", a "purely philological problem" and a "point of literary history". He maintains that the birth of historiography does not follow from the "self-consciousness of human groups." According to Veyne, historiography is a *"narrowly* cultural event that does not imply a new attitude towards historicity." We will come back to this point later.
6. See R. Lowie (1917, 167) who remarks that "Our own historical perspective is only a slowly and painfully acquired product of recent years."
7. This passage is found in book VIII of the *Odyssey*.

8. An astonished Englishman commented, "How strangely some words lose their primitive sense. By a critick was originally understood a good judge; with us nowadays it signifies no more than a Fault Finder" (quoted by Koselleck 1985).
9. The changing meaning of the word "revolution" is an example of this. It ceases to signify a circular movement with a regular return and now describes an irreversible, and therefore incomparable, upheaval leading to a future that must be both predicted and created.
10. Momigliano argues that if studies on the ancient Hebrews and Greeks' "conceptions of time" turned out to be true, Herodotus should have been born on the banks of the river Jordan and the Greeks would have waited for the Messiah. Momigliano also points out that Homer, saying that the oracle Chalcas "knows the present, future and past," foresaw the "discovery" of time in Greece by two centuries.
11. Paul Veyne (1971) takes issue with this point of view: "Whatever the age, 'primitive' no less than civilized men have always known that their destiny would in part made of it through their action." The reason, he argues, is that action does not encompass knowledge of the past. Better still, action does not make use of this knowledge. In 1873 Nietzsche criticized the German people's consuming passion for history in *Considérations inactuelles*. He asserted that "any action requires forgetting." According to Veyne this is a wrong requirement because forgetfulness is acquired at the moment of action. This is probably true of action, but what about its program?
12. As early as 1988 history exams were suspended in the former USSR, old textbooks taken out of circulation and new ones promised but never finished.
13. From the fact that "no two peoples live conceptually in precisely the same kind of time." A. I. Hallowell (1937, 647) incorrectly concluded, "It is impossible to assume that man is born with any innate temporal sense." The semantic experience of time (temporal concepts) is not the reflection of lived temporality (temporal sense).
14. Written history sometimes gives credence to myths and even enshrines them in school textbooks. For example, the Ceausescu regime fostered the myth that Roumanians descended from Dacia. As a result Roumanian archaeologists went to tremendous lengths to find traces of that ancient civilization.
15. Paul Valéry (1930) expressed similar views when he remarked that "History is the most hazardous substance ever developed by the chemistry of the mind." The historian Paul Veyne replied, "History is one of the most harmless products ever developed by the chemistry of the mind. It takes the value and the passion out of things..." (Veyne 1971).

5

On Some Uses of the Past in Native American Art and Art History

Christian F. Feest

In the following paper, I will discuss some of the changes that have occurred in the uses of the past by Native peoples of North America as well as by those who study them, especially in connection with the production of visual forms. I will argue that these changes in the perception of the past and of diachronic processes have in a large measure been the result of the creation of datable records of events and products.

Rare and Other Art Traditions

The past decade, in particular, has seen an increasing preoccupation with the visual productions of indigenous peoples by art historians. On different levels of analysis, this trend illustrates the increasing claim of modern nation states to the heritage of the indigenous peoples, and of a transformation of the subject matter of Native arts by assimilation to a set of modes of perception which place a central value on their historicity. Although the incorporation of Native artistic traditions is often based on an ideology of multiculturalism, this very concept is, of course, as much culturally constituted within the dominant society, as are the modes of perception and analysis, for which art historians generally claim universal validity.

On closer look, however, Western art historical discourse has origin-ated as part of the same historical process that has transformed indigenous visual productions into the subject matter of art history. In his *The Rare Art Traditions*, Joseph Alsop (1982) has demonstrated that the conceptualization of art in Western culture (as well as in a handful of other historic cultures) owes its origin to the practice of systematic collecting. Collecting is based on the assignment of an inherent value to form where the value is determined by the form's "rarity" or limited availability, which in turn can be defined on the basis of individual excellence or genius, antiquity, or foreign origin (or distance in space, time, and kind). Such collecting not only results in the disjunction of form and function, of art and crafts; but it leads to the preservation of visual forms under artificial circumstances, such as in museums. It also provides an incentive for the creation of markets, in which the value is expressed in economic terms (including super prices for the unique), which in turn encourages the specialized production of valued visual forms by a new class of artists, as well as the production of falsifications, which are inconceivable as long as man-made things have a value determined mainly by their usefulness. More importantly, the systematic preservation of forms provides the basis for reflections on now observable changes over time, including the reevaluation of past styles.

There seems to be no evidence for any collecting of artifacts based on the assignment of value to form in Native North America prior to an intensive exposure to the Western rare art tradition. While excellence of form was valued, it apparently never led to a disjunction from function. It would, however, be misleading to overlook other forms of collecting for which evidence exists in some Native American cultures. The accumulation and preservation of regularly displayed visual expressions of the privileges of kinship groups by various peoples of the Northwest Coast may serve as an example for the valuation of artifacts because of their *meaning*. Although such preservation did not lead to the side effects described for the Western rare art tradition, it may have offered carvers the opportunity to measure up to and be inspired by the achievements of the past (and help explain the remarkable stability of the basic principles of the highly formalized Northwest Coast style for more than two millennia). This tradition of preservation, however, did not necessarily inspire Northwest Coast people with a pronounced respect for old artifacts on account of their age. The objects obtained in 1778 at Nootka on James Cook's Third Voyage appear to have been mostly (by Western standards) venerable, old objects, which were traded to the English because they were damaged, old, or of foreign origin, and thus of lesser value.

Similar situations may be expected among other sedentary peoples, as in the Southeast, where Europeans caught a brief glimpse of the last vestiges of prehistoric chiefdoms and city states. There are seventeenth-century reports about the presence of treasure houses among the Algonquians of coastal Virginia, in which the rulers not only kept the tributes exacted from the commoners, but also artifacts valued for other than economic reasons (see Feest 1978). It may be assumed that these objects included products of exotic raw materials whose widespread estimation is well documented. At least in part, the value attributed to the *material* provided the rationale for the preservation of artifacts.

Such forms of collecting based on values associated with meaning or material do not so much correspond with the practice of contemporary European museums, but rather with medieval treasuries.

On the other hand there are, especially from the realm of ritual arts, numerous examples for the purposeful destruction of visual forms. Among the irrigation-farming Pueblo peoples of the arid Southwest and their Navajo neighbors dry paintings continue to be destroyed; Pueblo mural paintings in the kivas are whitewashed immediately after use, and masks are repainted for each appearance of the kachina impersonators (Wyman 1983, 32-33, 204-5). Zuni figures of the twin war gods (an artifact type much cherished for its modernist form by twentieth-century Euro-American art collectors) are left to the elements to rot and be replaced by new images (Merrill et al. 1993, 524-25). Even though such was not the case with painted Pueblo pottery, there appears to be no evidence that prior to the late nineteenth-century potters were inspired by the designs they must have encountered on old pots or potsherds.

Due to the indivisibility of form and function, artifacts were generally used until worn out, and then recycled or discarded. The hard soles of Plains moccasins were often made from pieces of worn-out painted parfleches, whose designs (or what had accidentally remained of them on the cut-out soles) were soon no longer visible.

Since the life span of artifacts could range from a few hours to many years, there were always enough contemporary models around, but generally few older examples (see Feest 1992a, 419-20). Thus, there was little opportunity, and probably also little interest, in reflections about the development of visual forms.

When visual forms of exotic origin first entered the Western art historical discourse in the nineteenth century, they were regarded—in keeping with the conjectural history approach favored by early anthropology—as representing early forms of the artistic expressions of mankind. It was assumed that they had little or not at all developed since time immemorial. What recent changes brought about by Euro-American influence were acknowledged, were seen as lamentable aberrations from the course of primeval purity. Directors of ethnographic museums were often reluctant to accept such evidence of "acculturation" into their collection and even discarded such items which had been inadvertently received from patrons willing to part with their travel souvenirs.

Such sentiments relating to the value of unblemished savagery were clearly shared by the modernist European and American artists of the early twentieth century, who found inspiration and legitimization for their own work in the assumed primeval nature of what was generally called "primitive art" (see Rubin 1984). These artists and their customers ultimately paved the way for the transformation of exotic artifacts, which by their incorporation into museums had already become artifacts of the Western culture of collecting, into non-Western art.

Although Franz Boas (1908) had used methods of internal reconstruction to demonstrate the stylistic changes in Alaska Eskimo ivory needle cases and although archaeology was compiling compelling evidence for such changes in prehistoric times all over the continent, the recognition of the historic nature of all Native American art was very slow in coming. One of the reasons for this phenomenon, it may be assumed, was the fact that the large ethnographic collections amassed by American museums in the late nineteenth and early twentieth century reflected mainly the work of a single generation, and thus were not conducive to the perception and study of changing visual forms.

Even those Native American artists, who during the same period of time began to be trained by White teachers to serve the evolving Southwestern regional ethnic art market, were encouraged to conform to certain, however constructed, expectations about their unfailing commitment to ancestral conventions.

The ultimate transformation of Native American artifacts into Native American art and as such into the body of the Western rare art tradition came only with their transfer from ethnographic museums, where artifacts were primarily used to illustrate culturally specific functions or, at best, the unity of form and function, to art museums, where they were considered and displayed as mostly self-explanatory formal statements. This was accompanied by a parallel move from flea markets with prices in the curio range to the major auction houses with prices in the fine art range, and by the gradual development of connoisseurship, which found its expression in the willingness to pay substantially higher sums for the older and rarer pieces.

This metamorphosis of artifacts into works of art was also marked by the interest ultimately taken in Native American art by art historians, who were gradually widening their perspective beyond the formerly narrow limits of their discipline to include, first, the arts of Asian and American civilizations, second, Western popular and trivial arts, and finally, tribal arts. Just as the rise of market values may be seen as a necessary function of the insatiable growth of the art market, which finally ran out of affordable Old Masters, the increasing art historical interest not only followed the lead supplied by the prestige accompanying the high prices, but also reflects the rapidly growing number of art historians who were overcrowding the limited research potentials of a closed canon. Be that as it may, the situation is well illustrated by the example of moose-hair embroidered birchbark items, which earlier in this century the director of the ethnographic museum in Hamburg had deaccessioned from the collection as "modern." Thanks in part to the Canadian government's Native art repatriation policy of the 1970s, such items today fetch prices of several hundred dollars and have become the subject matter of high-brow art historical discourse (Phillips 1991). Obviously, the Euro-American world has discovered the value of the Native American past.

It should be stressed that, to this day, visual forms produced by Native Americans are *not* the product of an indigenous rare art tradition, but of either one of a variety of other such traditions (which I have elsewhere defined as common, ritual, and craft art traditions; see Feest 1992b, 196-97; 1993, 11-15) equally defined by their side-effects, or of the professional *Western* rare art tradition, in which some, but by no means all Native peoples participate today. This becomes apparent if we look at the markets and institutions which define certain products as rare (or in the common usage of Euro-American art critics, "real") arts. The recent emergence of Native American-owned and operated museums may indicate a change in a new direction, although the current repatriation debate with its primary focus on reburial and return of objects to ritual decay illustrates the equivocal nature of the situation (Fuller and Fabricius 1992; Feest 1995). Because they have come to share the Euro-American perception of tradition as something surviving from the past, few, if any, of these Native American museums have started to collect the work of their "artists" in a Western sense.

Rare and Other History Traditions

For the sake of comparison and in order to provide cross-cultural perspective on the concept of "history," let us briefly compare the rise of what I will call "rare history traditions" (of which the Euro-American one will most concern us here) with that of the rare art traditions. Rare history traditions are based on the selective preservation of written documents, which by the very act of preservation become records of the past. Rare history traditions are thus based on the knowledge of writing by which events are reified rather than memorized, and by their ultimate disjunction from the context in which they have occurred. Rare history traditions also result in the establishment of archives, the rise of document forgery, and the development of systematic historiography.

The absence of this specific mode of looking at the past from the majority of the cultures of this world (see Müller 1993, 17) has given rise to the mistaken notion of a dichotomy between peoples with history and peoples without history, who live in world dominated by myth. This distinction is not really dichotomous, because it overlooks both the presence of strictly speaking non-historical uses of the past in societies in which rare history traditions are present (about which more in a moment), as well as the presence of non-mythical approaches to the past in societies which lack writing.

An often-cited example for a mythical, non-Western conception of time is Benjamin Lee Whorf's discussion of the different construction of time in the language of the Hopi of Arizona. Other than Indo-European languages, for example, the Hopi language lacks tense distinctions in verbs objectifying time into past, present, and future, it treats phases of cycles (such as seasons or parts of the day) as a separate world-class of "temporals," which cannot be pluralized or used with cardinal numbers such as nouns denoting physical objects, and it does not express duration through metaphors of space (Carroll 1956, 134-59). This was widely understood to mean that the Hopi were unable to distinguish between past, present, and future, and especially between the reality of the presence and the myths of the past. The representation of the mythical past in the ritual present is indeed a feature of Hopi ceremonial practice, but cannot be used as an indication of the timelessness of their thought. From a purely linguistic point of view, Ekkehart Malotki (1983) has since supplied all the evidence needed to refute the overdrawn conclusions of the Whorfians.

Among the stereotypes about Native Americans prevailing in North

America, one that is lovingly cultivated by Native Americans themselves, relates to the existence of a pan-Indian concept of time that differs from that of Euro-Americans. "Indian time" is indeed a favorite excuse by which not being on time is explained in terms of traditional culture, although it much rather is an act of indigenous resistance against the stressful regulations of time in Western industrial societies, than a result of the absence of a concept of time. "Mohawks were always on time!" Ric Glazer Danay, the Mohawk artist and Native American Studies professor tells his students who try to get away with being late by referring to "Indian time." It also hardly makes sense to contrast a Western progressive "linear" time concept with a Native American one that is "cyclical" and non-directional. Cyclical features are strongly present even in highly industrialized Western societies, whereas linear elements also occur in Native American constructions of time. Differences in this respect are quantitative rather than qualitative.

Even in the past, various Native American groups have made produced more or less permanent records of events. Some of these are, to use Jack Goody's (1977, 90-91) useful distinction, "event-dominated," whereas others qualify as "calendar-dominated." Event-dominated documents include Plains Indian pictorial war records which served to validate personal deeds of bravery in a social context; as they ceased to be of importance after the owner's death, they were not preserved beyond that point (see e.g. Vatter 1927; Ewers 1939; Brownstone 1993, 10-11). Historical markers, such as stone heaps constructed to commemorate important events, should also be mentioned here (Flannery 1939, 109; Feest 1974, 157). Wampum belts, whose generally abstract designs of white and purple shell beads were used by the Iroquois and their neighbors in the northeastern Woodlands to validate and commemorate mostly political statements or agreements, may be seen as portable historical markers, which were preserved and interpreted by specifically designated keepers of the wampum (see e.g. Speck 1919; Wilcox 1976).

Best known among the calendar-dominated documents from Native North America are the so-called "winter counts," best known from Lakota and Kiowa sources, in which a sequence of years ("winters") is established by a linear sequence of pictograms depicting the most memorable event of the time segment represented (Mooney 1898; Howard 1979; Wildhage 1988). In the same category must be placed the calendar sticks of the Papago of Arizona (Underhill 1938), and even the preserved chiefs' corpses of the southeastern Algonquians, which provided a permanent reminder of dynastic sequences, and which were kept in the same temples in which the priests maintained winter count-like records (Feest 1974, 157-58).[1]

Wherever they are found (and their distribution in Native North America was far from universal), such mnemographic records must have helped to stimulate more or less systematic reflection on the past. It should be noted, however, that such documents cannot be unequivocally "read" without the knowledge of an associated oral tradition. The same is true of mythographic records (such as the crest poles of the Northwest Coast [Barbeau 1950]), or ritual-dominated documents (such as birchbark scrolls or engraved wooden tablets [Dewdney 1975; Merrill 1945]). Such oral history traditions supported by non-writing records illustrate the fact that reflections about the past in non-literate societies are not necessarily of a mythical nature.

A brief look at some of the various classifications of oral traditions in different Native American cultures helps to underscore the importance of the need to differentiate between culturally specific oral genres (see Müller 1993, 15). Thus, the Cahuilla of southern California distinguish between "true stories" (including myths) and invented "tales" (Seiler 1970, 8), whereas the Ojibwa of the Great Lakes region differentiate between animate "sacred stories" and inanimate information on the lives of humans (Hallowell 1960, 56-57; see Ellis 1989). Among the neighboring Menominee the difference between the various forms of traditions was also spelled out by the compensation necessary for their delivery. Sacred myths demanded the payment of a substantial reward as well as tobacco offerings, invented stories could be had for a small token, whereas true events had to be told free of charge (Skinner and Satterlee 1915). In this case, the attribution of value depends upon the effort needed to preserve and reproduce the information.

But it would be equally mistaken to deny the validity of the distinction between the rare and oral history traditions (see Hochbruck 1991, 10-13) and their respective potentials. Preservation of historical knowledge even in the collective memory is limited by the capacity of the human brain; preservation in writing leads to permanent, immutable records—even if, as is commonly the case, *interpretations* of the documents change over time, the written records remain immutable, whereas oral traditions, because of their lack of reification and thus lack of distinction between form and function, tend to change with changing interpretations. The major difference is that rare history traditions leave a paper trail of changing interpretations, whereas oral traditions do not—except when recorded in contact situations with literate societies (see Richter 1993, 384-86).[2]

Just as Native American arts had been considered to be of timeless antiquity at the time of their admission to the art historical discourse, Native American societies were considered to be without history, passively living in mythic timelessness. Thus, their fatal encounter with Western Europe had seemingly made them "victims of history" and of historical "progress." It was only the rise of ethnohistory since the 1950s, using a blend of historical and anthropological sources and theoretical insights, which has restored Native Americans to their rightful place as *actors* in the historical narrative constructed by the Western rare history tradition. If mainstream history has been slow to accept this conclusion and to fully integrate it into its historiographic practice (see Richter 1993, 381-82), this cannot be blamed on inherent deficiencies of the rare history model (as increasingly claimed by Native American intellectuals such as Vine Deloria [1992] or Georges Sioui [1992]), but only on the stubborn ignorance of members of the profession.

The story does not end here, however. It has finally dawned upon philosophical historians or historians of consciousness, like Hayden White, that "in history, as in the social sciences in general, there is no way of pre-establishing what will count as a 'datum' and what will count as a 'theory' by which to 'explain' what the data 'mean'" (White 1973, 429; see Geertz 1991, 1). What is said here, in other words, is that "history" in the Western sense is not a universal, but a construct of our own culture. And so is "art," as we know it, without art historians having yet taken much note of the fact. Anthropologists should not be surprised, because this is what they have been claiming for some time. It is part of the paradigm of cultural relativism, that cultural constructions of reality are adequate to the needs of the societies which have come to share them, and that the only way not to get lost in this sea of relativity is the ethnocentric assertion of the exclusive or universal validity of one's own construction. Tolerance and respect for the otherness of other cultural constructs has indeed been cultural relativism's major contribution to a humanistic world view.

The loss of cultural innocence deriving from the recognition of the culturally constructed nature of "history" has finally led to what Danicl Richter (1993, 384) has recently called the "cultural zeitgeist traveling under the names of deconstruction, discourse theory, post-structuralism, and postmodernism," which claims (among many other things) that "documents that created white subjectivities cannot possibly tell us anything about Indian history." In denying not only the useful complementarity of the views from within and from without, but also of cross-cultural understanding, this attitude may ultimately best be considered solipsist.

The most important corollary of the culturally constructed nature of "history" is that the past is not necessarily conceptualized as "history." The past, which according to Max Weber (1981, 62-63) legitimates traditional authority by the postulation of a continuity from the past, can often be shown not to have been the past of history (see Hobsbawm and Ranger 1983)—but only within a rare history tradition based on the study of preserved written documents. The ethnographic record from North America supplies a number of interesting cases which allow us to study the mythification of historical events (see e.g. Kutsche 1963; Eggan 1967). There is ample evidence that the past of claimed tradition happily coexists with the past of recorded history in Western societies, whereas there can be no such distinction in what have been appropriately called "traditional societies."

By representing the past as the source of the legitimacy of their authority, these traditional societies have, in no small manner, contributed to the perception of their existence in a state of unchanging timelessness. Anthropology, as the Western scholarly discipline most specifically concerned with the study of "traditional" societies, has certainly helped to contribute to the misunderstanding of the problem involved here, by accepting the claims of tradition as historical facts. The word "tradition," as used in anthropology, thus often refers to cultural continuity rather than to claimed authority (see e.g. Willey and Phillips 1953, 146, who use it to integrate spatial and temporal dimensions). It would indeed be useful if the two phenomena could be clearly distinguished.

Somes Uses of the Past

None of the following examples illustrating some uses of the past in Native American art is particularly new. Drawn from a wide range of cases, they do not claim to represent all possible aspects of the question, but will hopefully elucidate some of the points made above.

One of the earliest documented cases of the resurrection of an already discontinued design style by a Native American craftsperson is the revival of Hopi pottery by the Hano potter Nampeyo (c. 1860-1942). The circumstances of this revival are generally known. At a time, when Hopi pottery had lost most of its traditional functions and had developed into a sloppily made ware for sale to low-budget tourists,

Nampeyo's husband Lesou was hired in 1895 to help in Jesse Walter Fewkes excavations of the ruins of Sikyatki. While it appears that Nampeyo had previously been experimenting with designs from Pueblo II and III pots, she now became interested in the fifteenth-century Sikyatki sherds and used them as an inspiration for a very personal new style of pottery (Hough 1917; Ashton 1976). Prehistoric pot sherds were commonly encountered in Hopi country, yet there is no indication that prior to Nampeyo anyone had ever before been inspired by their designs. It appears that the obvious value placed by White anthropologists on broken pieces of ancient pots made all the difference. This fact does not in the least belittle Nampeyo's achievement in creating a very successful style of pottery, highly prized by White collectors; it just demonstrates, how the value placed on the (pre)historic past by Whites served the Hano potter as an encouragement to use *this* past to legitimize a new tradition, which was not only picked up by some other potters of Nampeyo's days, but was further developed by several generations of her family, and used in easel painting by her relative Dan Namingha (see Barsook et al. 1974, 17-41). The success of Nampeyo's Sikyatki revival also led to similiar developments in other pueblos.

Just a few years before Nampeyo embarked upon her career, Tomah Joseph (1837-1914), a Passamaquoddy of Maine, had innovated northeastern Algonquian birchbark sgraffito by switching from the traditional floralistic-geometrial patterns to narrative drawings, partly based upon origin myths. Like in the Nampeyo case, the recognition of the possible value of, in this case, traditional *content* came from exposure to the White man's interest in it. In 1882, Tomah Joseph had served as one of Charles Leland's informants for his *The Algonquian Legends of New England* (1884), for which Tomah also provided illustrations in bark sgraffito, which were redrawn by Leland for publication (Lester 1993, 9). To identify this mythical past as "history," however, has been the privilege and mistake of the late twentieth century (Lester 1993, 4, 18, note 1).

Another Hopi case is that of Fred Kabotie (1900-1995), whose early work as a painter can readily be characterized as naive painting, within the usual range typical for the early Santa Fe School. His growing interest in past Southwestern traditions of painting is, for example, expressed in his 1949 book *Designs from the Ancient Mimbreños*, a volume with reproductions of prehistoric designs, in which Kabotie offered "the feelings and responses which come *instinctively* from one who has lived in that culture" (Tanner 1973, 226). While there is at least partial cultural continuity between the prehistoric cultures dealt with, the strong notion of continuity, of past as present, is remarkable. Even before that, in the late 1930s, Kabotie had been involved in the interpretation of the prehistoric murals excavated at Awatovi (Smith 1952, xvi). Kabotie later occasionally used the prehistoric mural style in his own works, as for example in "Germinator," a painting on buckskin. Clara Lee Tanner relates, how the Anglo press in reproducing the picture would relate how the artist "had killed the deer, tanned the hide, and painted the picture. With a twinkle in his eye," writes Tanner, "Kabotie ended his story—'And I *bought* that buckskin for $45.00!'" (Tanner 1973, 227-28). Clearly, the journalist had looked at the painting as traditional not only in style and subject matter, but also in its creation, whereas the artist drawing from his past-is-present tradition had fulfilled a commission within the framework of the Western rare art tradition.

Between 1935 and 1941 Ernest Smith (1907-1975), a self-taught Seneca painter from Tonawanda Reservation in up-state New York, produced a series of more than 240 paintings and drawings depicting traditional Iroquois life as part of a project financed by the Temporary Emergency Relief Administration. The set, which is preserved in the Rochester Museum and Science Center, includes scenes ranging from events set in mythical times to generic portraits of people in nineteenth-century Iroquois dress. Critical viewers will have the least problems with the depiction of the story of Sky Woman or of a mother dressed in beaded cloth costume holding a cradleboard; the first, after all, may be seen as a rendition of an inner view of an ongoing indigenous belief, the second as showing an historical reality accessible to the artist through personal observation. But what about the depiction of flint mining, hunting with bow and arrows, or even a lacross game with players not dressed in the fashion of contemporary lacrosse players, but in those of an imagined past? Although the Senecas had not mined flint or hunted with bow and arrows for at least two centuries, the prevailing idea was (and to a large extent continues to be) that Indians must necessarily be the best authority on any Native American subject matter. The fact that they are indeed generally not particularly knowledgeable about remote historic periods of their own people's culture does not make such fanciful depictions as Smith's less interesting. As perceptions of the past they are just as interesting cultural documents as the depiction of Sky Woman—one only should not expect them to be reliable documents for a historical ethnography of past centuries.

Gerald Tailfeathers, a Blood from Alberta, born in 1925, represents the sizeable, but often overlooked class of Native American painters, whose style—even less than the of Smith—displays no discernible trace of Indianness. Tailfeathers's use of the past is clearly limited to subject matter, which includes buffalo hunts, warfare, camplife, and other scenes from a traditional past. One might nevertheless describe this style as a traditional Blackfoot style of the twentieth century, especially since Tailfeathers (who for some years had de-Indianized his name to Gerald T. Feathers) had been inspired to paint by his uncle Two Gun, who himself had been a self-taught Western-style painter (Dempsey 1978).

Almost the opposite is true, on the other hand, for Randy Lee White, whose work has been described as a "one-man revival of the pictographic art used by the Plains Indians in Winter Counts and ledger drawings" (Houle 1982, 75). In fact, White has expanded the revived historic style of painting to produce paintings that are often non-traditional in subject matter. Born in 1951 on the Lower Brule reservation in South Dakota "of Indian, English, and Spanish heritage," White grew up outside the Native American community network. Because of this marginalization, his Lakota identity has been questioned, and he is one of the artists having problems passing the "Indianness" test of the American Indian Arts and Craft Act of 1990, despite having been "revealed as a living bridge, connecting past to present" (McCoy 1986, 33, 69). His work, which is featured in many books on contemporary Indian art, has also been characterized as "visionary" and "rooted in the culture of North America's Plains Indians" (McCoy 1986, 1). But is it a reflection of an ongoing tradition, or is the easily recognized style lifted from the past nothing more than a fig leaf to cover the artist's identity problem or even a marketing device to gain access to a legally protected market?

Other artists have also made use of the stylistic conventions of ledger art. Olivia Skenandore, who despite her name identifies as an Oglala, illustrates the use of different pasts from within the universe of Native American traditions. At least some of her works based on the late nineteenth-century Plains painting style are executed in the recent Navajo sandpainting-on-board technique, which Skenandore picked up as a student at the Institute of American Indian Art in Santa Fe. In addition, works like her "Warrior with Wife and Extra Horse" revive the traditional subject matter together with the style—what is untraditional is the "feminist" inroad on styles and themes formerly in the male domain. Conversely, Bob Boyer, a Cree from Saskatchewan, often uses Plains parfleche designs—a female art form—in his paintings. The lack of a discernible relationship between the designs and the titles (e.g. "Cahokia") may be interpreted as another indication of a constructed pan-Indian past, in which highly selective features of heterogeneous "traditions" are recombined (Houle 1982, 20).

No obvious relationship between the imagery and the painter's Navajo background is discernible in the paintings of Emmi Whitehorse. Yet, the artist has cited "the influence of her grandmother's shepherding and weaving—the 'causal equating of nature and geometry'" as a major influence on her work. "'As I move along in my carreer, it's like opening a door and stepping into another room,' wrote Whitehorse in 1985. 'But I always keep the imprint of my traditional values as I go'" (Lippard 1991). The situation is similar in the case of most abstract Native American painters, where the artists' assertions about the traditional roots of their work is usually more vocal than visual. One is reminded of Dorothy Dunn's claim that American Indians, after all, had invented abstract painting—at least as far as America was concerned (Dunn 1968: xxvi).

Is Randy Lee White's revival of ledger art more reminiscent of Nampeyo's achievement or rather of the mining of the "primitive art" resource by modernist artists of the Euro-American tradition? All three developments were made possible by the preservation and valuation by Euro-American culture of visual forms of expression of other cultures. The availability of such preserved forms to Nampeyo was limited to those of a tradition which in fact was ancestral to her own. The range of forms was much wider at the Trocadero Museum in Paris, when Picasso and his colleagues decided to invoke the "primitive" as a universally ancestral tradition. White and his contemporaries, however, not only have access to literally all that was ever created by mankind (including works of the Western rare art tradition), they now also have a choice of identities, ethnic or otherwise.

It can be argued that the traditional past has always served as an inspiration to the producers of visual forms of expression, even before they were categorized as "artists." It is, however, in the century since Nampeyo's Sikyatki pottery revival, that Native American artists' uses of the historic past have become very widespread. This is especially the case of artists of the younger generations, who aspire to succeed outside the narrow confines of the regional "Indian art markets," that is, in the world of "real art" (as mistakenly defined in universalistic terms by the Western rare art tradition), and obviously feel a special need—in the words of their colleague Robert Houle (1982, 5)—"to reaffirm one of the most important aspects of native cultures, the capacity to harness revolutionary ideas into agents of change, revitalizing tradition." In the late twentieth century, it is impossible, especially for those who leave their community to go to art school, not to be exposed to and make use of both he visual heritage of their own cultures and of the generalized, but impossible "Native American culture" as preserved by the Western tradition of collecting. For these artists, tradition is constructed through a combination of references to the experience of a living past, and often more importantly—or at least more visibly—to the constructed knowledge of a historic past. Those, for whom the authority of the past as tradition can no longer offer an unquestioned identity, must necessarily turn to the past as history as an alternative.

Notes

1. Brotherston (1990) is another compilation of data on Native American chronographic records. It errs, however, not only by accepting the largely fraudulent *Walam Olum*, once believed to be a Delaware epic, as genuine, but also by overinterpreting designs as chronographic in the absence of documentary evidence on a purely speculative basis.
2. For a different view of "representations of pastness" see Tonkin 1992.

6

Marketing Magic: Process, Identity and the Creation and Selling of Native Art

J.C.H. King

This paper takes an initial look at some of the native or native-style souvenir industries in North America. The issues behind the development of these industries are complicated, but of vital importance for a range of interconnected reasons. Part of this arises because of the way in which tourism may be seen as a major process which mediates between native and non-native people. Tourism, and tourists, penetrate much further into remote areas than for instance did any army in the nineteenth century. As a pervasive activity tourism engages the attention of, not merely aggregate native communities providing tourist facilities, but also that of the individual, home-based, artist or craftworker servicing that industry. In that old joke tourists travel away from home to see something different—and then complain when everything is not the same. Or, rather in the case of North America, the tourist complains if the apparently favourable stereotypes of natives are not to hand—in the form of souvenirs, museums and cultural experiences. For the tourist reality must always reflect expectations. In tourism souvenirs have a vital role, acting to condense reality and so strengthen by simplification. As a dominant industry, tourism provides a paradigm for the framing and freezing of history, enabling white tourists to experience, and in that sense, consume cultures. In this process the superficial attributes of form serve as promiscuous symbols onto which ideas of the other can be imposed. In North America of particular significance is the growth of the "generalized other," in which decontextualized symbols are associated arbitrarily to provide a simplistic model of Native North America.[1]

This essay considers a number specific contemporary instances in which native materials are today created by native and non-native organizations for the tourist market. The specific areas—the Northwest Coast, the Northeast, the North Carolina Cherokee—provide a wide range of industries in which highly simplified symbolic systems are arbitrarily employed to give meaning to composite souvenir forms. This association of ideas of the exotic, the savage, the native and the other, with industrial production by non-natives has its origin in nineteenth-century marketing and exhibitions. At this time, for instance, the Canadian economy was principally concerned with primary industries —with raw materials such as timber, mining, farming and fur production. It was quite normal practice for exhibits of say timber to be adorned with a native bark canoe, as at the London Great Exhibition of 1851, or for displays of furs to be set off by the standard inclusion of native skin clothing or kayaks. While some secondary industries cloaked their manufacturing activities in Native North American symbols, it was, from the end of the nineteenth century the tertiary or service industries that made most use of the native other. The opening up of railway tourism from the 1880s and of road tourism from the 1920s, brought a permanently reinforced association of the nature and wilderness with the native other. In particular the travel industry—and specifically the railroad—adopted native-motif imagery as a major component of its marketing strategy. The best example of appropriation of Indian symbols is that of the Santa Fe Railroad, a European-financed venture which failed in the 1890s. After bankruptcy, its marketing strategy was spear-headed by a "natural advertising genius" William Simpson (1858-1933) and a restaurateur of foreign origins, Fred Harvey (1835-1901). Places to eat, hotels and later tours—or as they were named "Indian-Detours" were set up to lure Easterners to the Southwest (D'Emilio and Campbell 1991, 7-12).

One aspect of this growth of tourism was the provision of native souvenirs, as for instance pottery in the Southwest of the United States. Generally in the nineteenth and early twentieth century tourists acquired souvenirs either directly from the artists, or through white curios stores, such as Ye Olde Curiosity Shop in Seattle and Winter and

Pond's emporium in Juneau (Wyatt 1989, 26). Similarly the Nome gold rush of the turn of the century stimulated the production of a great wealth of new ivory souvenirs by the Yup'ik and Inupiaq, which also fed into the nascent tourist industry (Ray 1977). In the Northeast tourism was much older, and centering on Niagara Falls, the St Lawrence river and New England, providing what is probably a seamless continuation from the eighteenth century. It seems likely that moccasins and baskets were produced, 200 years ago, in large numbers, for the use of local non-native people. In the nineteenth century with the opening of railways and the growth of Niagara Falls as the primary tourist spot, production turned to souvenirs designed for sale (Sears 1989, 17). In this century, the growth of the road system created analogous demand for souvenirs in other areas of the continent, for instance among the Eastern Cherokee.

None of these phenomena have attracted much attention until recently. But in the 1970s and 1980s tourist and souvenir arts came to be examined in their own right, but these accounts seldom placed these traditions in the context of the history of tourism, or of the native economies, or as a symbols mediating between the native and non-native worlds. Instead these descriptions emphasize internal native symbolic systems, seeking to contextualize tourist art culturally rather than to place it in the wider world. One significant affect of this was to endow these art traditions with a new-found status which had, perhaps usually, been previously lacking. The scholarship of art historians then combined with the rhetoric of indigenous revival to validate the whole process.

A related feature is the absence of historical case studies describing the growth of tourism in specific areas. Such studies would be important in order to identify the factors—both general and personal—which influenced the development of new traditions, what could be called neo-traditions. In North America the work of Graburn, as well as Graburn's own modelling of the process of creation of these arts provides the basic paradigm. It is yet to be fully imposed on the arts of the nineteenth century (Graburn 1976). Graburn's analysis of an existing and developing neo-traditions was complemented by the study of Haida argillite carving, initiated by Kaufman and continued, particularly by Sheehan (1981), and Macnair and Hoover (1984). In Northern and Northeastern North America the study of acculturated art forms focuses on porcupine quillwork, particularly for instance, among the Micmac and Oddawa, and on beadwork among a great range of people from Canada, New York and New England (Nicks

1982; Canada House 1985). In the Southwest equivalent studies have been made on the creation of neo-traditions in Navajo rug weaving from the end of the nineteenth century (Rodee 1977; James 1988).

The secondary elaboration of this scholarly process diversified in two directions. Firstly it began to focus on biographical and occasionally autobiographical accounts of individual artists, usually but not always, identified by name: for instance potters, basket-weavers and carvers. The second direction in which this process moved lay in the creation of models for the analysis of whole traditions of, among others, beadwork and embroidery. The purpose of these extended accounts was to provide coherent explanations of meaning from the Native point of view. Inherent in these discussions is however a basic dialectic between good and evil, immorality and morality. Tourism can be seen, in a sense, as the final insult at the end of the process of colonization, and souvenir arts are the symbol of this insult. Yet the developing interest in souvenir arts chooses to invert this reality and, as a consummate fiction, raises these arts to a new status.

More useful are studies of the role of tourist arts as a medium for communication between native and non-native society, as exemplified by Lee's account of tourist arts in Alaska (Lee 1991). In some specific areas, such as jewelry, the scholarly process has been highly varied. In Northwest Coast silverwork, for example, analysis is made of the work of individual artists, while for the jewelry of the Southwest studies emphasize the broad outline of the art form rather than any attempt to personalize the work of individuals. In basketry the opposite has often happened, with researchers identifying the output of single weavers, and also outlining their relationships with the dealers and collectors who acted as patrons, although some studies combine both processes (Bates and Lee 1990). Finally it should be mentioned that the situation on the Plains is in some ways entirely different to that existing elsewhere. Beadwork and craft production is centered on the production of costume for Plains, if not for pan-Indian performances. Whereas contemporary Navajo textiles, or Haida argillite, or Northeast splint basketry are designed for non-native use in the art market, powwow costuming is designed for use—i.e. for consumption rather than for collectors or museums. In some sense, this Plains native use of native art is paralleled in Northwest Coast carving, although in that case it seems likely that the vast majority of articles created are sold for tourist or collecting purposes. A significant issue here is the extent to which studies of historic material culture and of contemporary artists are increasingly seen as important, while the general situation, of non-native control of souvenir production, is, with its profound economic and cultural effects, ignored.

Of major interest is the nature of the contemporary development of new material culture traditions in relationship to the economics of art production. Two aspects are particularly significant. One relates to the way in which North American tourist industries—in the Southwest, Southeast, and Northeast provide a vast, but poorly recorded demand for articles of native origin. This unquantified demand is very largely met by industries which may or may not have some native input, in design, creation, marketing and retailing. A particular issue is of course the appropriation of native designs, or art traditions, by non-natives and the supply of this market by business which while identifying themselves as Indian, or Eskimo for instance, have no substantial native involvement. On the Northwest Coast, while the tourist industry is economically highly significant very little of the huge quantities of native-type souvenirs sold, except for the notable exception of silk-screen prints, are produced with native involvement. During the current period of rapid economic change brought about by the decline in fishing and forest products under the influence of the Canadian-US free trade agreement (NAFTA), employment opportunities in remote communities have suffered, placing further emphasis on the importance of home-based production of souvenirs and other crafts. An issue behind of all this is the extent to which labelling of native art is effective in protecting indigenous interests in this area.

The purpose of this paper is to introduce a range of situations under which native goods are produced, marketed and sold. The status of the artist of international repute is of course significant in this. But it may be that the role of individual craftspeople producing native and non-native goods at home or in factories has within the community a greater cultural and economic significance. This affect arises through the process of tourism and the resulting transfer of simplified cultural values. Underlying it all are the lost economic and cultural opportunities which occur as a result of the alienation of souvenir industries from native control. At the most fundamental level a whole range of art products including carving, jewelry and basketry are created at home by individual artists. These goods may be made seasonally, and may be part-time and or full-time occupations. While basketry, for instance, on Vancouver Island, among the Nuu-chah-nulth, or among the Yup'ik in Southwest Alaska, or the Cherokee in North Carolina, is clearly under the control of each individual person, only among the Cherokee is there significant retailing and marketing of baskets by native-controlled organizations. Very rarely, today in North America, does the individual craftworker sell his or her product to the final consumer, although there are numerous instances of individual native-owned stores, and indeed directories may be produced of native artists. While many native communities possess native owned stores, these are often primarily directed toward the selling of high art—the finest things that that particularly community may produce. Most materials, whether Cowichan sweaters or Northwest Coast jewelry or Yup'ik and Inupiaq ivory carving are sold to non-native stores. A second and rather different type of relationship exists where non-native organizations employ native people to produce goods on demand. On the one hand this may simply be a gallery-owner commissioning an artist to create specific works to order. A more general process is that in which medium sized businesses, which may or may not be native-owned, employ natives to mass produce souvenirs. A third aspect of this exists when native-type products are mass produced overseas, for instance in Asia.

Northwest Coast Souvenirs

In Seattle mail order firms provide a mixture of manufactured goods for the tourist industry to the North. Since the 1950s this type of organization has probably come to dominate and replace the individual native artist producing basketry and totem poles for local stores. Indian Arts & Crafts, Inc., founded in the 1950s, is one of these businesses that provides materials for the US tourist trade on the Northwest Coast, in the Pacific Northwest and in Alaska. The 66 page catalogue (IAAC 1992) offers a plethora of materials including everything from T-shirts, jewelry and native-style ornaments to wood masks and totem poles. Significantly much of the material is probably of Asian origin, including many of the toys that are entirely non-native in concept. There is little attempt in the catalogue to emphasize the native component of the selection of goods offered for sale. Natives are however employed on the premises in Seattle to carve masks and other items. Several pages of Northwest Coast style masks, and other goods, are included in the catalogue: particularly moulded totem poles, cast totem reproductions, totem boxes and argillite items. The first page illustrates soapstone figurines—the stone is from Washington State carved in Canadian Inuit style. The rubric accompanying the photographs is: "Each piece is hand carved by Native Artists such as Keith Willis, Eddie Omnik, Ben Sacelamana, Peter Kunnuk, Rick Thomas,

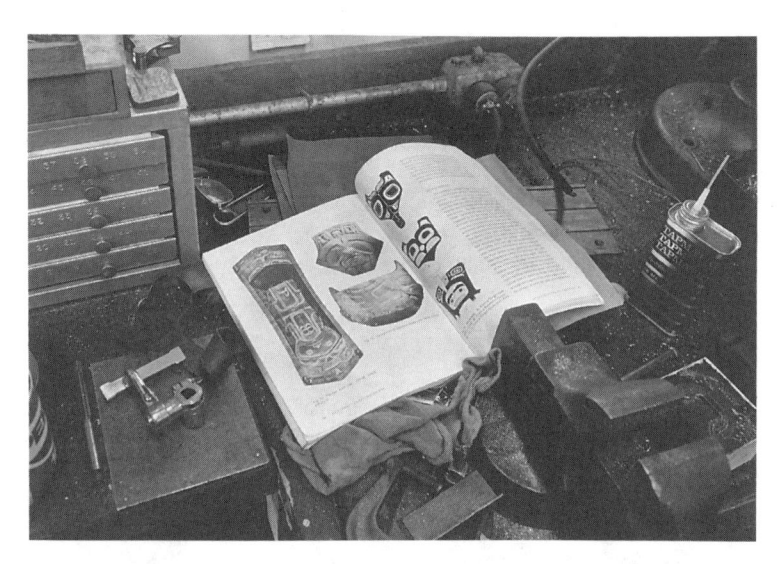

6.1. Bill Holm's book open at the page illustrating the Northwest Coast horn bowl used in flattened form to create a brooch. Whole Earth factory, Seattle, 1980s (photo J.C.H. King).

6.2. The wood maquette and metal dye taken from the illustration of the horn bowl for the production of a brooch. Whole Earth factory, Seattle, 1980s (photo J.C.H. King).

Pat Mezzenna, Glenn Tingook, Olaf Piscoya, etc."

A second Seattle-based company is called West Earth. This produces a wide range of silver jewelry and other metal souvenirs. Included here are some observations about the way in which a new product line was being created in the 1980s. Of particular interest was the use made of Bill Holm's book *Northwest Coast Indian Art: An Analysis of Form* (1965). At the time of my visit in 1983 a carver was working on a wood maquette copying a design from the end of big

6.3. A Nuu-Chah-Nulth design under discussion between the owner of the jewelry factory Whole Earth and Ron Hamilton, historian and artist from Port Alberni, B.C., 1980s (photo J.C.H. King).

horn mountain sheep horn bowl. The form of these bowls is generally rounded—and indeed voluptuous in effect—with horizontally flanged ends. The photograph in Holm's book shows the flanged end in such a way as to make the split representational design stand out. It depicts a mammal, perhaps a bear with one creature in the mouth and another between the ears (1965, 88). The factory artist flattened the design to create a new more or less hexagonal form in wood, in low relief, perhaps 15" square. Relatively little attention was paid to formlines. From this maquette he created a small steel die from which to create two-dimensional broaches bearing no relationship to the original bowl. Objects as well as literature were used as source materials for new products. The West Earth catalogue for 1983 is interesting for a number of reasons. Unpaginated it contains 20 or 30 illustrations and Xeroxes of economically-priced jewelry. Featured at the beginning are "two new North Coast Indian sterling bracelets" designed by Barry Herem. The illustrations include numerous designs loosely derived from Northwest Coast prototypes. One, bracelet number 725, was copied from an Edensaw beaver design also included in Holm's book (1965, 90). Some of the vaguely Tlingit-style bracelets were endowed with non-native names such as "Lovebird" for an eagle. Much of the other jewelry offered for sale consisted of Hawaiian trinkets, mostly devoid of Polynesian motifs except for the occasional spoon adorned with a dancing girl or an eighteenth-century Hawaiian nobleman. Other lines featured include earrings, charms and pendants and numerous items illustrating the signs of the zodiac. The visit to the show room was made with the Nuu-Chah-Nulth artist Ron Hamilton, who commented that he had seen some of these non-native bracelets in native use, where they no doubt assume an authentic identity.

The Cherokee

The second tourist area is that of the Cherokee reservation in the Great Smoky Mountains, in North Carolina. This area was opened to visitors in the 1930s with the construction of highways. Roosevelt made a visit in the late 1930s which was publicized in the early literature. Tourism was accompanied by the development of performance arts; these include the Ball Game, the initiation of the pageant *Unto These Hills*, and eventually the construction of Oconaluftee Village, where basketry, pottery and other traditional and neo-traditional arts are practised. Also included in this category are the activities of individual natives, for instance practising the business of posing for photography with tourists. Tourism in Cherokee is accompanied by a professional Museum with historical and cultural displays. The business of arts and crafts is conducted at three levels of industry. Most significant is Qualla Arts and Crafts Mutual, Inc., a co-operative specializing in basketry, sculpture and other traditional arts. Perhaps the most important continuing tradition is that of creating double-weave river-cane basketry. This is accompanied by oak splint and honeysuckle basketry, traditions which are paralleled by non-native people in the Appalachians. The 1993 edition of the 16 page Qualla mail order catalogue contains illustrations of a hundred or different objects. Apart from the basketry there is a double-page spread of masks with some detailed explanation:

> Mask making is another tribal custom that almost drifted into extinction. It was the duty of the tribe's medicine man to carve the various masks that were used to scare away sickness, prepare for war, or aid in the hunt... (Qualla n.d., 8)

6.4. Tourist at Cherokee photographing his partner with Chief Henry, 1990s (photo J.C.H. King).

Another double-page spread features sculptures carved in local woods with mid-century realism, and pottery. Five pages feature basketry and three pan-Indian beadwork. The final two pages include miscellaneous materials such as finger woven book marks, chopping boards and imitation eagle feather dance wands.

While Qualla Arts and Crafts is native-owned, the two major industries in Cherokee are non-native. Most prominent is The Cherokees. This major business was set up at the suggestion of the Cherokee themselves during 1955-6 by P K Ferree from Knoxville. He had originally worked in the leather industry, manufacturing, among other things, moccasins. The company moved to the Cherokee Reservation because of reduced labour costs. Today they employ 93%

native labour, 200 people in a factory of 60,000 square feet, have a turnover of about $5m, and issue a catalogue. Each year they use 1200 lb. of racoon tails, 12000 lb. of feathers, and 300,000 rabbit skins from Europe. The current catalogue (No 20) is 32 pages long. Six pages are devoted to moccasins and boots, and a further two to other types of leather goods. Two pages are for feather works —head-dresses made from ready-dyed domesticated turkey. Most of the materials are designed for children, providing toys for those who learn about Native

6.5. Cherokee manufacture of drums, North Carolina, at The Cherokees business, 1990s (photo J.C.H. King).

America only in primary schools. It is easy to deride things like cardboard drums, pipes, blow-pipes, boomerangs, totem poles and the like; and yet millions of dollars feed into the local economy through this company. According to the publicity material "A considerable percentage of Capital Stock of the company is held by members of the Cherokee tribe." However the market is a highly competitive one, particularly vis-à-vis Asian imports. The customers are very prominent in the entertainment industry, and ensure that the Cherokee name is widely known nationally and internationally. They include the Atlanta Braves (the baseball team), Disneyworld and Eurodisney, and a fast food chain. The essential marketing strategy is quite simply that these things are Indian made. The Qualla materials are tagged with labels registered by the Indian Arts and Crafts Board guaranteeing that they are genuine handicrafts, from a certified Indian enterprise. The Cherokees business simply issues its own tags: "If it bears this tag, it's Cherokee Indian made...your assurance of a quality-crafted product."

While a factory making such things may be vital to the local economy, and, in the wider world, in providing a native identity, this is not the largest craft factory on the Cherokee Reservation. The quilt factory of Barclay Home Products is very much bigger than the previous two organizations. This large business occupies a 300,000 square foot factory, with 500 employees, and 70% native employment. Turnover in 1993 was $50m a year, and is increasing. The factory had been built in 1955, and was reorganized under present management in 1986. It is the largest patchwork factory in the world, making New England-style quilts. These are sold to mail order firms such as J C Penney and Sears; there is no Asian competition, and the quilts are marketed without any indication of their Cherokee origin. This is of course in complete contrast to the traditional and neo-traditional goods sold by Qualla Arts and The Cherokees. The significant common denominator here is the native input of high quality craft labour, and the low wage-rates.

The Northeast

In the tourist trade on the Northwest Coast, and on the Cherokee Reservation, most souvenir materials are provided without significant professional native design input, and with only a very modest degree of native control or investment. The materials created in factory environments may be vigorously marketed as native, although of course without the explicit labels provided by the Indian Arts and Crafts Board. In Northeastern North America a similar situation exists, but with the addition of the production of materials, which while native in origin, do not seem to depend in marketing strategy on their native label. One example of this type of production lies in the series of native-organized factories on the reserve at Villages-des-Hurons, outside Quebec City. A number of business are located there which created a plethora of different products. They include snow shoes,

6.6. Huron making commercial moccasins, Québec, 1986 (photo J.C.H. King).

canoes for northern use, and a series of souvenir-products rather analogous to some of the material created by The Cherokees factory: tomahawks, moccasins and such things. The snow shoes and canoes are however made for use. All over Northeastern North America splint baskets are also made by Iroquoian and Algonquian people, and while they may be marketed as native products seem likely—if only because of the production volumes—still to be employed in the utilitarian usages indicated by the designs. Another Iroquoian product made and sold in open competition with Asian products is the lacrosse stick. While these may be crafted at native-owned work places they have to compete with mass-produced examples, for instance imported from Asia.

The North

In Northern North America, that is Alaska and Northern Canada, the situation is comparable to that elsewhere, but with significant differences. As on the Cherokee reservation local co-operatives oversee the marketing of native products, particularly art and clothing. The most prominent organizations are the Canadian co-ops with their southern warehouse outlet and marketing facilities for distributing prints and sculpture. Two examples of these are the Fédération des Coopératives du Nouveau-Québec with a new multi-million dollar facility at Baie d'Urfée outside Montreal, and Dorset Fine Arts in

Toronto. Dorset Fine Arts, and other Inuit organizations issue annual print catalogues, as does Ocean Pacific Graphics in Victoria BC, for Northwest Coast artists. The selling of Inuit art is underwritten by a secondary market, including the sale by auction of prints and sculptures. This circumstance is neither featured in contemporary native—and specifically Indian—art where, for instance, paintings, sculpture and basketry are not auctioned in New York since, apparently, the demand for such materials is not consistent. Apart from the selling of Inuit art, primarily sculpture and prints, but also basketry and textiles, clothing is the main product created in the north and sold by mail order catalogue and at centers of tourism. In much of the North clothing is still home-produced, using more often in Canada home-tanned skins; in Alaska much of the native-obtained stock of skins is sent out of the state (The Cutting Edge in Bethel is an example of such a store) to New York for tanning, and reimported with exotic non-Alaskan skins for native and non-native use. In some parts of the north, such as New Quebec and the Northwest Territories home-tanned moose skin moccasins are made and sold locally. For the most part mukluks, kamiks, parkas and other items of modified-traditional clothing are created from commercially produced materials. They are sold alongside traditional items such as quilled moccasins. Examples of traditionalist marketing of Northern products are provided by the Cree Indian Center at Chibougamau, Quebec, which does not issue a catalogue, Treeline Trappings (1986), and Yukon Native Products (1986), in Yellowknife, which do publish booklets. A white-organized business Arctic Trading Company from Churchill, Manitoba, sells a mixture of traditional and modified traditional clothing, along with entirely traditional items such as kayaks (1985,1990). In character, although in standards of design or skill, these catalogues are not radically different from those produced by southern businesses such as Caribou Clothes, from Mountain View, Alberta.

In contrast, the production of more entirely traditional goods such as basketry, and porcupine quillwork is much less organized. This type of product is often featured as embellishments in retail establishments selling clothing produced in large quantities. Items such as sample porcupine quillwork belts are only created in very small volumes, and do not command prices commensurate with the traditionalism and skill.required in the making. Instead they provide the magic of the traditional, sanctified by the association of the native with the environment, to enable high volume products to be marketed and sold. Similarly in the Arctic there is little or no non-native market for traditionally prepared seal skin boots. Without the expression of high value monetary attached to such things, there is little incentive for younger natives—brought up in a market economy rather than the community or familial one—to learn how to make such things for sale and to maintain the skill.Continued production of boots relates only to the maintenance of cultural values.

Conclusion

The purpose of these few brief comments is to try to bring together ideas about tourist arts with some of the context of the dominant souvenir industries. These industries are significant, both economically, and in the way they influence and perhaps determine the response of the non-native tourist to the native. Although the souvenir industries act to articulate the native and non-native worlds, the native artist and souvenir producer is not usually part of a conscious process of marketing native identities through tourist art. Central to the whole business is that of labelling, and the production of Indian crafts by white North Americans and Asians. One attempt to assist this process lies in the production of guides to native artists (for instance Johannsen and Ferguson 1983), another comes through legislation. In 1992 Congress passed a new Indian Arts and Craft Act. This provides for the FBI to investigate labelling infractions. Individuals may be fined up to $250,000, and Galleries $1,000,000 for selling non-native materials claiming them to be native made.[2] But it is not clear who should be required to prove native ancestry, and what standards of proof should be enforced. If $800m worth of Indian crafts are sold each year, it is reasonable to attempt to reduce the estimated 20% or so that are imported from Asia. Yet further difficulties arise when individual enterprises are examined. The materials may be native produced, in non-native circumstances as among the Eastern Cherokee; or they may bear native designs adopted from authentic sources but produced in non-native factories. Underlying of all this is the reality that no one, particular if native, is in charge of their own identity, and there are few published accounts of native discourses on tourist art. The challenge for native artists is, therefore, both to benefit from the widespread currency of favourable stereotypes, and then to improve on them. None of these issues are simple, but their examination may provide a better understanding of how to influence the design and study of native-style products. Without appreciation of the souvenir-industries, and their affect through tourism on white North America, the rather different effects of scholarship, and the growth of native empowerment in museums, will bear only a secondary influence on changing perceptions of the native world.

Notes

1. This account is derived from MacCannell 1992
2. See *The Economist*, September 5, 1995.

7

A Tradition of Invention: Modern Ceremonialism on the Northwest Coast

Michael Harkin

Authenticity and Authority

The notion of "invention of tradition" is a useful one, to the extent that it draws our attention to the ways in which key cultural symbols may be deployed and manipulated through time for political ends. In Hobsbawm and Ranger's (1983) volume on the topic, Cannadine's fine article on the British monarchy's uses of symbols of the past stands out as an exemplary analysis of this sort. During the Victorian and Edwardian eras, in response to the increasing size of the British Empire, and the need for symbolic and ritual means to reign over this far-flung territory, legitimating symbols of tradition were not so much "invented" as refined and carefully framed. During the preceding Georgian era, rituals were slipshod and the monarch was despised rather than venerated.

The changing role of the monarchy is to be seen against the background of rapid social and technological change within English society itself. One example is modes of transportation. As the British populace came increasingly to rely upon trolley, bus, and bicycle for transport, the horse-drawn carriages employed by the monarchy became obsolete. This very obsolescence was, in a sense, a symbol waiting to happen (Cannadine 1983, 124). It needed only ritual framing in public ceremonies, such as coronations and royal weddings, to become what it is now considered to be: a "thousand-year-old tradition," which, among others, lends grandeur and stability to the British state (1983, 161).

Two crucial points can be drawn from this analysis. First, traditions may be authentic, in the sense that they move people affectively (and move them to action), despite the fact that they may be "artificially" constructed and framed. In part, this is because symbols are selected for their perlocutionary potential (see Levinson 1983, 236). Thus, gilded carriages were bound to play on the nostalgia, on corporeal and emotional levels, of urban strap-hangers. It also played into an English structure of the *longue durée*, the valorization of rural, pre-industrial modes of production. Properly framed, the state landau could not but be a powerful symbol, evocative of past glories and future stability in a rapidly changing world. The pragmatic power of the symbol derives from its ability to condense incipient emotional states.

To be effective, constructed symbols must be drawn out of a fairly limited repertoire. We must thus contest the use of the term "invention," implying as it does creation *ex nihilo*. It seems clear rather that this phenomenon involves the selection and ritual framing of latent symbols, which are already present within the culture. These potential symbols may be latent for a variety of reasons, because they have never been framed as symbols and are drawn out of the realm of praxis (as in the case of the horse-drawn carriage), or because of a historical discontinuity. A related point here is that symbolic re-framing of obsolete symbols inevitably changes their meaning; they come to stand largely, if not primarily, for the historical culture from which they are drawn. We see this especially clearly in Native American deployments of archaic symbols. On occasion, the meaning of "tradition" all but overwhelms the specific meanings attached to them.

The second point is that such framing or re-framing of symbols is always political. Shared symbols unite social groups, giving them a sense of identity and solidarity, and making them capable of unified action (Durkheim 1915, 225). Those successfully wielding such symbols are invested with authority, which is indeed an effect of certain types of communicative acts (Lincoln 1994, 1-13). Of course, not all attempts at constructing authority are successful, no matter how powerful the symbols wielded; authority is constantly challenged by competing discourses (1994, 74-89).

Tradition and Invention in Native American Cultures

One of the most powerful of these "corrosive discourses," as Lincoln calls them, is the challenge to the authenticity of the symbols and the legitimacy of their wielders. It is within this framework that we may situate the North Americanist branch of the "invention of tradition" school, who have exaggerated the basic model to the point of it becoming a grotesque game. In particular the work of James Clifton and his colleagues (1990), which attempts to unmask the "invented Indian" beneath recent attempts on the part of Native groups to gain greater cultural, political, and economic autonomy, is a political discourse. We are told that modern Indians wearing buckskin and dancing in powwows are posturing urbanites, motivated by a desire for personal and political power (Clifton 1990a, 31-32).

The political motive among Native American leaders, activists, and neotraditionalists is certainly present, as I have argued, but the idea that this should be surprising or inappropriate is extremely naive. Political activism of one sort or another involving Indians and Whites dates back to the beginnings of European presence in the New World: at least to Malinal and Cortès. What is doubly (perhaps cynically) naive is the posture of many contributors to this volume that they are uncovering "the truth" and are not themselves politically motivated.[1]

Piece by piece, key elements in the "dominant narrative structure" of the American Indian are exposed as "false" by dedicated scholars who tell us that Squanto may have learned his fish-fertilization technique from Europeans, or that Indians did not really worship Mother Earth (Ceci 1990; Gill 1990). The former is more a commentary on a Euro-American, not a Native American myth, which provided justification for large-scale European settlement in the New World; the latter is a nominalist critique of the idea of a personal deity that could be termed "Earth Mother," and says little about the fundamental religious attitude of Native American groups toward nature. Yet behind these ephemera is a dominant narrative structure that portrays the modern American Indian as inauthentic and the "real" Indian, located in the past, as vanished.

This narrative plugs into the oldest story line in the history of colonialism: the disappearing savage. This is often coupled with a desire for the Other, who is unattainable (Berkhofer 1978, 99). We see this most clearly in the visual record of the exotic. In photographs and films from the 1860s to the present we see the depiction of colourful, vibrant, often nude, and thoroughly primitive humans, whose very primitiveness seals their fate in the "modern" world (Edwards 1992). Like Barthes' famous description of seeing a *Paris-Match* photograph of a "black Frenchman" at the barber shop, such pictures embody and reinforce political mythologies (Barthes 1972, 116-17).[2]

The myth of the disappearing savage provided the story line for thousands of films, ranging from the obviously biased Hollywood westerns to "scientific" ethnographies (Berkhofer 1978, 96-104; Morris 1994). On the Northwest Coast alone, hundreds of films were made depicting Native people as residing in the past, or alternatively in "islands of no history" as Morris (1994) calls them. We may rue it or celebrate it, but there is no denying that these people are doomed. Such ideas motivated figures as diverse as the anthropologist Franz Boas and Duncan Campbell Scott, the Canadian Deputy Superintendent of Indian Affairs, who wrote sad romantic poetry about the disappearance of the Indian, while enforcing policies designed to ensure precisely that outcome (Cole and Chaikin 1990, 92). What is involved here is the "denial of coevalness," the assumption that real Indians cannot possibly share the same time, space, and political-ethical universe as the metropolitan elite (Fabian 1983). Thus, it is with ironical amusement that Clifton notes that among the Menomini with whom he worked were those who held advanced academic degrees (Clifton 1990a, 13).

The denial of coevalness also denies historical dynamism to tribal cultures. Their past is seen as static, devoid of history, until Promethean Europeans arrive on the scene. Authenticity is read as a product of that "long sleep;" anything new must, by definition, be inauthentic. Ideas of discontinuity are thus emphasized and exaggerated, making it impossible within this discursive universe for the contemporary Indian authentically to practice his tribal religion; we hear only of frauds and charlatans (Kehoe 1990). At the same time, this adds to the authority of the anthropologist or historian who becomes the sole guardian of "real" tradition.

While discontinuities are not to be denied, the greatest of these, the dying off of Native populations at the time of contact, were for most groups far in the past. Political and cultural pressures from Whites—the reservation system, allotments, termination, English-only education, television— have been powerful forces for assimilation, fairly successful with some groups, less so with others. As I have argued, the idea of authenticity should not be linked with continuity, especially not continuity of manifest cultural practices. Rather, authenticity is a measure of the effectiveness of symbols, and especially their ability to constitute and motivate a group.

Is this pragmatism a radical new reading of authenticity? I think not. In fact, it is one that is implicit in many cultures. In Northwest Coast cultures the potlatch is a means of testing the authenticity of claims precisely by means of determining who will support them. The strength of claims, such as claims to titles, is measured by the ability of the claimant effectively to manipulate symbols, to persuade with references to myth and genealogy, to achieve a "conversational" accord among the assembled community (Seguin 1985). This has always been the case in these cultures, and this general context for marking authenticity has permitted new symbols and practices to be deemed authentic.

In an interesting case reported by the anthropologist Margaret Seguin, a Tsimshian hereditary chief held a feast in January 1980 to mark his adoption by the Raven clan. This adoption gave the chief membership in all three village tribes, an unprecedented move. The chief was no longer seen as affiliated with a single clan, opposed to chiefs from other clans, but as a paramount figure in the community, who united the clans in a new trinity, a three-in-one whole (1985, 94). This is to be seen against the changing political situation, in which the relevant opposing entity is not another Tsimshian clan or community, but federal and provincial government. It is worth quoting from Seguin's conclusion:

> The Raven Feast of Chief Billy Clifton presented a new kind of claim couched in a traditional form. A "new tradition" has been forged. This new tradition celebrates the unity among members of the village, and is incarnate in the person of the Chief who participates in all three clans ... Symbolically, the three have become one, and low has become high ... I would argue that the symbolism that has been used is distinctively Christian, not as a replacement of traditional symbols, but as an interpretation of them. (Ibid)

"New tradition" is not an oxymoron within this system, for it is precisely the function of the feast or potlatch to confirm publicly the authenticity of claims. As a vital institution, it is charged with reconciling old and new, with constituting communities of agreement, and potentially of action. As such, it is the social enactment of the theoretical model of authenticity that I proposed above.

A Brief History of the Potlatch

The potlatch or feast (a term more often used by Natives when speaking English, which refers to any sort of ceremonial presentation, large or small) never really disappeared from the Northwest Coast, despite efforts by missionaries and the Canadian government to effect such a cessation. The infamous Canadian Potlatch Law existed in some legal form from 1885 to 1951. During most of this period the law was procedurally unenforceable or was simply not enforced. Only in the 1920s was the Department of Indian Affairs, under Duncan Campbell Scott, truly devoted to ending the potlatch on the Northwest Coast.

Around Christmas 1921, Kwakwak´wakw Chief Dan Cranmer gave a huge potlatch. Although the Kwakwak'wakw were accustomed to operating in secrecy, word of this potlatch leaked out to the authorities. In February 1922, thirty-four people were prosecuted by the Royal Canadian Mounted Police and the local Indian Agent, William Halliday (Cole and Chaikin 1990, 118-19). All were convicted. In lieu of threatened prison time, the community gave up its entire store of "potlatch goods," including, of course, masks and religious objects associated with the Winter Ceremonial (1990, 120-21; U'mista Cultural Society 1975).

This did indeed have a dampening effect on the potlatch, although it certainly did not eradicate it. On many parts of the Northwest Coast, especially in the north, the potlatch continued unabated. Among the Kwakwak'wakw of Alert Bay, the potlatch did indeed vanish for forty years. Even after the potlatch law was dropped from the Indian Act in 1951, the Kwakwak'wakw would wait twelve years for their first potlatch (Cranmer-Webster 1992, 36). By this time, the younger people no longer spoke Kwakw'ala and many "did not know that what they were seeing was much different from what their grandparents had known in better times" (ibid.). However, after 1963, many more potlatches were given, as families reactivated titles. In 1979, initial repatriation of artifacts was made; part of the confiscated collection was to be housed in the new museum of the U'mista Cultural Centre, which opened in 1980 (1992, 35). Since repatriation, potlatches have come to include historic and modern artifacts.

While potlatches have become larger and more frequent, and ritual performances more elaborate, there is considerable outside criticism that the modern potlatch is inauthentic, because it is different from the pre-1922 potlatches. Cranmer-Webster directly addresses the criticism that historic and modern potlatches are not the same: "How could they be? The world in which we live is vastly different from that in which our grandparents lived ... If a culture is alive, it does not remain static" (1992, 36).

Clearly, the assumption that cultural practices must be static to be authentic would only be applied to "tribal" cultures. Were the same standard applied to Western culture, almost nothing could be deemed authentic.[3] Institutions such as the Catholic Church, the French legal system, and the American university would be made illegitimate by the application of such standards.

The potlatch remains a vital institution, even, perhaps especially, in places where it was absent for two generations. When speaking of the potlatch, we are speaking less of a discrete institution than of a general institutional framework for bestowing legitimacy and authenticity. It has been compared to Western legal institutions for good reason (U'mista Cultural Centre 1975). It is less a symbol of tradition than a means of validating traditional symbols.

The Revival of the Dance in Waglisla

The first Heiltsuk potlatch in 50 years was held in Waglisla (formerly Bella Bella) in 1977 (Hilton 1990). As at Alert Bay, official opposition forced the termination of potlatching. However, at Bella Bella, much of the opposition to potlatching was internal. Bella Bella was an intentional community, founded by Methodist missionaries and Christian Heiltsuk Indians with the expressed purpose of fostering material and spiritual progress (Harkin 1993). A key element of this program of "improvement" was the termination of traditional Heiltsuk cultural practices. Even within this mission community there was resistance, but the last public potlatch was held in the 1920s. Smaller, private ceremonies bestowing names continued to be held, as did Christmas celebrations at which gifts were given away to non-family members (Harkin 1985-87).[4] Moreover, neighboring communities such as the Oowekeeno and Nuxalk (Bella Coola) continued to hold potlatches during at least some of this hiatus. However, the Heiltsuk themselves discontinued potlatching for an even longer period than did the Alert Bay Kwakwak'wakw.

When the potlatch resumed in 1977, only the older community members could remember attending a potlatch in their own community. While the highest ranking lineages managed to hold onto their titles through uninterrupted possession, many middle-ranked titles were unclaimed. As in Alert Bay, very few children spoke the Native language or fully understood the meaning of the potlatch.

Against this background, the revival of the potlatch was somewhat experimental. With the model of Alert Bay, where potlatching had been on the increase for fourteen years, there was good reason to think it would be successful in Waglisla. In fact two propositions were being put to the test. First, that the specific claims to titles at that first potlatch were legitimate and authentic. Secondly, that the potlatch itself remained a valid mechanism for determining legitimacy and authenticity.

Generally speaking, both propositions were accepted by the community. By the mid-1980s, potlatches and feasts were widely considered to be the appropriate means to validate claims to titles, to commemorate the dead, and to perform dances (Harkin 1985-87). All segments of the community, including the United Church[5] minister and congregants, participated. Elders, of different ranks and lineages, drummed and sang. Although occasional mutterings could be heard about specific titles and honors claimed by individuals, no one challenged the institution of the potlatch itself, nor the appropriateness of individuals hosting a potlatch to validate *some* title (Harkin, 1985-87).

As with the Kwakwak'wakw, the modern potlatch is a departure in many ways from the historic potlatch. It is no longer financed by the elaborate system of loans and lineage support that Franz Boas described (see Cranmer-Webster 1992, 36). It is usually paid for by an individual, although I was present at one multi-day potlatch that was co-sponsored by several members of a family. Numerous other differences between modern and historic potlatches could be mentioned: duration, types of gifts, and the dance performances held during the potlatch.

While the revival of the potlatch as a context for creating and affirming public meanings was relatively unproblematic, other aspects of modern ceremonialism were not so readily accepted. Especially the revival of Winter Ceremonial dances, which are performed at feasts and potlatches, created considerable controversy within the community. Several distinct areas of resistance were encountered. As with the hosting of potlatches, questions were raised about the rights of individuals to perform dances. A more important and general critique came from many members of the community, who objected to the revival of the dances on religious grounds. As I mentioned above, Waglisla was a mission community, and Christian values continue to play an important role in collective life. Since missionaries and ministers had preached out against the Winter Ceremonial as a type of satanism, some of the elders shared that view. Especially those associated with the Pentecostalist Church, which had been established in Waglisla in the 1950s, took a hard line against the dances, and refused to participate in the potlatch for this reason.

Eventually these objections were overcome. In part, this had to do with general trends on the Northwest Coast, and a more liberal attitude towards historic culture displayed by both Whites and Native people. Equally important was the work of Native intellectuals to reinterpret historic culture in the context of Christianity. A Kwakwak'wakw Anglican priest by the name of Ernie Willie, who was pastor at the Waglisla United Church in the mid-1980s is one such intellectual.[6] The Rev. Willie reinterpreted the *hámac'a* (Cannibal Dance) in terms of Christian sacrificial imagery, and the historic wedding ceremony in terms of personal and familial responsibility (Harkin 1985-87). The work of such intellectuals paved the way for devout Christians to tolerate, if not actively support, the revival of the dances. This reconciliation was certainly made easier by the fact that many of these dances bore little resemblance to the historic dances. Thus the *hámac'a* does not even pretend to bite people, and there is no staged cannibalism, although the costuming and movements of the dance are quite similar to those recorded by Boas (see Rohner and Rohner 1970, 102).[7]

Indeed, these dances have been reconstructed at least in part from textual sources. At several of the Heiltsuk dance performances I attended, professional Kwakwak'wakw dancers acted as advisors to ensure the formal accuracy of some elements of the dance. This gave some of the performances the air of a semi-professional entertainment, rather than a powerful religious ritual. This great shift in the meaning of the dances has not gone unnoticed; elders remarked how different these performances were from the ones they had attended as children. Are we to take the view then that because of historical discontinuities, and the resultant shift in meaning, that these dances are "inauthentic" traditions? In order to answer that, we must look more closely at the role of dances in modern potlatches, and the significance of potlatches in community life.

Dances are but one element in modern potlatches. A full-scale potlatch, which certainly not all of them are, begins with the dedication of a gravestone and commemoration of the dead in late afternoon. This is a somber affair, which is completed with the ritual "sweeping away" of sorrow (Harkin 1985-87). This is followed by dancing, dinner, and the giving away of goods. At one potlatch I attended a wedding was also performed. Dances are thus not the only important element of a potlatch, but they are quite important, and represent, in terms of time, significant portion of the evening's activities.

Until now I have spoken of "dances" without distinguishing among the several types presented at a modern potlatch. These distinctions are important. In historic Heiltsuk culture the Winter Ceremonial was divided into two distinct series: the *λúeláxa* and the *caíqa*. The *λúeláxa* was notable for its restrained, formal style. The dance steps were gradual, stately, and repetitive. The dancers were inspired by "heaven" and the ancestors who dwelt there, symbolized by eagle down. Headdresses, rather than masks, were worn, emphasizing the fact that the dancers danced as themselves *qua* titled noblemen and chiefs, and were not possessed by an alien spirit. The general meaning of the dance had to do with purification of the community and the representation of rank structure. The *λúeláxa* performance was traditionally associated with the largest distributions of food and goods of the Winter Ceremonial; to some degree this association still holds.

The *λúeláxa* contrasted with the *caíqa* series of the Winter Ceremonial, which had many elements that I have termed "carnivalistic" (Harkin 1996). The *caíqa* was a rite of passage, marking the transition between childhood and adulthood, and adulthood to old age. It also marked the calendric transition from the productive portion of the year (*bákʷ'en*) in which humans were free to pursue normal activities, to a time in which spirits held reign and, coincidentally, most food species disappeared. Cosmologically, it was thought that the world flipped over in the wet, dark, short days of late fall and early winter. Society was made to imitate this transformation.

During the *caíqa*, dangerous forces were loosed upon the human world: death, disease, cannibalism, and incest are among the themes represented in these performances (Harkin 1996). Dancers were "excited" or "possessed" by these dangerous spirits, which led them to engage in extremely antisocial acts including theatrical and possibly real anthropophagy, and certainly biting the arms of spectators. Chiefly and noble titles were replaced by *caíqa* names, which often had obscene or humorous meanings. Like carnival, *caíqa* led to its antithesis, which was the *λúeláxa*. The *λúeláxa* represented the restoration of chiefly authority, and the "healing" or "setting right" of society as a whole, and the reascendancy of cosmos over chaos (see Berman 1991, 666).

In modern potlatches the *λúeláxa* dances are performed by hereditary and elected chiefs. Dressed in full dance regalia, complete with eagle down, they command considerable respect. Although it is impossible to know for certain, due to a paucity of sources on historic Heiltsuk culture, these performances seem to embody the main elements of the historic ones. By contrast, the *caíqa* performances are extremely abbreviated and include none of the dangerous elements of historic performances, although the traditional *caíqa's* inversion of the social world is marked by wearing button blankets reversed. These performances are not feared at all, but are rather considered to be the most entertaining of all the dances. While this attitude retains elements of the older carnivalistic ethos of the *caíqa*, it would be impossible to argue that it evokes substantially the same response from the audience, which I think would be true for the *λúeláxa* (Harkin 1985-87).

In addition to the *caíqa* and *λúeláxa*, a class of dances called "play dances" are performed by groups of children. These dances are drawn from the lower-ranking Winter Ceremonial dances, and probably were never taken terribly seriously. Now, of course, they are excellent opportunities for parental photographs. They are also an important element of young children's introduction into ceremonial life.

The interplay of different dance types, and the interplay of dance and other potlatch elements creates a dramaturgical structure that oscillates between entertainment and efficacy, as Richard Schechner (1977, 75) describes it. The more "serious" moments of the potlatch invoke a respectful and unquestioning attitude on the part of the audience, and do elements of ritual "work," such as the purification of the community, the representation of sociological structure (rank, clan, age, and gender), or the transformation of an individual's place in the community. The *λúeláxa*, the commemoration of the dead, formal potlatch speeches, and, to some degree, certain of the *caíqa* dances have ritual efficacy, while the play dances, many of the *caíqa* dances, the food, and the music, have entertainment value. These moments invite audience participation, even criticism, and are enjoyable, not solemn events. The entertainment features of the potlatch frame the potlatch temporally, as entertainment activities such as *lahel* gambling and drinking alcohol at private homes follow the potlatch itself (and, over a several-day potlatch, may precede it as well).

This framing of the potlatch by entertainment features is not a modern innovation. Pre-1920s potlatches involved similar features, which was one reason they offended the sensibilities of Victorian and Edwardian Canadians (Harkin 1985-87; Fisher 1977, 132-139). In fact, we see in both modern and historic potlatches a nested structure, in which serious and playful moments intertwine, creating a spectacle of counterpoint. At the broadest level the potlatch is a performance of identity, in which group and individual identity is represented, transformed, and confirmed (Schechner 1993, 103). This performance is effective, powerful, and, by my definition, authentic because of its dramaturgical enactment of key symbols which retain their hold on their audience.

The Canoe Journey: The Construction of a New "Traditional" Performance

The modern potlatch is an effective vehicle for representing individual and group identity. However, the social world outside the community has changed considerably; new identities, new political strategies are required. As Seguin noted for the Tsimshian, the important sociopolitical opposition is no longer between "sides" of the village, but between village and government, Native and non-Native.

In the contemporary period, Native groups are fighting against the Provincial and, to a lesser degree, federal government (and in some cases, other Native groups) over land claims and resource use rights (Cassidy and Dale 1988). In this period of political and economic flux, the need for alliances among Native groups and a Native "common front" have been sharply felt.

Arising out of this context (although not instrumentally so), a young Heiltsuk man named Frank Brown planned and organized a long-distance canoe trip from Waglisla to Vancouver's Expo '86. In doing so, he was attempting to elevate the canoe, usually called by the Heiltsuk word, *gélw'a*, to the status of a key symbol of renascent Heiltsuk culture, and pan-tribal unity (see Ortner 1973).

We are reminded of Cannadine's description of the British Monarchy's use of the state landau in similar fashion (Cannadine 1983, 124). An obsolete mode of transportation is drawn out of the realm of praxis, where it scarcely continues to exist, is ritually framed, and becomes a symbol of a new sociopolitical order. Like the landau, the canoe was a latent symbol of an historic culture that had disappeared. It came to represent the entire range of material and ideological culture of the precolonial Heiltsuk; or more accurately, it was a vehicle for feelings about that disappeared world. These feelings are condensed and mobilized by such symbols, which make them politically potent.

Ritual is a key element in activating such symbols. The "baptismal" ritual of the canoe as symbol was held in July 1986 on the eve of the trip to Vancouver. The ritual consisted of a Christian prayer and a paddle song sung by elders. On the 400 mile trip to Vancouver, the canoe stopped in at several reserves, where the crews were regaled with traditional welcome songs and dances. The most well-publicized of such greetings came when the canoe landed in Vancouver Harbour and was greeted by Salish chiefs, who, as hereditary owners of the territory on which the city of Vancouver now sits, had the right to do so. The political dimension of this, in the context of land claims, is obvious. Speeches by Heiltsuk hereditary chiefs expanded on this political theme, in front of television cameras. Speeches were punctuated with *λúeláxa* dances, lending ancestral validation to the speeches.

The national publicity of Native grievances against the government was only part of the success of the canoe trip. It also succeeded in depicting a positive and traditional image of the Heiltsuk in the national and provincial media, which was a radical departure from previous depictions of the Heiltsuk (e.g., NFBC 1975). Perhaps more important were the contacts made with other Native groups, including many with whom the Heiltsuk had had little or no previous contact. Historically, permission to beach canoes on a tribe's land was extended only to allies. This symbolic alliance of major British Columbia First Nations is a fact of potentially great political significance.

A *Gélw'a* Feast was held in November 1986 to honor those who had contributed labor to constructing and paddling the canoe, especially Frank Brown, who had organized the project. At this feast hereditary chiefs danced and gave speeches. New rituals were invented for this feast, including one in which the paddlers lifted the one-ton canoe and made a circuit around the hall. Historic rituals were performed as well, including the masked dance of the *p'g"is*, an anthropoid sea monster, representing power coming from the sea. Many other historic dances were performed, including the dance of the "tamed" *hámac'a*. After the dances, each paddler was given a name. A small distribution of goods was then made to each of the paddlers, and small souvenir fabric patches were given to everyone (Harkin 1985-87).

This feast represented a significant departure from other feasts and potlatches. For one thing, the food was brought in by the "guests" in potluck fashion, rather than provided by the host. Another important difference was that those receiving names did not distribute goods themselves (or have their families distribute goods), but were the recipients of goods. This was partly a response to the practical problems presented by this novel situation, where a group of unrelated young men were being honored by the community at large, and not by their own families. This new format was also an aspect of the innovation of the canoe project itself. As with Chief Billy Clifton's feast, the young paddlers were being situated within a larger sociological context than would be the case at a traditional feast. As representatives of the community as a whole, it was incumbent upon the community, and not an individual or family, to honor them.

This new-style feast was less than entirely successful. The attendance was fairly poor, reflecting among some community members questions about the legitimacy of the honoring and bestowal of names upon the young men, and their right to speak for the community as a whole. However, this attitude changed over time, as the canoe journey became an increasingly important feature of Native life on the Northwest Coast. In July 1989 the "Paddle to Seattle," timed to coincide with Washington State centennial festivities, drew dozens of canoes from Native groups in

British Columbia, Washington, as well as Maori from New Zealand. Frank Brown, leading the Heiltsuk canoe, used the opportunity to invite the tribes to a rendezvous in Waglisla in 1993 (Smith 1993; Neel 1994, 1995). This week-long Quatuwas Festival organized by Frank Brown and hosted by the Heiltsuk attracted hundreds of Native people. It included a formal welcoming ceremony and a potlatch. All the Heiltsuk hereditary chiefs participated in these ceremonies, which were well-attended by the community. By now, the indigenous canoe festival enjoys wide support not only in Waglisla, but throughout the Northwest Coast. Another festival is scheduled for summer 1997 in Washington State (Neel 1994, 18).

Conclusion: "To Create a Ceremony is to Create the Future"[8]

The success of the canoe festival as an "invented" ceremony belies the notion that new traditions are bound to be perceived as inauthentic and false. While there is some precedence for the ceremonial canoe journeys in historical culture: in wedding, war, and potlatch expeditions, and, more recently, in organized canoe regattas held in Washington State until the 1930s, these elements have been recombined into a new and vital ceremony (Smith 1993, 11). Strong emotions are summoned by the appearance of these canoes, as if from out of the past. Heiltsuk elders spoke of the days of their youth and the ancestors they remember (Harkin 1985-87). One Tulalip elder was rendered almost speechless by the sight: "I could see the old people again. . .I don't want to dwell on it. It is too moving to me" (Smith 1993, 14).[9]

Such strong emotions, and the blending of personal and collective experience, are markers of the pragmatic value of the canoe as a symbol and the canoe festival as a ceremony. Their ability to harness labor-power, money, and media exposure testify to the political potential of such new ceremonies. Within the pragmatic model of authenticity I presented above, it is clear that the canoe festival is an authentic ceremony. Although it was new, it was constructed out of cultural fragments in the manner of *bricolage*; individual signifiers all had pre-established meanings. These meanings were altered in the new contexts. A canoe became not an obsolete mode of transport but a symbol of, on the one hand, historic culture, and, on the other, the revitalization of contemporary culture. As such, it is a "new tradition" in a real and unironic sense.

Notes

1. It should be pointed out that this species of argument—that the modernization of Native societies delegitimizes Native claims to sovereignty or unique status— is made on the left as well as the right. Animal rights activists argue that Inuit use of animal resources, especially seal, is not justified by their traditional culture, since that culture has been irreversibly altered by capitalist and technological penetration (Wenzel 1991, 53-58).
2. Barthes' photograph portrays a related political mythology: that of assimilation. It is the "liberal" reading of the Vanishing Savage myth; the savages vanish, and in their place are black Frenchmen or red Americans.
3. Indeed, certain strains of postmodernism proclaim just that (e.g., Baudrillard 1988). However, this is ultimately an absurd position which allows no space for culture.
4. The line between officially approved ceremonies during the "dark years" as Cranmer-Webster (1992, 36) calls them and modern feasts is often very fine indeed. In May 1955, the community held a banquet at which Dr. Darby, the missionary of long standing, was not merely present but was the guest of honor. Drummers drummed and sang. Hereditary chiefs made speeches, as did other luminaries. The chiefs gave gifts of a carved pole and staff to Dr. Darby. On a previous occasion, in 1944, Dr. Darby was the honored guest at a similar ceremony, where he was awarded the highest title in the community, Wauyala (McKervill 1964, 148-149).
5. The United Church is the successor to the Canadian Methodist and Presbyterian Churches and, as such, is the "official" church of the Heiltsuk community.
6. The Rev. Willie was posted at Waglisla because the community wished to have a Native pastor, despite the denominational difference.
7. Some scholars have argued that these modern dances are identical to those of the nineteenth century, a curious position, which must be explainable by their desire to affirm cultural continuity. Bill Holm thus states with reference to the Heiltsuk Winter Ceremonial: "Tolmie's 1834 description of the Heiltsuk version ... describes very well the dance as seen today" (Holm 1977, 19). As I have shown, and others have argued, authenticity is possible despite considerable changes in performance and symbolism.
8. Quotation by Frank Brown quoted in Smith 1993.
9. The power of this image of the canoes, and their association with the "old people", is certainly connected with the Salish belief that ghosts travel by canoe to the Land of the Dead (Miller 1988).

8

The Berdache as Metahistorical Reference for the Urban Gay American Indian Community

Massimiliano Carocci

The social network of gay American Indians dates back to 1976, when the first gay and lesbian Native American support group appeared in San Francisco. Since then the number of groups with the same orientation has increased to the current number of seven across USA and Canada.[1] Through information gathered between 1991 and 1993 among members of three groups based in San Francisco, San Diego and New York, I was able to evaluate how the ideas of Indianness and sexual diversity overlap to generate the ideological premises that keep the gay American Indian community united.

In order to comprehend the metahistorical dimension of the berdache and its relation to sexual diversity as it is used by the gay Indian community, it is necessary to take a look at the construction of the idea of Indianness as the basis of the pan-Indian movement. We can in fact recognize the factors that created the idea of "berdachism" in the historical circumstances that originated pan-Indianism. The idea of Indianness can be traced back to the 1920s. During the next fifty years the pan-Indian movement developed the concept of Indianness as a model of cultural identification, unity and strength for the various Native American groups living in cities (Ewers 1964; Lippard 1990; Orlando 1991).

The movement was spurred on by millenarian phenomena as well as by political goals. The concept of Indianness is based on white/Indian relations rather than on the opposition of different tribal backgrounds. The reason for its existence thus lies in the affirmation of one's identity by means of a public image proposed in social fora as a response to the inadequacy of former models.

The strategy of Indianness indicates to each individual a self-cognitive order system expressed in the sequence tribal identification/ethnic identification, or vice versa, according to the social forum that requires such definition. In public fora such as urban powwows, the tribal identification appears as a contour to the "pan-Indian" or "inter-tribal" denominations that characterize such events as being purely Indian. Today's urban Indian society is made up of families of mixed descent, resulting in the need of relating to more general categories that can include everyone (Orlando 1991).

In the pan-Indian movement, the category of Indianness has to do with ethnic and cultural identification. In contrast, the gay Indian community uses the category of berdachism to deal with sex and gender identification. In both cases, an abstract category represents diverse realities, ideologically supporting a social environment suitable to the widest range of people with the same cultural identification. A parallel with the pan-Indian movement can be drawn with the gay Indian community. The latter draws its strength and unity from the use of general categories such as berdachism in much the same way as the pan-Indian movement used the concept of Indianness to inspire a sense of belonging to the Native American population.

Berdachism nominally stands for the practice of cross-dressing among Native Americans that implies a gender-mixing status in any of its institutionalized forms. Occasional forms of transvestism that occur in traditional societies generally are not considered berdachism if they do not satisfy these conditions.[2]

To distinguish the contemporary meaning of berdachism from its use in the past, I have to point out two different stages of interpretation of the phenomenon. Since the beginning of the colonization, and for the next three centuries, the word berdache has always been associated with sodomy. Gender-mixing was never considered to have the same social dimension it does today. The use of these mutually interchangeable categories almost always had moralistic undertones, implying negative judgement that sometimes led to extreme political actions.[3] When repression did not occur, berdachism was ridiculed to reaffirm the code of socially orthodox behaviour as opposed to alternative ones considered deviant.

Many words are derived from the Persian *bardah* or *bardaj* that describe negative aspects of sexuality. The original word meant "sultan's sex slave". The Italian *baldracca* or *bagascia* derived from it is still used for "old whore," and the Neapolitan *bardascio* designates a male prostitute. The French used this word more extensively on the American continent to comprise a wide variety of realities including transvestite shamans, war slaves obliged to wear women's clothes, effeminate men, etc., independent of the social/cultural context in which they were found. The indiscriminate use of the word berdache by explorers led scholars in more recent years to revaluate its specific meaning, so that now we are able to contextualize the various functions of cross-dressing and gender-mixing to redefine the boundaries of the phenomenon.[4]

In the past, berdachism was a widespread practice among the North American tribes. Today's urban gay Indians assume it as the role model for the sexual differences necessarily bonded to the ethnic identity by the concept of Indianness.

Moreover, the institutionalization of practices linked to berdachism (ritual roles, cross-dressing, sexual inclinations) and the faculties attributed to berdaches by indigenous populations (power to foretell the future, to handle corpses, to mediate with supernatural worlds, to bring luck, etc.) make it a totally Native American phenomenon. This further legitimizes the urban gay Indians to use berdachism in such a way as to guarantee both a cultural identity and a place in contemporary society. Given the berdache's gender-mixing status as the main feature of its role does not exclude the cultural specificities found in each individual case. The berdaches' role differed from tribe to tribe in tasks, occupations and ritual obligations that were linked to the mythological lore. His/her cultural activity was performed within and according to the specific tribal context.

The gay Indian's current use of berdachism as a category becomes a tool to give cultural depth to sexual alternatives (lesbian, homosexual or other). This term thus tends to lose the connotation of historical specificity that distinguishes the scholars' use of it in reference to ancient berdaches. The meaning given to berdachism by contemporary gay Indians neutralizes contextual differences into an all encompassing category that de-historicizes it as a real practice, thus rendering it metahistorical, in other words "beyond history."

The place held by berdaches in past societies was officialized by the functions attributed to them through the symbolic states of "mediator" and "caretaker." These two states interweaved with each other, proportioning the nature/culture, inside/outside opposition expressed in the contexts in which berdaches operated. As spokesmen/women of their tribe, they virtually became the symbol of the inside/outside relationship. In a similar way, naming children or burying the dead linked nature to culture in the transition from life to non-life and vice-versa. Likewise, the care of orphaned children demonstrated their role as mediators between culture and nature in the function of teacher and storyteller. Consequently, berdaches were considered the keepers of tradition even when creating art because their products and techniques were regarded as the best examples of the material lore. Berdaches' opinion on their culture and mythology was fundamental if not indispensable.[5]

Today, the role of the berdache as a keeper of tradition is a focal point around which lesbian and gay Indians have started a socio/cultural debate with political connotations. This aspect is so important that the legacy claimed earlier on by certain intellectuals of the gay Indian movement has been integrated into contemporary gay Indian culture. In many cases, this legacy is consciously in keeping with its historical antecedents. Often lesbian and gay Indians have occupations that, interpreted through the lens of tradition, assume a meaning that emphasizes the relation to the past. AIDS buddies, social workers, teachers and artisans embody the very idea of berdachism, characterized by membership in the two symbolic states of mediator and caretaker. The AIDS buddy figure for example, clearly epitomizes the two symbolic functions in one of the younger generations of gay Indians' most widely preferred occupations.

A Diachronic Approach

Notwithstanding the several living examples of berdaches, the temporal dimension of berdachism is the past. In an urban setting, the lack of direct, constant bonds to tribal culture generates a unilateral cultural progression that puts tradition behind, in opposition to the present of modern life. Tradition and traditional, in reference to the berdache are used to relate social norms, cultural behaviours, and spiritual values that remained unchanged until the nineteenth century or so it is believed. "Behind" and "past" shape the modern cultural behaviours with no negative connotations. On the contrary, they balance out often overwhelming contemporary influences.

From this clearly emerges the syncretic nature of the phenomenon, which eventually tends to shorten the spatial/temporal distance separating modern gays from berdaches of the past. Urban gay Indians effectively revamp past traditions by reinterpreting the old berdaches' spiritual powers and social roles.

Despite the spatial and temporal distance that separates berdaches from modern gays in the cities, the metahistorical dimension expressed in gays' use of the word legitimizes the presence of lesbians and homosexuals in today's Indian society for the younger generations and validates the cultural consistency of sexually diverse people with tradition. Awareness of this legacy keeps the social network that underpins the gay Indian community united.

The process of reinterpretation of past berdaches' spirituality and social roles, generally passes through a first stage of rediscovery and reappropriation of berdaches' characteristics in which not all gay Indians self-identify. In traditional thought for instance, masculine and feminine are considered cultural features rather than biological differences, gender is related to occupation and sexuality does not define individual's position in the social structure. None of the Native American languages refer to sexual habits in terms of berdaches (Roscoe 1987). The ability to assume cultural and social behaviours of both sexes was thus perceived as a third gender, halfway between male and female with strong spiritual connotations.

Gay Indian people with traditionalistic inclinations feel entitled to adapt this perspective to their case once they become familiar with these concepts. This process totally depends on the particular educational, environmental and familial background. In fact, not all gay Indians necessarily express their sexuality through a cultural framework pertinent to their ethnic belonging. Often, sexual inclination can be the only element guiding them in the process of self-identification; this leads them to embrace the Western model in so far as the sexual preference clearly expressed in the term "homosexuality" is in no way sufficient in Native American thought to define the gender category symbolized by the berdache. Eventually, we can say that the contemporary Native American lesbian and gay population falls into three main categories: the traditional berdache, the modern berdache or two-spirited person and the Westernized lesbian or gay man.

It must be noted that this distinction is based on individual self-identifications which reflect a cultural spectrum conceptualized on the opposed categories of tradition and innovation as the extremes of a time span with all the degrees of difference in between. Since the time span is conceptualized on these two extremes, reservation and city will necessarily be the spatial correspondent of the opposing points being the actual spaces where the real berdaches (traditionalists) and anti-traditionalists (Westernized Indian lesbians or gay men) dwell.

Despite an evident level of innovation in the material life of the reservations, people brought up according to tribal values and spirituality are considered the real berdaches as they are close to the origin of Indian cultural categorizations. Next to traditional berdaches proceding towards modernity, two-spirited people stand somewhat in between tradition and innovation extremes as they resume the cultural and spatial transition between reservation and city. It is nonetheless important that most two-spirited people experience both worlds due to particular personal antecedents such as family removals, adoptions and split families where one of the parents lives on the reservation and the other in the city. These people are conditioned to make the transitory process their own cultural dimension in which they need to revaluate past traditions if they want to claim an Indian identity within the urban context. The moment of self-identification as Indians in the city conditions two-spirited people to a movement backwards in search of role models for sexual identity. This syncretic nature of the two-spirits phenomenon thus lies in the very same essence of pan-Indian urban culture that creates a new cultural identity by bringing together forms of different places from different times.

Strategies of Survival

As a consequence of the persecution and repression of homosexuality and cross-dressing by missionaries and federal agents, berdachism lost its role in the social and religious life of native peoples. "Relocation" and "allotment" policies during the '50s and '60s imposed a cultural isolation on many families, fragmenting the social framework that supported the existence of these practices (Williams 1986; Roscoe 1988). Where Euro-American influence was stronger, it would replace absent Indian role models. The traumatic impact on Indian culture led to changes in berdaches' cultural expressions and confined their sexuality to a totally private dimension in a closed familial environment. Their former socially acknowledged position expressed in rituals, blessings and dances that made public their sexual relations has now been replaced by private confessions on one's sexuality.

The traditional berdache exists in those tribal contexts that still resist the dominating Western ideology. In spite of this, some gay Indian men from the city prefer to be addressed as berdaches, claiming that this term better suits their case, evidently stressing the charisma that such identification carries with itself. This does not exclude the possibility that old fashioned berdaches might live in cities although they are totally alien to Western lifestyles. The berdache figure embodies a sacredness that is closely tied to his/her personal relation to land, family and myth that can exist only in tribal contexts where his/her presence is justified within the boundaries of tribal histories, in direct connection of funding mythologies and language that define their gender. Apparently, a public dimension of such a set of relations does not find a place in the mutated socio/cultural framework that once sustained berdaches by mean of rituals, kinship obligations and ceremonial tasks. Their existence in the tribe therefore is seldom discussed and their sexual habits are regarded with distance and reserved respect. A personal talk to a Crow elder made me realize that issues regarding "Bades" (i.e. male berdache in Crow) were not "public business." Traditional berdaches are generally addressed with the proper tribal denomination for their role and are never associated with Western codifications.

The term berdache, commonly used until now, is being slowly replaced by lesbian and gay American Indians with a new category known under the name "Two-spirits" or "Two-spirited people." This is widely preferred over berdache because it emphasizes the spiritual aspect of sexual diversities. Its use restores the traditional habit of thinking according to three gender categories, in which the third one is the intermixing of the other two (Roscoe 1994). Furthermore, its meaning is inter-tribally intelligible as a pan-Indian category opposed to berdache, a term imposed by the West. The word berdache may be used to explain the cultural reference and the source of inspiration for the gay pan-Indian movement. Through the link with the past, two-spirited people make their sexual life part of a set of values culturally consistent with their ethnic identity. This is why among them, contact with family and land is highly esteemed as a genuine need to maintain a precious sense of belonging. Two-spirited people are the contemporary urban version of the berdache, which is linked to a rural environment (reservation) and to an uncontaminated lifestyle. Since the dominant thought system is Anglo-Saxon, Indians need to use white-centered categories to describe themselves when talking about gender alternatives, even when addressing to an Indian audience. "Gay" and "homosexual" have a descriptive and ontological function. When addressing an audience unfamiliar with the two-spirited concept, they may call themselves gay. Otherwise the word gay reflects a concept which is distinctly alien to traditional Indian beliefs. The gay category describes a lifestyle with codes, behaviours, aesthetic standards and values that are not part of traditional Indian reality.

Leading a private homosexual life is certainly possible on the reservation, but an outspoken homosexuality or lesbianism faces ostracism and disapproval within the tribe. Traditionalists tend to judge it on the basis of its detachment from old Indian values; more Westernized Indians apply to it the strong moral stigma imposed on sexually diverse people derived from Western values.

If, to some extent berdachism on the reservation is still tolerated, it is due to the commitment to the preservation of traditions that individual berdaches pursue in the social sphere, although their sexuality may never be acknowledged publicly. In the reservation, a better acceptance of a different sexual inclination seems to appear only at a familial level when there is support of at least one traditional member of the family, generally one of the grandparents. Very seldom is tradition strong enough to connect sexually diverse orientations to old gender classifications and patterns, especially where old languages are no longer spoken. Indulgence towards diverse sexual inclinations by some members of the family is useless towards the creation of a traditional cultural model in young people if the social environment is no longer prepared to accept homosexual and/or lesbian orientation as one of the possible connotations of a particular gender difference. We could say that the more a person feels supported by traditional culture in regards to his/her sexual preference, the more it is difficult to move towards a Westernized model, but this is now very rare. Such an explanation should be enough to justify the reduced presence of traditional berdaches in the reservations. Gay as a system of cultural reference probably would not affect younger generations if language and cultural context offered a valuable model for the integration of sexual diversities to refer to, but obviously cultures do not develop themselves in vacuo. So being gay cannot be reconciled with being Indian as long as being Indian means following traditions; the two terms exclude each other. This is why those who do not identify with traditional values and embrace an Anglo-Saxon lifestyle are normally considered gay, either within and out of the reservations. They do not use the native language or Indian categories to define themselves and therefore are seen by two-spirited people and traditionalists as lacking the spiritual part originally connected to the third gender difference. In other terms, they are cultural outsiders who reject or do not acknowledge their link to Native American cultural identity. This is particularly true in the cities where sometimes Native American culture among gays is absent or ethnicity needs to be proved if not rediscovered.

Among several urban Indian gay men, I realized that few reduced contacts with traditional lore had no effect at all in the formation of individuals' Native American identity. In the city some parents consciously abnegate their American Indian culture and even hide their ethnicity to their children. Sometimes poor economic conditions or little education do not allow the child to develop an interest in or any attachment to traditions. In some other cases, people of mixed descent know about their Native American ancestry only casually.

Very often when educational standards are low, children from interracial couples tend to adjust their cultural identity towards a model which is perceived stronger and more secure, a fact that evidently puts Indian culture at the bottom of the social scale. Nevertheless, despite the official classifications or appearances that may denote a high blood quantum of African-American or Hispanic ancestry, many young people take pride in the Native American heritage so that cultural affiliation becomes more a political choice than the product of the process of inculturation (Epstein 1978).

A Question of Language

Certainly the city, as opposed to the reservation, offers better outlets for an outspoken homosexuality due to the presence of a gay subculture that sustains homosexual relations, creates social networks, sets points of reference and generates self-confidence. The more the gay culture goes mainstream in urban life, the more urban Indian population is willing to accept the presence of lesbians and gays among them. This perspective helps young lesbians and gays coming from the reservations to face their sexual diversity and ethnicity. Nevertheless, it is the concept of Indianness that seems to offer a useful ethnic identification in the city's social forum of cultural confrontations. Tribal identification is far less important in such stage, although lately there is an increasing tendency to show one's tribal origin rather than using the terms Indian or Native American.

On the reservation where the opportunities for sexually diverse people's integration are minimal, more Westernized Indians reject homosexuality on the basis of the lack of appropriate cultural references, as if integration of alternative sexual relations was never recorded among third gender people's practices. The general attitude in regard to homosexuality/lesbianism shown on the reservation is to deny their existence. Naturally, lesbianism and homosexuality as we know them today never existed, as such conceptualization derives from Western bourgeois environment, but this is not the argument used to defend Indians' pretended unfamiliarity with same-sex practices. More traditionalists on the contrary, may accept these practices more or less compromisingly as long as they can be related to former models of integration. We can not forget that even today's most traditional elders have difficulty to revive part of the past traditions as they too have been affected in many ways by white hegemonic culture through education, missions etc.

In the city the process of acceptance seems to be reversed. Those modernized Indians who left the reservations to be more accepted as gays and lesbians now feel the need to be less Westernized and become more traditional, having discovered through the Indian centers, that tradition can actually offer an appropriate answer to their quest of identity. In this way the social, political and cultural work carried on by the gay groups within the American Indian centers, helps the rest of the Indian population to familiarize with the presence of gay and lesbian Indians. The process of self-acceptance and social acceptance of sexual diversities seems to restart from where it actually ended, that is, the Westernized forum of pan-Indian modern culture.

Evidently, on the reservation there is no cultural osmosis between Westernized and traditionalists, otherwise we would witness to a revival of berdachism forms on a wide scale. It must be also said that Western and traditional cultural patterns operate quite separately on the reservations, for they share no common code to be used at least as far as sex and gender issues are concerned.

In the city, the overall use of English language for instance, makes possible to match the different realities of Native Americans through a single common code that certainly helps to systematize the complex homosexuals' cultural/sexual identity as it is being made. Interestingly, two-spirits phenomenon creates in the city a new culture of gender difference that blends tradition and innovation opposites on the basis of sexual orientation (homosexuality/lesbianism), ethnic belonging (Indianness) and shared language (English). Making sexual orientation the basis of a new third gender actually differentiates two-spirits from the past berdache tradition. It is as the process of the cultural construction of gender of the past had shifted from spirit to sex to from sex to spirit. A reverse has taken place.

Reshaping Paradigms

The sources (Callender and Kochems 1983; Whitehead 1981; Williams 1986) show how in order to become berdaches one should follow personal inclinations in dreams or visions and performing opposed gender tasks, that were interpreted as powerful supernatural indicators of third gender status. Nonetheless, acknowledgement of one's sexual inclination is now the only condition on which a third gender is created. Third gender spirituality can be claimed by today's two-spirits who consider themselves the contemporary version of berdaches, even if homosexuality was formerly only one of their characteristics.

The condition for the ongoing cultural osmosis process between what is past, antecedent, traditional, Indian, and new, modern, non-traditional, Western, is made possible in the city probably because the cultural void experienced by urban ethnicities is being progressively filled by contents that assume their meaning by way of reinterpretation of old concepts in a new context. This potentially dismantles the problematic old-new dichotomy, creating room for new meanings beyond the sharp differences that characterize reservation life. This fierce optimism is rather tangible in the aims and activities carried on by the gay Indians taken as example.

Each of the three urban support groups tries to guarantee processes of cohesion and identification as opposed to mechanisms of individual isolation and competition. They tend to recreate a family-type bonding between the members, especially important for those that have no point of reference in the city. The average age is between 25 and 35. Basically all cultural areas are represented within each group, with a large number of people coming from the Western reservations in the groups of San Francisco and San Diego. Many members are of mixed, inter-tribal descent, which has a particular relevance in shaping each group's identity on pan-Indian ideas. This does not exclude a particular interest in the activities that ought to be carried on in the reservations, although the groups are mainly involved in activities strictly related to urban life. Communal gatherings are held on a regular basis to discuss and compare the different experiences of the members and to allow the development of new strategies that can affect both reservation and urban realities.

The re-emergence of the berdache figure in the urban setting fits in with that part of the gay Indian movement's philosophy concerned with rediscovery of spiritual values and historical references aimed at familiarizing people with a common heritage of sex and gender issues.

In fact, many projects have been started to create pan-Indian values regarding sex and gender alternatives. Groups engaged in anthropological and historical research are working together to readapt original berdache features to modern needs. The highly spiritual character of ancient berdaches is a striking example. Two-spirited people put a big emphasis on individual and communal spiritual practices that obviously, in an urban context, differentiate themselves from historical antecedents. So for instance, as berdaches took care of dead, the sacredness of this office is now reformulated in the care of AIDS patients and generally people that need social or medical assistance.

Each group has its base in the American Indian center of the city that offers spaces for meetings, spiritual events, video festivals, rehearsal rooms and libraries. Some activities are in collaboration with the centers, other are sponsored by private non-profit organizations. In 1988 for instance, the San Francisco group published the first anthology of essays by lesbian and gay Native Americans about the historical and anthropological relevance of the berdache from an emic point of view. The book, primarily aimed to a gay public, challenges the general Indian population to deal with lesbian and gays.[6] Other books and activities brought gay American Indians into the media spotlight and spurred discussion and interest beyond academic fora. The New York group collaborates with other minorities in the monthly magazine *Color* and publishes a newsletter with news from the gay Indian front, poetry and information about their current activities. In recent years there has been an increase in the production of literature and poetry, especially by lesbian writers who seem to have found in these forms a way to be visible and participate to the cultural exuberance that surrounds the phenomenon. Christos, Beth Brant, Paula Gunn Allen, Barbara Cameron and Janice Gould, to cite a few, have won the interest of the larger gay population in addition to Indian audiences.

Educating the Indian population to respect sexual differences and the gay population to embrace cultural pride is also pursued with the help of videos and documentaries,[7] archives, school lectures, slide shows and the massive presence of gay groups in official events. Other cultural activities include arts and crafts courses, drum and dancing groups and spiritual gatherings.

Style Politics

The syncretic aspect of the metahistorical dimension of the berdache figure emerges from these totally new cultural forms. Especially in parades and gatherings it is evident how material culture expressions often reflect the blend between tradition and innovation carried on at an ideological level, because traditional elements from different origins are formally brought together through aesthetic codes to express the idea of Indianness as a pan-Indian category. The colourful mass of elements displayed in clothing during parades has on an outside viewer the effect that something Indian is happening. Decorative elements of particular areas can be casually worn independent of the ethnic background of the wearer that may pair them with modern or old motifs for purely aesthetic reasons, to match colours, shape or subject. The syntagmatic relation between the clothing pieces clearly expresses the post-modern melange of Native American elements condensed in the concept of Indianness. The same process of mix-matching various elements in a casual fashion is much more reduced in the reservation's official events where traditionally set canons are more rigid.

In cities such canons may vary altogether, as Indianness needs to be expressed in any possible way, whereas on the reservation, Indianness is taken for granted. The mixing of old and new, or the blending of decorative elements from different areas, become the condition to show Indianness imposed by the confrontation of a large variety of ethnic backgrounds and mixed descent people that need recognition and self-identification.

The latter tend to adopt fashion elements of the Plains tribes because they are generally perceived to better express the idea of Indianness. Original costumes denote a particular tribal identification, but often simple fashion devices are sufficient to manifest ethnic belonging. Jewels, feathers, t-shirts with Indian motifs, a folded blanket carried on the arm or a feathered fan constitute a mark that symbolizes ethnicity more than one's presence in the Indian section of the parade. Sometimes, two-spirited people express their status of modern berdaches by wearing clothes combinations that denote gender mixing.

For two-spirited women this is more difficult than for men, because the introduction of trousers, cowboy boots, man's hats and bandannas into women's wear does not contain any gender-mixing connotation as such items are widely accepted, even among reservation Indians. A more visible marker of their third gender status can be their tendency to interiorize male gender positions and attitudes stressed by a particular set of codes in body language, walking, sitting and posture. On the other hand, women who prefer to dress in their tribe's traditional clothes very seldom wear men's garb on women's to indicate their third gender status.

Two-spirited men in parades and public happenings sometimes mix more strikingly opposite gender codes by overlapping skirts on trousers, or wearing women's shawls on their jackets and flamboyant earrings. On such occasions, clothing as a marker of gender difference seems to be less considered among women than men; in every day life anyhow it is for both totally unimportant. Some people naturally develop more than others a particular taste for extravagant clothing and tend to manifest openly their desire to be noticed. Generally, two-spirited men and women translate the opposite gender's behaviour into mannerisms that have become an exclusive feature of their position.

The extreme freedom in blending and reinterpreting diverse cultural expressions from the American Indian past and present is also displayed by the example of women's only drumming groups and women's only sun dances, recent innovations on traditional themes viewed by spiritual leaders with some suspicion. Such changes in gender related tasks are noticeably recent.

Although women's only societies have been historically recorded across the Plains area, women's drumming is quoted in the sole exception of Mandan women's "White Buffalo" society (Bowers 1950). With the information available so far on the topic we are not able of knowing whether women's societies in the past included female berdaches in their rituals and dances, but in some cases even controversial interpretations of historical data can justify modern expression with concrete antecedents.

Paula Gunn Allen (1986) sees the Sioux's dummy baby dance related to the Anuk'ite cult as an institutionalized form of acknowledgement of women's berdache status. Such cases can lead to think of a separate social sphere in which female-to-female relations avoid-ed male cultural hegemony. This is to say that for as much as these facts may never be proved they constitute reference cases upon which two-spirited women can base their cultural speculations and activities.

A case opposite to this is constituted by women's only sun dances where no actual reference can be found in the past. Although male berdaches are reported to have had a specific role in sun dances, the privilege to attend the session given to a women's only crowd and the two-spirited nature of the event seem to be difficult to establish as a new version of an old ceremony, notwithstanding the pledger's claim to have been instructed during vision quests. Women's sun dances are kept as close as possible to the original versions. They invite two-spirited women and lesbians of other ethnic groups to participate under the Native American women's supervision, but the exclusion of men and the direction of lesbians are so criticized in respect of traditions, that in some cases, the rituals have to move away from the reservations to be performed in more neutral environments such as private properties.

Other ritual elements are mainly derived from Plains tribes' religious practices. Purification with sage, vision quests and sweat lodges are rituals usually integrated into two-spirits' spiritual life, although it is common habit to follow individual practices that change from person to person. The high regard for spiritual issues has led many two spirited people to perform their rituals in private. Also, communal gatherings that involve strictly religious practices are closed to non-Indians to prevent external factors from disturbing or influencing the sessions. They underscore the political attitude that values self-determination as the main tool to preserve the heritage.

In opposition to the privacy of religious life, most of the political work is carried on together with other minority groups such as Latinos, African-Americans, Asians and Pacific Islanders. Collaboration between these groups focuses public attention on common issues such as discrimination, marginalization, lack of services and representation in the media. The feeling of being misrepresented or hardly represented within the urban gay culture is a common denominator among the minority groups that condemn the ethnocentrism of the white majority and their information monopoly. The strategy of proposing their own categories, cultural behaviours and aesthetic standards raises interesting issues such as stereotyping derived from white biases. Gay American Indian groups are against most of the standards commonly set within the gay subculture, a fact exemplified by the rejection of the term gay to describe their lifestyle. Rather, ethics and morals evolve around the pervasive spirituality accorded to the third gender that for its unicity draws a discriminatory line between Native Americans and others. Consequently, they claim an alternative cultural niche complementary to the mainstream gay culture.

The emergence of a gay American Indian community is a new phenomenon that involves part of the homosexual/lesbian Indian population. Its particular cultural niche within the larger gay subculture draws inspiration from traditional elements that, appropriately de-contextualized, are adapted to abstract categories suited to contemporary needs of sexual and cultural identity. In defining a proper gay Indian identity the use of categories such as Indianness and berdachism overlap on an individual level in the form of a cultural identification. Making sexual preference the condition to establish a new third gender category reverses past berdache's gender construction based on supernatural causes. Two-spirits' city based activities also make possible an inversion in the process of acceptance of sexual diversities among modern reservation Indians who seem to disapprove or reject entirely homosexual/lesbian relations and cultural references as alien to pre-reservation Indian cultures. Eventually, the berdache's room for the acceptance of sexual diversities can be reintroduced as a past reference for a concrete relevant feature of modern Indian culture. For now, the berdache's cultural relevance is circumscribed to the gay Indian community's cultural framework. In its functional use for educational, political and cultural purposes, berdachism connects realities distant in time and space to create an original reinterpretation of traditional cultural characteristics transposed to a modern background. By reorganizing the fragmented traditional lore in a unique cultural pastiche, berdachism is substituted for particular histories, thus bringing the gay Indian's cultural identity into the innovative metahistorical perpective. Pointing out valid cultural options to younger generations it also challenges Western society to reinterpret its own sex and gender categories. The unicity of the final result is expressed through the cultural products inspired by ideas structured on the opposition of two extremes, traditional versus non traditional, old versus new, in which two-spirited people bring together tradition and innovation inheriting the mediatory function once held by the berdache in dealing with opposite categories, to impose once again its proper cultural efficiency.

Notes

1. The list of American Indian lesbian and gay groups updated to 1993 include Nations of the Four Directions, San Diego; Gay American Indians, San Francisco; Tahoma Two Spirits, Seattle; American Indians Gay and Lesbians, Minneapolis; Weh Wah & Bar Che Ampe, New York; Gay and Lesbians of the First Nations, Toronto; Nichiwakan Lesbian and Gay Indians, Winnipeg.
2. I have attended a powwow in Rosebud (South Dakota) during which some men took the garb and style of the women's butterfly dance. This case of cross-dressing/acting cannot be considered a case of berdachism because it is totally detached from the institutionalized sacred duty traditionally attributed to the status of the Winkte (Sioux for male berdache).
3. Jonathan Goldberg (1992) gives an interesting interpretation of the Spanish repression of the New World sodomites.

4. In 1955, Angelino and Shedd started to contextualize the phenomenon but the last extensive reports that include female and male berdaches are to the best of my knowledge Callender and Kochems (1983); Roscoe (1987); and Whitehead (1981).
5. A berdache informant from Rosebud reservation (South Dakota) is officially recognized by the Lakotas as one of the experts on his tribe's traditional lore. Examples of historic berdaches confirm this case. See for instance the Navajo Kinipai in W.W. Hill's article "The Status of the Hermaphrodite and Transvestite in Navajo Culture" or "Weh Wah and Klah, the American Indian Berdache as Artist and Priest" by W. Roscoe. Today the process of defining an urban Indian gay culture, creating new categories and re-evaluating the berdache figure is made difficult by the relationship with the official interlocutors of the tribes of origin, who have the last say on what can or cannot be considered original, and therefore legitimate.
6. See *Living the Spirit* edited by W. Roscoe (1988).
7. Here is a list of videos and documentaries updated to 1993, by and about gay American Indians, berdaches and berdache-related topics produced by or in collaboration with one or more native groups. *A Light on the Path* by Massimiliano Carocci and Marco Puccioni; *Her Giveaway* and *Honored by the Moon* by Mona Smith; *Two Spirits and HIV* by James Wentzy; *Two-Spirited People* by Lory Levy, Michael Beauchemin, and Gretchen Vogel.

9

The Reification of Aboriginal Culture in Canadian Prison Spirituality Programs

James B. Waldram

Introduction

Members of cultural minority groups often do not have the luxury of simply living as cultural beings. Frequently, the threat of forced or inadvertent cultural change looms large as they attempt to coexist alongside, and in some cases under the domination of, larger cultural groups. A good example of this are the Aboriginal[1] peoples living in Fourth World contexts, such as in Canada and the United States, who have experienced substantial colonization and over a century of policies designed to eliminate their traditional cultures. Hence, for these peoples, "culture" tends to become considerably more reified as the need to protect its most central, tangible, and significant elements grows.

Part and parcel with cultural oppression comes political oppression, and one symptom of this is the extent to which members of cultural minority groups are represented within the justice systems of the dominant culture. In Canada, as in most countries with indigenous populations, Aboriginal peoples are over-represented throughout the various components of the national and provincial justice systems. This fact is particularly evident when incarceration rates are examined. For instance, within the prairie provinces of western Canada (Manitoba, Saskatchewan and Alberta), where Aboriginal peoples constitute only 5% of the general population, they constitute 32% of the federal penitentiary population.[2] The data for provincial incarceration rates are even more telling: Aboriginal incarceration rates range from 17% in Alberta to 60% in Saskatchewan (Pasmeny 1992, 403).

In the early 1980s, Aboriginal inmates began to demand access to traditional religious services in penitentiaries. While the many Christian denominations were well represented through the prison chaplaincy programs, Aboriginal inmates wishing to follow the traditional spiritual path were denied access to their ceremonies, religious paraphernalia and spiritual leaders. Political protests by a handful of inmates at Oakalla and Kent Institutions in British Columbia in 1982 and 1983, involving both spiritual fasts and legal action, resulted in the development of a new policy to allow Aboriginal religious services in federal prisons (Couture 1992). Nevertheless, actual services have developed slowly over the years.

While many Aboriginal inmates have become involved with the traditional services offered, many others have not, and the degrees of involvement are extensive. It is important to appreciate the cultural diversity that exists in Aboriginal Canada. This diversity is best viewed as operating along two dimensions. The first represents the traditional Aboriginal cultures themselves, as they exist in the 1990s as continuities from the past. Despite over 300 years of colonialism in Canada, there remain many Aboriginal peoples who can still be described as "traditional." That is, they retain facility in an Aboriginal language as their first language, with relatively poor grasp of English or French (and in some cases, no understanding of these European languages). There are still many Aboriginal communities in remote areas of the country, some of which still lack road access. Hunting, fishing and trapping remain important cultural and economic activities. Other Aboriginal peoples retain elements of their traditional culture but have also become more integrated within the culture of the national society. This represents the second dimension of cultural orientation, that is, the degree of integration within or familiarity with the Euro-Canadian culture. Bicultural Aboriginal persons are very common; in effect, these are individuals able to operate within both their Aboriginal culture and the national culture. There also exists many Aboriginal people with no knowledge of their heritage Aboriginal culture. These individuals typically were raised in Euro-Canadian foster or adoptive homes, often in urban areas. In essence, the cultural orientation of Aboriginal peoples in Canada today runs the broad range from traditional in the Aboriginal context to more-or-less completely Euro-Canadian. Individuals of all types of cultural orientation find themselves incarcerated within the federal and provincial correctional systems. How they experience and react to various prison Aboriginal programs depends, in part, on their individual cultural orientation.

Beginning in the fall of 1990, research into the cultural aspects of treatment programming at the Regional Psychiatric Centre (Prairies) in Saskatoon, Saskatchewan was commenced. The RPC is a federal correctional facility and forensic hospital, designed to treat federal offenders (those with sentences longer than two years). The RPC houses a variety of offenders, from those considered "insane" under the law, to sex offenders and those diagnosed as "personality disordered," including those convicted of armed robbery, assault, and homicide. Approximately one-third of the patients at RPC at any given time are Aboriginal.

Subsequent to the RPC research, the study was broadened to include inmates at three other federal institutions in Saskatchewan and Manitoba, and one provincial institution in Saskatchewan. In total, since 1990, over 90 Aboriginal offenders have been interviewed using an open-ended, tape-recorded format, and another 250 with a structured instrument. Elders have also been interviewed, and the researcher has participated in many of the prison spirituality programs. The data presented in this paper are derived primarily from the first RPC study, although subsequent research has served to verify the observations made at that time.

In this paper, I wish to examine how Aboriginal "culture" is conceptualized and understood by these offenders within the context of various Aboriginal-oriented prison programs. It is evident from the research that a fractured, incomplete and somewhat stereotypical model of Aboriginal culture is being presented to and/or internalized by many of these individuals, many of whom are anxious to learn as much as they can about their heritage.

My argument in this paper is that, within the prisons where inmates are serving very long sentences, Aboriginal "culture" has come to be defined within the context of a fairly narrow set of beliefs and practices. Further, these beliefs and practices, referred to in their totality as "spirituality," have taken on an eclectic, pan-Indian flavour. Indeed, since many of the current prison Elders seem to have lived an avowedly unspiritual existence in the past, they have come to acquire spiritual knowledge only late in life, and often have had to travel beyond the boundaries of their own culture to acquire knowledge.[3] As a result, I would argue that the Aboriginal offenders, as inmates, are heavily influenced by the view of "culture" and "spirituality" they receive in prison, and that while in many cases these programs have helped them solidify their own identities, in some cases identity conflict has been generated.

Prison Aboriginal Programs

It has been only a decade or so since Aboriginal cultural awareness and spirituality programs started to become available in most federal prisons in Canada. There are many facets to these programs, and they tend to vary from one institution to another. In general, the programs tend to include both cultural and spiritual education, available to all inmates (including non-Aboriginals) on a voluntary basis. Spiritual leaders, usually Elders, are contracted to provide services to the offenders, including personal and spiritual counselling. They also conduct spiritual ceremonies and sweatlodges, and provide cultural information to inmates.

Many of these Elders themselves have experienced problems similar to the inmates: they may have had alcohol or drug problems in the past, and may have done prison time. Frequently, they have discovered their own spirituality later in life. In this sense, they are not the same as traditional, reserve-based Elders. Many prison Elders seem to have at least two important characteristics: they can provide empathy to the inmates, by virtue of having lived similar lifestyles; and they are able, and willing, to undertake spiritual activities within the many restrictions of the prison setting. Nevertheless, Aboriginal spirituality is highly individualistic, and each Elder brings to the prison not only the teachings of his or her own culture, but those of other Elders they have interacted with. Even within a particular cultural tradition, there is great variability in terms of the spiritual "gifts" and teachings given to, and therefore offered by, Elders. Furthermore, there is also variability in the kinds of services they are willing to perform within a prison. Some, for instance, will not bring sacred objects such as pipes into prison, others will not bring sweetgrass, and so on. Typically, a given institution will have only one Elder on contract, with the result that the services provided are entirely dependent upon the approach of that one individual. Hence, it is quite common to see a Cree Elder working with a Dene inmate, or a Saulteaux Elder running a sweatlodge ceremony the Saulteaux way, but with Cree, Blackfoot and Dene participants. Some Elders will pray in their own Aboriginal language during ceremonies, and hence are often not understood by many other participants. "Culture" as it is being offered under these circumstances adequately represents neither the total richness of the Aboriginal cultural experience nor even the total richness of Aboriginal spirituality. The prison acts as a cultural filter in this process. Yet, some Aboriginal inmates come to mistakingly believe that, through participation in such selected spiritual activities, they can become culturally competent "Indians" (or, in some cases, improve their existing competency).

For the inmates, being "Aboriginal" is an important, positive status which both identifies them and separates them from the other inmates. Native Brotherhood organizations exist in most institutions, and serve to develop Aboriginal solidarity around cultural, political and social issues. Subtle, and sometimes substantive, pressures are often brought to bear upon Aboriginal inmates to participate with their "brothers" in a positive recognition of their Aboriginality. Involvement with Elders and attendance at spiritual ceremonies is the most profound demonstration of this solidarity. While many become involved in these activities to develop their own sense of spirituality, and to help themselves heal, others become involved for more secular reasons.

Pan-Indianism in Prison Spirituality Programs

Over the course of this research, three Elders were involved at the RPC, one Dakota, one Stoney and one Saulteaux. Their teachings varied with the individual, but it became clear that they were presenting a fairly similar view of Indian spirituality, centered on the Medicine Wheel, tobacco, the sacred pipe, the sweatlodge and the use of sweet grass. The symbols used were typically those of the Plains cultural groups of which these individuals were members. So while there were differences, such as the direction in which the sweatlodge faced, where the Elder sat within the lodge, and the colours of the sacred cloth used, the basic principles were similar. Indeed, the Elders often reiterated their views that the fundamental principles of Aboriginal belief systems were essentially the same. Inmates from different cultures were encouraged to be open-minded and learn the Elder's ways for the time being, and when released to seek out Elders from their own cultural traditions.

In the research, it became evident that the various spiritual items and activities formed a cultural trait list, against which many Aboriginal offenders compared their own cultural upbringing. Furthermore, these traits seem to have come to represent the most integral parts of

Aboriginal cultures. According to one traditional inmate:

> All he [the Elder] talked about was our culture, sweatlodges and stuff like that, and about Elders, prayers, sweatlodges and stuff like that.

Another inmate, a Metis, described his introduction to Indian culture as follows:

> Well, I have been involved with the Native Brotherhood ... and I have been involved with the Elders and the sweats. I got involved in the pipe ceremonies and sometimes we have powwow. So I guess in fact, what I have got into is more of the Native [Indian] culture rather than the Metis culture [Bicultural].

A third inmate described his home environment:

> There was Indian culture. There was a lot of medicine bundles in my home. A lot of drums, a lot of Indian artifacts. So I grew up with a lot of culture [Bicultural].

A fourth inmate very clearly related Indian "culture" to religion and spirituality:

> The sweats is like keeping up with your culture. Like when you go to church, it's the same thing [Traditional].

One Aboriginal offender, a Christian, took the equation of Indian culture to spirituality to its extreme, and refused to become involved:

> I don't get involved in any Native programs ... Because some of the things I don't believe in ... Sweetgrass, I don't believe in that. I don't believe in what they call "praying to the grandfathers" ... and I have my own faith in what I believe in ... Christianity, that is what I believe in, and I go to church, but I don't participate in any Native culture [Euro-Canadian].

In general, there was very little criticism of the Elders' methods and teachings by Aboriginal inmates. Indeed, despite the great cultural variability exhibited by the Aboriginal participants, there was clearly an attempt to seek more fundamental principles within the teachings that tempered cultural differences (see Waldram 1993). In their comments, we clearly see efforts to define a pan-Indian perspective:

> But to me, our religion is all the same anyway. It doesn't really matter, you know, what tribe you're from. We still all believe in the same thing, that we're from different tribes but we're all the same [Bicultural].

> Elders, I guess I respect them because the Native people, they almost do the same thing. A little different, but almost the same everything [Traditional].

> It is the same way, with just different culture and that's all. Different. The Elder uses Cree and I'm Chipewyan. That's the only difference. But all our ways and everything is the same [Traditional].

> And they [the Elders] all came from different tribes or nations. And their focus was toward the great spirit or creator of the universe but their teaching was also similar or interrelated in one way or another. And the ceremonies are more or less similar in a lot of respects although there might be some different elements involved [Bicultural].

However, one individual was critical of the pan-Indianism of some Elders, and in particular their apparent eclecticism:

> Some of the Elders are pretty good. Not all are level. Some of them are just a bit off ... Like they've got things kind of scattered about, and they give me a piece of this, a piece of that ... They give you something from one area, then they go to a totally different area and give you another thing [Traditional].

As noted above, the spiritual programming is strongly based on Plains Indian traditions. One inmate, born to Gitksan parents (a northern British Columbia hunting and fishing people), but who was raised extensively in non-Indian foster homes, found a sense of pride in being Indian while watching a prison powwow:

> When I'm at a powwow, it makes me glad. When I see the dancers, the singers, it makes me really proud being an Indian ... I want to be a dancer, an Indian dancer, you know, make my own sort of costume thing, dancing suit ... [But] I am still trying to identify who I am, where I came from [Euro-Canadian].

As this inmate suggests, his identity is being reshaped by his introduction to a Plains Indian form of dancing, despite the fact that this was foreign to his ancestral culture. Another individual presents an even more dramatic case. This individual is from a northern Northwest Territories Dene community, but has been heavily involved in Plains-style prison spirituality for ten years. He is renowned for his teepee making skills, dances Plains-style powwow, and practices a Plains-style spirituality. He acknowledged a solid up-bringing in Dene culture, including spending a great deal of time on the traplines and out hunting, but suggests that "spiritually, it [his upbringing] was empty." In terms of his identity, he states:

> The central belief system that I have is of the Cree culture... My cultural upbringing is Dene so those two are definitely combined. I definitely combined those two in comprising my identity [Bicultural].

In contrast, Inuit offenders seem to be beyond the influence of the Plains-style spirituality programs. While they often attend many of the more secular and social Aboriginal activities, such as powwows, they rarely avail themselves of Elder services or participate in sweats. This is no doubt due to their strong Inuit cultural orientations and well developed sense of "otherness" with respect to those Aboriginal offenders from more southern cultural groups.

A few offenders directly challenged the spirituality services provided, suggesting that there was more to Indian culture than spirituality. Noted one:

> They do have programs in Indian cultures, but look at all that ceremonial stuff ... Not everyone is into Indian religion, not every Native. Like me, I am not really into that, you know [Bicultural].

And another stated:

> All he [the Elder] talked about was our culture, sweatlodges and stuff like that, and about the Elders, prayers, sweatlodges and stuff like that. But maybe there could be something like Native skills in here, about living and survival and stuff like that [Bicultural].

Most, however, seemed content to simply absorb whatever lessons the Elders were willing to impart.

Perceptions of Cultural Competence

This brings us to the other theme of this paper. Some Aboriginal inmates, particularly those raised in an Aboriginal cultural context, are actually coming to view their own cultures as somehow deficient because they presently lack, or may historically have always lacked, certain of the spiritual traits identified earlier. Furthermore, some of these individuals are beginning to openly question their own cultural competence in either or both of the Aboriginal and Euro-Canadian cultural milieus.

One offender, a traditional Ojibwa from a northern Manitoba community who was raised on a reserve, stated:

> When I was brought up ... I didn't even know what Native culture was ... I didn't understand it ... Nobody even told me about it, you know. Maybe if I was brought up in a culture way, if I understand what life is all about, maybe I would have understood the meaning of Indian religion, because kids that are brought up in their culture, Native culture, they follow it.

This individual had spent a major portion of his early life in an Aboriginal community, yet clearly felt he had not been enculturated. Another inmate, a Northern Ojibwa from Northwestern Ontario, also suggested he knew little of his culture despite being raised in a reserve context and heavily influenced by his grandmother:

> I only know a little bit [about my culture], not very much ... It was just more or less the foundation of your grandmother, of how she lived, and how you respected things toward her and your auntie. When they speak Indian to you, like it just makes you feel down to earth [Bicultural].

The following inmate, a very traditional Cree man from northern Alberta, had spent most of his life in the bush or on the reserve. He expressed a deep discomfort in being around large numbers of people, preferring the solitude of the trapline or his prison cell. Yet, his feelings that his upbringing was culturally inadequate are clear:

> I never really learned about nothing deep down Native, just that we were staying in the bush and surviving, and staying in the reserve and how it is. But I never really learned about nothing like the Elders and stuff like that. Sweatlodges? I never even heard of sweatlodges before I came to [prison]. Never seen one. I never seen pipe ceremonies. There was no powwows where I came from. So I have seen all this stuff since [I came to prison] [Traditional].

This individual, in part, is comparing his own culture, a northern subarctic hunting culture, with that of the Plains Indians and their powwows and pipe ceremonies, and his is not faring well. He seems to feel cheated. Consider the following comments from a Dene offender from the Northwest Territories who is clearly questioning his own cultural competence despite lifelong residence in his community:

> In that prison I got involved with my Native spirituality, got involved with sacred circles, Native sweatlodges and pipe ceremonies ... There was something that was missing, knowing that I was a Native person and there was no culture in me. No cultural background grown up with ... Where I come from in the Territories I never heard them do stuff like that [Bicultural].

Again, the lack of certain traits, including those traditionally defined as of Plains Indian origin, has resulted in this individual viewing his own Dene culture and his cultural upbringing as somehow deficient.

Another offender seemed to feel there was little "culture" on his reserve because certain aspects of spirituality had gone underground:

> I don't think anybody on the reserve back then was into Native culture because the ceremonies and stuff that they had, was always hidden. Always in the background. I went to rain dances when I was a kid. I knew about medicine and stuff like that. But I didn't know about the spiritual part of my culture [Bicultural].

The situation for those Aboriginal offenders raised within a Euro-Canadian cultural tradition is somewhat different than for the others quoted above. These individuals, lacking knowledge of any Aboriginal culture from a firsthand perspective, are wholly dependent upon the cultural education they receive in prison. Their own cultural incompetence as "Aboriginal" peoples is self-evident and explicitly acknowledged, and they often become very involved in working with the Elders and in Aboriginal political activities within the prison. But they do not seem to question the validity or comprehensiveness of their Euro-Canadian cultural upbringing; rather, they seek to augment that with what they can learn of Aboriginal culture. In this sense, their involvement with the prison Aboriginal spirituality programs is less problematic.

In general, then, "culture," as understood by many Aboriginal offenders has come to be equated with "spirituality." Most Aboriginal offenders feel that spirituality was lacking in their communities and in their upbringing. This is due in part to extensive Christianization; indeed virtually all of the traditional offenders had been raised (at least superficially) in the Anglican or Catholic churches. Furthermore, in some areas of Canada, certain religious ceremonies were outlawed for many years, with the result that some have disappeared entirely from specific communities. But offender feelings that they are culturally incompetent because of a lack of spiritual knowledge is also due to the subtleness of much Aboriginal spirituality, especially when compared alongside certain visually-appealing Plains Indian ceremonies. For instance, some offenders clearly fail to see the inherent spirituality involved in living off the land, particularly in northern areas; some even fail to view themselves as culturally "Indian" despite growing up in Indian communities in remote areas.

In many ways, Aboriginal offenders are coming to view Aboriginal culture, reified, as spirituality. They speak of "practicing" their culture, "getting into" their culture, or "following their culture," and stress the fundamental values of spirituality, such as the need for prayer through the use of sweet grass and sweatlodge ceremonies, and the need to live a certain kind of lifestyle, one that is free of alcohol and drugs and respectful of others. Spirituality, as they are coming to understand it, is a plan for leading one's life. And an individual with little understanding of that spirituality is often considered, or considers himself, to be culturally incompetent.

This situation is problematic for a number of reasons. The form of spirituality to which they are being exposed is generally Plains Indian in orientation, but in a much broader sense it is eclectic and suggestive of an emerging spiritual pan-Indianism. This means that this spirituality is not intrinsic to any specific Aboriginal culture, and hence many cultures will appear deficient by comparison. As a result, individuals who have been fully enculturated in their particular Indian culture may doubt their "Indianess," and may develop a negative attitude toward their own people and culture. An identity crisis may well ensue. Furthermore, there is the risk of growing dependence on the spirituality services of the prison, which are offered on a scheduled basis, and which are rather reductionist (usually the result of the prison context and/or the limitations of particular Elders), such that when the inmates are released, they may find it difficult, and confusing, to "practice" their culture on the street. Indeed, they may be shocked to realize that spirituality has not the same overpowering significance on the lives of most Aboriginal people on the outside as it has in prison.

Conclusion

The Aboriginal culture and spirituality programs are having a profound effect on offenders who participate. They are serving an important mental health function, by providing a mechanism to cope with the stresses of prison life, and by helping individuals who are suffering from identity problems which have resulted from the many years of colonization and oppression by a settler society (Waldram 1993, 1994). Gerald Vizenor (1990, 312) has referred to various Aboriginal spiritual programs in general as "pan-tribal fundamentalist movements," an expression which is well-suited to the Canadian prison context. However, the evidence presented here suggests that some offenders are internalizing a fractured, reductionist view of what constitutes Indian "culture." Through a process of reification, conditioned by the prison environment and its many restrictions, and enhanced by the relative lack of spiritual knowledge of many inmates, "culture" is being internalized as a limited number of spiritual or religious traits, such as the sweatlodge, sacred pipe, medicine wheel, and sweetgrass. To be an "Indian" is coming to mean to be spiritual, to practice both the ceremonies and the values in everyday life. The spirituality programs particularly allow those Aboriginal offenders who lack knowledge of their heritage cultures to reconnect with their Aboriginality, and attain status within the prison Aboriginal community by mastering, at least on the surface, a relatively small portion of the overall Aboriginal cultural complex. Individuals raised in traditional environments, on the other hand, who would be well-integrated within their Aboriginal cultures, nevertheless find something new in these prison programs since spirituality in general tends to have played a less prominent role in their pre-prison life than other aspects of their culture. Some of these offenders may experience identity confusion as a result of their involvement, by questioning their own "Indianness" because of their lack of prior exposure to this unique form of spiritual education. In so far as some individuals become devout, even zealous, followers of Aboriginal spirituality, the likelihood that they will spread this "pan-Indian fundamentalism" upon their release from prison seems great.

Acknowledgements

The author would like to acknowledge the assistance of the staff at the Regional Psychiatric Centre (Prairies) in Saskatoon, the Elders and especially the inmates. The research was undertaken under contract to the Correctional Service of Canada; however, the views expressed in this paper represent those of the author only.

Notes

1. The term "Aboriginal," in upper case, is used to encompass the three main groups recognized in the Canadian constitution as the "aboriginal peoples:" the Indian, Inuit and Metis peoples. Current literary trends dictate that the term be upper-cased as a proper noun.
2. In Canada, persons convicted of criminal offenses and sentenced to incarceration terms of two years or more normally serve their time under federal jurisdiction in penitentiaries; sentences under two years are normally served at provincial correctional centres.
3 Aboriginal elders acquire spiritual knowledge in a variety of ways. Education, through work with the elders, is particularly important. Certain spiritual activities, such as fasting, sweatlodge ceremonies, and participation in the Sun Dance are also important. Elders stress that this process of learning is life-long, and they tend to defer readily to their own mentors on spiritual matters.

10

Avocation Medicine Men: Inventive "Tradition" and New Age Religiosity in a Western Great Lakes Algonquian Population

James A. Clifton

Considerations

One issue underlying the selection of a theme for this conference,[1] I believe, is the substantial tension (marked by ambivalence among social anthropologists) about continuing use of the shopworn notion of "tradition."[2] This approach-avoidance equivocation is surely exacerbated by recent developments among social anthropologists about the morality of relationships with the subjects of their studies. Especially so in the United States and Canada, many of our colleagues have convinced themselves that a prime directive for their involvements with other folk must include the assumption of a helping or advocacy role, a stance defined as a near absolute of professional ethics (AAA 1990, Part I).

As for the intellectual stress associated with the use of "tradition" as a quasi-theoretical constructum, I offer an unpretentious suggestion. Perhaps we are in process of confronting another of those classic dislocations that stem from using colorful "explanatory" locutions drawn from the nomenclature of everyday European and American life, together with the heavy burden of their accumulated semantics, as if they represented theoretically sophisticated, meaningful ideas." Race," "Custom," and other such powerful European-American folk notions anthropologists have long since discarded in favor of more productive, penetrating questions and forms of explanation. Why not discard "Tradition" as well, substituting therefore a series of theoretically pertinent queries for which we can obtain empirically grounded answers?

However, as anthropologists well know, discarding key ideas licensed by prolonged usage is no simple matter. The time encrusted convictions used by historians, sociologists, anthropologists and other scholars are no exception to this rule, whether such were originally simply borrowed from a folk lexicon, as is true of "tradition," or not. So, for some years there has been much tinkering with the notion of "tradition," efforts to perpetuate its core denotations by clarification, by rationalization, by qualifications such as "invented," and by attempts to resolve its "dilemmas" (Handler and Linnekin 1984; Hobsbawm and Ranger 1983; Linnekin 1983, 1991). In contrast there have been some productive efforts to step entirely away from this antiquated folk idea, by deliberately formulating fresh areas of inquiry and interpretation, accompanied by new forms of explanation (Boyer 1990).

Regarding the contribution of advocacy posturing to perpetuation of the notion of "tradition," I have an equally modest proposal. One of the greatest difficulties in abandonment of this old folk constructum is that it has acquired invigorated popularity among several publics with whom anthropologists must contend. In the so-called post-colonial, post-modern world of mass culture, where the fad for what is called "multi-culturalism" has achieved high official and popular standing, any performance or thing that can be called "traditional" has achieved quite extraordinary appeal. Since anthropologists must also deal professionally with their specialized publics, those who are the subjects of our observations (and advocacy), we are dealt a double blow. For as many have observed, our native publics now talk back forcefully, using the nomenclatures theyhave learned from dealings with Europeans and Americans. Prominent among their borrowed lexicons is "traditional," commonly reified and defined as an important collective goal, toward which indigenous groups should properly strive—whether in the form of reconstruction, resurrection, or sheer (if disguised) creativity and inventiveness.[3]

Here the consequence for anthropologists is not so much intellectual as it is emotional stress. This is so because here we find much role confusion and conflict, always certain to raise tempers. This role conflict is caused by the inconsonant demands, on the one hand, of the temporary "insider" imperative of keeping in the good graces of native publics, and, on the other hand, the "outsider" ideal of nonpartisan, objective truth-telling. Even for those academics who ordinarily avoid the assumption of an advocacy role the demands of their special indigenous publics cannot go unheeded; so some conflict is unavoidable. For such professionals, the conflict is commonly expressed in (and, hopefully, resolved by) extensive intellectualization and rationalization.[4] In contrast, for those much involved in praxis, whose livelihood and careers are entirely dependent on loyal services delivered to native clients and employers, detachment and objectivity may be denied as meaningful ideals. For such practitioners, protests that all observations and depictions are subjective, politicized, or indeterminate may be substituted for the rigors—and the sometimes considerable risks—of truth-telling.[5]

Among all the world's supposedly "indigenous" categories, North American Indians are in a particularly anomalous position. In this region, the *We* and the *They* have been so long intermingled and mixed that it is often difficult to tell *Us* and *Them* apart. Social boundaries, aside from juridical ones, are commonly difficult to define, and when asserted can appear capricious. For such reasons, most likely, arbitrary cultural markers of group identity have acquired particularly powerful salience. Necessarily, such identity signifiers have to be acquired or constructed, publicly broadcast, and legitimized if they are to serve in differentiating *Them* from *Us*. One common tactic for legitimizing such identity markers is to attach to them the affect loaded qualifier, "traditional." There is regnant a certain social ethic in this respect. It is required, and politically chic, for example, to accept unquestioningly everything said, done, or claimed by persons defined as "Indian" as authentic cultural things and ways handed down from generation to generation from time immemorial. Moreover, often enough anthropologists are called on to validate such assertions of ethnic distinctiveness.

These are the concerns and assumptions under girding my remarks in this essay. I will illustrate my views in the traditional anthropological style of empiricism, by some eye witness description followed by a hopefully analytic commentary.

The Green Corn Rite: Promise and Performance

A few years ago I was asked to witness and participate in an allegedly "traditional" rite to be performed by a small community of Western Great Lakes Algonquians, a ritual long in disuse but now being restored, so I was told. My host, who telephoned the invitation, was the self-styled "Medicine Man" of this small community. In our discussion, it was he who used the word "traditional," not I. Clearly, his tender suggested, my special part in this performance was to be that of an officially sanctioned anthropological observer. I was expected to place my stamp of scholarly authenticity on this rejuvenated performance of an allegedly age-old ceremonial, it was plainly indicated to me.

I have elsewhere expressed my views on the historical transformation of the last century's surviving Great Lakes Algonquian ritual specialists, in all their variety, into the generic Medicine Man of today's scene, a novel role that is part of popular American culture, and part of our public culture as well (Clifton 1994a, 1994b). There is no reason to repeat myself here. My host, this particular alleged Algonquian Medicine Man, also indicated that he and his colleagues were resurrecting this important communal ritual, identified as the "Green Corn Ceremony," whose performance had been prohibited for many decades by "the powers that be." Thus a standard motif was part of the preparations for this performance: the struggle against oppression or victimization, accompanied by a declaration of historic suppression of native ritualism. Such assertions are prominent in the rhetoric of contemporary Indian public figures, who reflexively feed such shibboleths back to audiences attuned to respond positively to them.

Some biographical and culture historical background are in order. Although it is now the vogue to identify individuals like my host as "aboriginal persons," I have grave difficulty in seeing him as aboriginal anything. In his secular, work-a-day life, he is a university educated, graduate degreed, monolingual, full-time professional man long productively employed in the larger, non-Indian community. However, most of his ancestors did come from the nineteenth-century Algonquian population from which the membership of the modern assembly derives its distinctive collective identity. Nevertheless, whatever cultural knowledge he has acquired—including the script for this Green Corn Ceremonial—cannot have come from generation-to-generation oral transmission. This is so because early in this century his Great Grandparents set his Grandparents on a different cultural track, deliberately so, orienting them to a social life as assimilated Americans, rather than as Indians. That script could not have come otherwise from in-group transmission, as well, because there is no independent evidence that the ancestral communities ever performed such a rite. I characterize him, and others like him, as avocational Medicine Men, since this role is a sideline for him, not a time, energy, and identity consuming (i.e., properly shammanic) vocation.

My host, the Medicine Man, was one of those many thousands of Americans for whom the status of Indian began acquiring a much increased value and luster starting in the late 1960s. His moment of ethnic awakening came in college, where his professors patronized him effusively, and where he was also encouraged to adopt a politically activist stance, to proclaim and defend his Indianness. Since then he has increasingly asserted leadership aspirations within his own community, while, on the outside before non-Indian audiences, he has adopted the role of cultural broker, regularly explaining the "traditions" of his people to non-Indians. His recently proclaimed stance as Medicine Man interactively services both these intertwined facets of his career, advancing his prestige as ambitious political leader within, and enhancing his position by plaudits from others without.

As a matter of civility, I will leave the exact location and the identity of this small group unspoken. This makes little difference, since the same processes and developments I will discuss are generic; they can be checked in numerous other contemporary Indian populations like this one.

In referring to these Algonquians, I use such words as "community" and "group" hesitantly, with substantial qualifications. Not for well more than a century have they constituted a cohesive, geographically situate local community. For at least that long, neither have they been a face-to-face, regularly interacting primary group, as their ancestral band communities once were. Speaking sociologically, today these Algonquians constitute a secondary group, a voluntary association of persons who live scattered widely across the whole Great Lakes region, and much of the rest of the United States. The central basis for their association consists of claims of descent from names on government sanctioned, written lists of ancestors who were the recipients of annuity payments well more than a century ago.

They do have a formal charter, that of a legally constituted nonprofit corporation organized under state law. In this charter, they identify themselves grandly as a "Nation." In the usage of the federal bureaucracy, they are one of many allegedly Indian "descendency groups" seeking official recognition. Speaking anthropology, there is a kinship basis for their association, a set of partially interlocked bilateral descent groups. However, there are no recognizable boundaries to these ancestor based descent groups, since for more than a century this population has intermarried extensively with non-Indians. Hence, as is common among modern "Indians by definition," the ethnic status of all non-Indian ancestors is ignored. In the racial categories of American public culture, which these Algonquians express, "one drop of Indian blood" overwhelms all other varieties.

The whole of the membership of this association are not known to one another. In fact, the whole membership is not even known on a personal basis to the cadre of several dozen individuals who do regularly come together to promote the affairs and to advance the interests of their "Nation." Instead, the names and last known addresses of those affiliated with the association, whether or not they know of it or themselves assert membership, are listed in a computerized database.

Politically, these Algonquians are not one of the corporate tribal entities officially recognized by the United States. That is, they are not as yet protected clients of the state, although they aspire to attaining that special status as "citizens plus" soon. They are one of the some 104 applicant organizations waiting to have their claims to Indian political status "clarified" by the federal bureaucracy or courts, or by Congress.

Economically, these Algonquians have recently fallen onto persistent hard times, in common with other chronically unemployed and under employed skilled working class Americans in the Great Lakes rust belt. But for some eight decades, generally, they had known abundance, and confident economic expectations, except for cyclical economic downturns whose vicissitudes they shared with others in the region. Their prosperity came mainly from employment in light industry and manufacturing, in large plants long since abandoned, sharply down sized, or transported to Mexico and Brazil. Most of the adult men in their middle years had decades of participation in industrial unions, especially the United Electrical and the United Auto Workers, and more than a few had served as shop stewards and union officials. Today, their expectations for a prosperous future are tied to hopes of windfalls from tax-exempt enterprises of their own, particularly high stakes bingo and casino gambling operations, ventures which would enable them to prosper from exploiting the minor vices of other Americans. Such a privileged economic status will be theirs if or when some branch of the federal government legitimizes their status as a separately recognized tribal entity, and moves them into the Indian estate stratum of American society.[6]

For going on two centuries now, these Algonquians have been practicing Christians, with much of their social life tied to the congregations of the denomination their ancestors converted to early in the nineteenth century. An exclusively English speaking people, fully exposed to the deluge of images and enticements of American mass culture, like other Americans they are responsive to the numerous fads and fancies which sweep the land, including that variety of nondenominational spirituality called New Age Religion, as well as the current craze for palatable multicultural performances.

The setting for the evening performance of the reborn Green Corn Ceremonial was rural exurban, the remnants of a Great Lakes area farmstead—comprising five acres, large, well-maintained house, some dilapidated outbuildings—the home of my host, the Medicine Man. In size and quality of housing, it differed little if any from that owned by other neighboring American skilled working-class and professional men, who also regularly commute thirty to sixty miles to their places of employment, if they have steady employment now. About five dozen people had mustered, mainly adult men and women in their thirties and forties, with some small children. There were no adolescents present, and few elders, which I found particularly surprising—for an assembly billed as traditional. By-and-large, the gathering comprised but one bloc of the factionalized middle-aged leadership cadres who form the core of this association's active members. There were interesting absences, I realized, including the Medicine Man's political rivals and those Algonquians so staunchly Christian they would have nothing to do with such "heathen" rites. All the adult women, the small children, and the few elders, were inside the spacious house, organizing the evening's potluck dinner. All the adult men were outside battling the elements, struggling to get their ritual act together.

A severe thunderstorm had blown in utterly disrupting their plans. I found the men congregated in and around the Green Corn ritual structure, a lozenge shaped sapling framework of none too substantial construction, covered by a huge, heavy old canvas tarpaulin. This covering, I learned, had been salvaged from an abandoned factory, where it originally had been used to protect newly completed industrial equipment from the weather. With the wind gusting at 40 or more miles per hour, the lightning crackling around, the rain and sleet pouring down, it was a feverish scene. The whole structure threatened to blow away like the mainsail of an America's Cup racer, and the men—who (I thought) should have been calmly preparing their ritual acts—were rushing around struggling unsuccessfully to hold the structure together. In this, later in the evening, they failed, and efforts to perform this supposedly just renewed Green Corn ceremonial ended abruptly.

There was something culturally errant about this scene, I noted. By analogy with the practices of their ancestors, and by the practices of the few contemporary kindred communities where there is still substantial continuity of knowledge and practice from an earlier century, these

Algonquians should not even have tried to subdue these awesome forces of nature. For those others, I reflected, even to attempt an important ritual in the face of such a storm was anathema. By their screed, such foul weather was clear evidence of the displeasure of the Thunders, a particularly bad omen. In a more pragmatic vein, those predecessors had the sense to stay in out of the rain, more so to avoid the real risks of lightning strikes. But these American working men, determined to get on with a ceremonial, stubbornly persisted in their efforts to subdue the forces of nature.

In such frustrating circumstances there was little time or energy left for ritual thoughts or deeds. Nonetheless, for at least one there was time for some courtesies. As I approached the Green Corn sanctum, I was accosted by a party previously unknown to me, who identified himself formally as the "Assistant Medicine Man." I was the Guest Stranger, he indicated. He would play Host and Tutor. At this point I must rely on texts. These were his words. "This is our *Sacred Green Corn House*," he intoned, most seriously." Here is our *Sacred Fire*." "When the weather lets up, we will bring in our *Sacred Drum* and then we will sing our *Sacred Songs*." His English intonation was such as to demand, rendered in print, capital letters, or bold face, or italics, or all three. My reaction was more disquiet. I had never before heard such vehement, overly compensatory declarations from a kindred Algonquian ritualist, one who knew what he was doing, a believer-practitioner who was confident in his ritual knowledge.

Shortly, I broke away, leaving the Assistant Medicine Man to take hold of a flapping corner of tarpaulin. Perhaps I was too abrupt, maybe impolitic, for as it happened he was keeping a disciplinarian's eye on me for unorthodoxies or discourtesies. In any respect, falling back on what I had once been taught about the appropriate ritual courtesies, I managed to commit what he saw as a horrendous gaffe. I no longer carry a pouch of *kinikinick* in my pocket for such occasions, so I employed what I was once advised was, and had often used as a proper ritual substitute. Field stripping the tobacco from a cigarette, I balled it up in my palms, expelled my breath upon it, expressed a sotto voice welcome to "The Maker of All Things," and cast my offering upon the fire. Whereupon the Assistant Medicine Man rushed up with stick in hand, exclaiming angrily, "We don't throw cigarette butts in our Sacred Fire," then fishing the offensive stuff from the embers. Now I was really confused.

Later the storm tossed Green Corn chapel collapsed. So, too did efforts to perform the ceremony. The Medicine man, my host, offered to substitute therefore that old standby, a Sweat House rite. For the more than two dozen adult men involved, given the limited sweat house facilities available, this required much standing in line in the storm. In the interim, with no Green Corn rite to observe, I had to fall back on verbal queries. Later discussions with my host fleshed out what information I was able to obtain in that manner.

This can be briefly summarized. None of the adult males who came to participate in this ceremony had ever previously been involved in a Green Corn ritual. Indeed, excepting my host, none had ever previously heard of the Green Corn ritual as something that was part of the heritage of this association, although a few had vague recollections of the Green Corn religion as being authentically Indian, for Indians of some kind. None arrived knowing what they were to do, how they were to do it, why they should do so, or what they would accomplish by their acts. But all arrived with high if vague expectations. What they experienced from the start, in the middle, and in the end was confusion. I use "confusion" deliberately, for this is the English word regularly employed by kindred Algonquians who do know their scripts and parts when some ritual act is misperformed. These well instructed, experienced, knowledgeable kindred ritualists assert that exactitude is requisite, precision in deed engendering predictability. Confusion, for them, is what a communal ritual is aimed at eliminating, among whatever other important aims their rituals may have.

There was one exception to this general unawareness, I have suggested: my host the Medicine Man. He had in his mind (and in fact on paper) the script for a simple Green Corn ceremony, a script he intended to use in guiding his congregation through their first performance, sans rehearsal. I will come back to him and the question of the mode and path of communication of the tenets of this Green Corn ceremony momentarily.

Meanwhile, I can report that, in the absence of a satisfying, successful sacred ceremonial, a badly needed secular rite was efficiently conducted. While their men were outside fighting the elements, the women remained indoors preparing the meal. By twos and threes, as they returned from the sweat house reasonably well warmed, they were seated and indulged, a welcome and much needed repast laid before them. If their spiritual wants had been frustrated, their physiological and their social needs were sated. And so, after much cold, wet, unrewarding labor, that was enough to restore a semblance of good spirits to this instant congregation.

With this description in mind, I can proceed to some queries and analysis. The questions are few, simple, and straightforward. How and where did my host, the Medicine Man, acquire his knowledge—the script for—this Green Corn rite? It was not via intergenerational transmission over the decades within the association, I have indicated. There was no ancestral prototype for this ritual to be so communicated. Moreover, there was at least a two generation deep hiatus in the transmission of any substantial cultural knowledge within my host's ancestral kindred, a gap that was in substantial part, at least, self-determined through decisions made by Great Grandparents and Grandparents.

A way toward pinpointing the mode and channels of this communication consists of biography. My host, the Medicine Man, had experienced a proper middle-class, suburban American socialization at the hands of his parents, skilled blue collar and clerical workers. Pushed by family to elevate himself, he became a super achiever. Outside his formal schooling, where he excelled, as a youth his unusually strong needs for recognition and prestige were realized in the Boy Scouts organization. There he advanced to the status of Eagle Scout, and was eventually elected to the Scouts' elite fraternity, the Order of the Arrow, which once steeped its novices in things supposedly Indian, before such practices were defined as offensive to minorities and became politically tabooed.[7] It was in a hometown Chapter of the Order of the Arrow that my host was exposed to and participated in a secular rite called the Green Corn Ceremony. This ceremony is not generic to the Order of the Arrow nationally or even regionally; it was unique to this one chapter of that fellowship. The innovator, the Master of this chapter of the Order, was not Indian. His prototype for the Green Corn rite had come from a little knowledge acquired in a university anthropology course about Indian cultures. A professor had lectured him on the characteristics of some Eastern Algonquian religion, a first fruits rite I presume. Once selected as Master of the Order of the Arrow chapter he elected to encourage a worshipful sense of awe, mystery, thanksgiving, and in-group solidarity among his charges through teaching them the ways of the Green Corn, as he reconstructed them to fit the constraints of a scouting organization. In this way, a little classroom instruction *about* coastal Algonquian ritual knowledge and behavior was converted, innovatively, through cognitive processes of identification and substitution,[8] into a script *for* performance by a troop of senior, elite Scouts. It was in this context that my host, not yet a Medicine Man, mastered the forms of the rite.

It is useful, for emphasis, to track the chain of communication of knowledge of this Green Corn ceremonial. Eastern Algonquian horticultural societies once practiced, and I suppose their few survivors may still practice, Green Corn rites. Knowledge about these rituals was obtained by ethnographers, and set into print. A university teacher, with no firsthand observational experience with the eastern rites, used this secondhand printed version to prepare lectures for his students. One of his students, who later became head of an Order of the Arrow chapter, used his memory of these lectures to devise a ceremony for his elite Scout troop. In turn, one of these Boy Scouts, who subsequently assumed the role of Medicine Man for a Great Lakes Indian population, used his memory of instruction in and experiences with this in-group ritual to contrive an ostensibly "renewed" ceremonial for "his people."

Analysis and Explication

In this manner, along this chain of transmission, what was (and still may be) a sacred ritual for one community, was converted into secular knowledge by members of an academic profession, thence refashioned into a secular performance for a brotherhood of American youths, then once again refashioned, this time as an innovative, hopefully sacred ritual, and presented to an audience of eager, if untutored participants as an allegedly meaningful part of their collective heritage, one only distantly related to the eastern originators. I suggest that this type of complex pathway of communication of supposedly "traditional" heritage to modern Indian groups in the United States is not at all uncommon. A fair amount of the substance of performances, public displays of knowledge of "Indianness," is borrowed from, and with much creative elaboration is transported back and forth into, the vast inventory of Indian things in American popular culture.

Speaking an older dialect of anthropology, I will say that what we have here is an interesting example of diffusion, in a culturally complex, multiethnic society, where in recent years protestations and displays of ethnic identity have achieved an unusually strong cognitive, and affective, salience. Now, was this process of communication "traditional"? Certainly, it involved (at least at several communicative junctions) the oral delivery of information or instruction. Equally so, speaking plain English, the Indians involved — the Medicine Man as well as his congregation — alleged that this was a "traditional" affair.

However, following the line of inquiry suggested by Pascal Boyer (1990), I will suggest that what happened that evening was not the product of a "conservative mindset." On the contrary, the entire affair was plainly if abortively innovative. Neither was the event an expressive projection of a shared, underlying "worldview." As I will indicate in closing, these Algonquians do share much in the way of worldview about themselves and their place in American society, but it does not include a logic of presumptions about the supernatural that would make sacralized sense of this performance. Moreover, how the ritual expert, my host, acquired his knowledge of the Green Corn ceremony is not especially pertinent—not to his communicants. The biographical truths about his experience, if they were confronted with them, would simply be denied or rationalized away. Being Indian in the United States, today, is in New Age lingo being "into denial" in a big way.

For my host, the Medicine Man, the proximate prototype for the associative sequence that led to his innovative efforts was, in fact, the teachings of his Scout Master, who served him as a respected, surrogate Grandfather. However, his efforts to model and to advocate the acceptance of this innovative ritual resulted in near disaster. Although there are powerful wants among his congregation for ritual activities like this, I doubt that any departed that night with a reasonable degree of satisfaction. The Green Corn rite, I understand, has not been attempted again since. I doubt it will be. Forty years ago my respected ancestor, Homer G. Barnett, taught us of such matters that some innovations may allege an advantage over existing practices where none in fact is felt by potential acceptors. In such instances, efforts to promote the acceptance of an innovation "create a want instead of filling the void when a real want goes unsatisfied" (1953, 364).

That want among these modern Algonquians remains powerful and unsated. What then, was the substance of the happening I witnessed some years ago? What interesting and instructive social happening lay behind the choice of words used by key participants to characterize it?

This small Great Lakes population asserts a distinctive ethnic identity, and this claim is confirmed by many others. These others constantly clamor for displays of their distinctive Indianness. And within, among these Algonquians, there are strong needs to know and to show. Yet their particular history as a group, and their individual biographies, have long since separated them from that mass of cultural detail which might allow them, confidently, to believe and behave as they wish they could do. Let me offer a heuristic hypothesis: *I presume that ethnic identity abhors a cognitive vacuum.* The efforts of my host that evening were aimed at instilling some meaningful, satisfying content where there is much too little among a membership which strongly desires to be as well as to claim to be distinctive. That this one event was unsuccessful is no predictor of the future. There have been and will be numerous other innovative efforts to fill in the cultural voids among these Algonquians.

In the last decade or so, the adjective "invented" has increasingly been prefixed as a qualifier for "tradition" by historians Hobsbawm and Ranger (1983). In the thinking of these neo-Marxist scholars, there would seem to be a distinction between genuine or authentic and spurious or inauthentic "traditions." They do not seem to appreciate that, whatever else may be true of them, all things or practices called "traditional" invariably have histories—every one was at some time or another in the past invented—whether or not those histories are recoverable and knowable. For Hobsbawm and Ranger, the object of elucidating the histories of those selected items they call "Invented Traditions" seems to be an application of orthodox Marxist discourse, an exercise in discrediting the symbols and rituals of empire and market capitalism.

Ideological preoccupations aside, clearly, appending "invented" to "tradition" is an apparent oxymoron, and in ordinary street parlance, unfortunately, can readily be seen as an effort to insult practitioners or to diminish the merit of a performance. I find Hanson's extended discussion of this issue compelling and persuasive (1991), but I prefer a different solution than the one he suggests. I have identified the process I witnessed as that of inventive tradition making, trying to call attention to the creative processes involved. That certainly was what was going on that stormy night as these Algonquians worked at infusing their group identity with satisfying, public meaning. Casting my thinking in that mode, I believe, allows us to link these particular cultural processes with other, related more general ones.

About my small part in the affair of the Green Corn rite, the intimation that I should come and stamp the performance as credible and faithful to the past, I do not regret being unwilling to conform to that expectation. For I am not convinced it is proper for an anthropologist to serve as an authoritative agent of an ad hoc Bureau of Cultural Authenticity. My preference is for the primary role of observer and analyst. I think I understand what these Algonquians are trying to accomplish, and I empathize, but I see my professional task as an effort to know, not to patronize or to advocate.

Notes

1. This is a revised version of a paper delivered at the 14th American Indian Workshop, Collège de France, Laboratoire d'anthropologie sociale, Paris, June 4, 1993. I am greatly indebted to Dr. Marie Mauzé for inviting me to participate in that stimulating conference.
2. I note that while Seymour-Smith's *Dictionary of Anthropology* (1986) does contain an entry for "Tradition," one that differs little from what is found in

any desk dictionary, the Kupers in their desk size *Social Science Encyclopedia* (1989) do not bother to include such an entry. This may express ambivalence, or greater British disdain for such obsolescent terms.
3. For further discussion of my observations and thoughts on these matters, see Clifton 1993, 1-37, and 1990, 1-48.
4. Although he by no means claims to have uttered the last word on the subject, in my judgment Alan Hanson has offered the most intelligent, relatively detached discussion of these issues, particularly as regards his own efforts to cope with Maori reactions to his scholarly writings. See Hanson 1991.
5. The defenses of practitioners vary considerable. Daly and Mills (1993) for instance, expressed outrage when a Canadian court refused to accept their expert testimony on behalf of native clients because of the taint of partisanship, and quite pragmatically recommend revising the American Anthropological Association's *Code of Professional Responsibility* so as to avoid this undesirable outcome. In a not particularly sophisticated alternative, McClurken (1990) declares the inevitability of bias in such "expert" testimony (favorable or not, depending on which adversary is being "served"), confesses his own culpability, and extols the virtues of faithful performance as a "Friend of the Indian."
6. For a discussion of the estate variety of social stratification in the United States as applied to Indian political entities, see Clifton 1994c.
7. I am informed by local Boy Scout officials that the regional organization will no longer allow the lads to wear "war paint," unless a particular Scout can deliver written evidence that "he has Indian blood in his veins." American racial inanities, and the confusion of cultural and biological causation, go on apace.
8. For an extended discussion of the intrapsychic processes of innovation, see Barnett 1953.

11

All the Old Spirits Have Come Back to Greet Him: Realizing the Sacred Pole of the Omaha Tribe

Robin Ridington

Introduction

Marie Mauzé introduced a workshop on "Tradition: Continuity and Invention in Native North American Societies," with a question. "How" she asked, does "a society, a minority or a group experience its relation to the past in the present?" (Mauzé 1993). This paper describes how the Omaha tribe of Nebraska responded to its renewal of contact with a sacred object from which it had been separated for more than a century. This object is *Umon'hon'ti* (the Real Omaha), their Sacred Pole. Omahas continue to regard him as a living being; a person who stands for all the people of the tribe. Once a symbol of tribal unity, he now challenges the tribe's understanding of its present identity in relation to its past

The Pole came into Omaha life as a solution to problems caused by the dislocations in early historic times. Now, in the words of elder Lawrence Gilpin, "All the old spirits have come back to greet him." Omahas are not universally comfortable with the presence of these spirits among the people of today. Many are fearful and ignorant of past tradition. Fortunately, the tribe has access to ethnographic documentation of the Pole's use, in nineteenth-century ceremonies of tribal renewal, through the writings of Alice Fletcher and her Omaha co-author, Francis La Flesche. Omahas today are debating how best to experience both the Pole and the information about him. This paper describes events to which I have been witness, using transcriptions and translations of Omaha commentary.

The real Omaha in Tribal History

> My son has seen a wonderful tree.
> The Thunder birds come and go upon this tree,
> making a trail of fire
> that leaves four paths on the burnt grass
> that stretch toward the Four Winds.
> When the Thunder birds alight on the tree
> it bursts into flame
> and the fire mounts to the top.
> The tree stands burning,
> but no one can see the fire except at night.
> (Adapted from Fletcher and La Flesche 1911, 218)

With these words, an Omaha elder interpreted his son's visionary experience of a miraculous tree he had encountered directly beneath the "motionless star" around which all the other points of the night sky turn. This encounter took place, perhaps in the late seventeenth or early eighteenth centuries, when the ancestors of the Omaha tribe of Nebraska were still united with ancestors of the Ponca tribe, after having split from others of the five Dhegiha Siouan tribes (Omaha, Ponca, Kansa, Quapaw, Osage). The Omahas were originally part of a loose confederation of Siouan villages living in the Ohio Valley. Alice Fletcher and her Omaha collaborator, Francis La Flesche, documented Omaha oral tradition as it was known in the late nineteenth-century. They report that the the tribe consciously sought to form a system of government that would hold the people together as they moved from their original homeland:

> The Sacred Legend and other accounts tell the story of the way in which a central governing body was finally formed and all agree that it was devised for the purpose of "holding the people together" (Fletcher and La Flesche 1911, 201).

A tribe on the move has an inherently more difficult problem keeping itself together than one that is settled on a common territory, particularly in the absence of a centralized governmental authority. The Omahas of proto-historic times probably governed themselves through a system of complementary clans and sub-clans distributed throughout a loose alliance of neighboring villages. Prior to that, some of their ancestors may have participated in the Mississippian system of chiefdoms which were "kin-based societies with strong clans that provided chiefs and subchiefs" (Conrad 1989, 93). Perhaps because of diseases that swept through Mississippian territory in early historic times, many of the former chiefdoms had become decentralized. By the time they appear in the written record, they were held together by their clans, rather than by hereditary chiefs.

Fletcher and La Flesche suggest that "it was prior to the cutting of the Sacred Pole that the Omaha organized themselves into their present order" (1911, 73). By this they mean that the system of complementary clans was already in existence when the son of a chief discovered "a tree that stands burning." Omaha oral tradition makes it clear that finding the Sacred Pole provided the tribe with a powerful new symbol of its identity. It was a symbol appropriate to the Omahas' recognition of their place in the rapidly changing flow of history. Rather than looking to a single chief to stand over them, the Omahas looked to the Pole to represent a common but movable center shared by all. The Pole's power within the tribe is concentric rather than hierarchical. He represents a center they share, not a ruler who stands over them. He stands for a spiritual rather than a temporal authority. He gives supernatural sanction to the complementary opposition of Omaha moieties, Sky People and Earth People. Earth and Sky clans representing the power of thunder flanked the entrance of the Omaha camp circle. According to the legend that Yellow Smoke, his last keeper, told Fletcher and La Flesche:

> ... attention was called to the tree from which the Sacred Pole was shaped by the Thunder Birds coming to it from the four directions and the mysterious burning which followed, all of which caused the Sacred Pole to stand in the minds of the people as endowed with a supernatural power by the ancient Thunder gods. (1911, 229)

Later, at the height of Omaha control of the Missouri River trade, trading chiefs did obtain considerable power, but they did not reestablish hereditary positions of authority like those of the former Mississippians. Their power was personal rather than mandated by member-ship in a noble family. Chiefs, like Blackbird of the late eighteenth century, achieved great power within the sphere of trading, but did not overthrow a form of government which granted spiritual authority to the Sacred Pole and the seven pipe-bearing clans (Barnes 1994). Although the trading chiefs became influential and wealthy secular leaders and powerful shamans or prophets, they had little to do with the priestly functions of the seven pipe-holding chiefs and the ceremonies conducted by the keepers of sacred objects. The ceremonial duties of these men were hereditary within their clans and had to do with the preservation and renewal of the tribe as a whole. In this they were supported by the authority of the Sacred Pole. Fletcher and La Flesche write:

> In the process of governmental development it became expedient to have something which should symbolize the unity of the tribe and of its governing power—something which should appeal to the people, an object they could all behold and around which they could gather to manifest their loyalty to the idea it represented. (1911, 217)

That object was the Sacred Pole, known to nineteenth-century Omahas as *Waxthe'xe* "sacred, mottled as by shadows, bringing into prominence to be seen by all the people" (Fletcher and La Flesche 1911, 219). Contemporary Omahas call him *Umon'hon'ti*, "The Real Omaha," and *Washabe'gle*, "The Shadowed One." Each year prior to 1875, when the practice was abandoned, the Pole was painted with buffalo fat and ochre in a solemn renewal ceremony that Omahas believed would restore the tribe's internal balance, as well as its relationship with the buffalo and other features of the natural environment. When the buffalo disappeared in the 1870s and the tribe abandoned this ceremony, they turned away from the Pole as a symbol of tribal unity.

In 1888, Francis La Flesche approached the Sacred Pole's last keeper, Shu'denathi (Smoked Yellow or Yellow Smoke) with a proposal. La Flesche was the son of an Omaha woman, Ton'inthin (Elizabeth Esau) and Inshta'maza (Iron Eye, or Joseph La Flesche), himself the son of a French-Canadian trader and a woman of Ponca tribe. He was one of the first Native Americans to become a professional ethnographer. Francis began his written descriptions of Omaha culture in collaboration with Alice Cunningham Fletcher, a researcher and writer from Harvard's Peabody Museum. In 1911 when their great work, *The Omaha Tribe*, appeared as the Twenty-seventh Annual Report of the Bureau of Ethnology, he had become Fletcher's co-author. La Flesche reports his conversation with Yellow Smoke in that publication:

> "Why don't you send the 'Venerable Man' to some eastern city where he could dwell in a great brick house instead of a ragged tent?" A smile crept over the face of the chieftain as he softly whistled a tune and

tapped the ground with his pipe stick before he replied, while I sat breathlessly awaiting the answer, for I greatly desired the preservation of this ancient and unique relic. The pipe had cooled and he proceeded to clean it. He blew through it now and then as he gave me this answer: "My son, I have thought about this myself but no one whom I could trust has hitherto approached me upon this subject. I shall think about it, and will give you a definite answer when I see you again." The next time I was at his house he conducted me to the Sacred Tent and delivered to me the Pole and its belongings. This was the first time that it was purposely touched by anyone outside of its hereditary keepers. (1911, 248-249)

So it was that in 1888, *Umon'hon'ti* came into the care and keeping of the Peabody Museum. In 1988, a century later, Omaha hands once again touched their Sacred Pole. Tribal Chairman Doran Morris, a member of the Honga clan who is Yellow Smoke's great-great-grandson according to the Omaha system of reckoning kinship, and Eddie Cline, a former tribal chairman, wept as they held *Umon'hon'ti* in prayer in a little courtyard outside the Peabody Museum. They wept because of the break in ceremonial order caused by his long absence from his people. They wept for the Pole's century of confinement. They wept for joy at his release. And they wept to see him refreshed by sun and wind after so many years within the walls of the "great brick house." Doran Morris later described his experience as follows:

I felt that power. I always thought that as a man I never cried. I felt sad a lot of times but when they brought that Pole out, boy it just overwhelmed me. Shivers up my spine, and I just started crying. That's what happened.

Fletcher and La Flesche reported that "if by any chance a mistake occurred during the ceremonies connected with the Sacred Pole," members of the Honga clan responsible for the Pole and its rites, "lifted their arms, held their hands with the palms upward, and, standing thus in the attitude of supplication, wept" (1911, 232). Doran's tears that day were spontaneous, but were also clearly the correct response to the Pole's hundred-year separation from his last keeper. Eddie Cline also wept. In his prayer of greeting to the Pole, Cline began:

This is a living tree. This is a living person as far as we're concerned. Maybe, to some of you, it's just an old piece of wood, but the teaching ... it was there for the People to see, to become a part of, to touch, and to be tied to it—what kept the Tribe together—that's the teaching.

Cline began his prayer to *Umon'hon'ti* in Omaha as follows:

> Aho! *Wakon'da.* [Most Holy Spirit]
> You have created everything good.
> This *Umon'hon'ti.*
> He is a living spirit [*Umon'hon'ti Ni'kie.*]
> He has a body, the wood.
> Because of him I am offering a prayer.
> *Dadeho* [Father].
> This day the chiefs [the tribal council]
> the head of the Leaders [the Honga Clan],
> my grandson, are here.
> As you see him, know him.
> Pity him, whatever his thoughts.
> This tree has been living, standing.
> Whatever his thoughts, make them possible.
> Make his good thoughts possible.
> *Dadeho Wakon'da.* [Father, Most Holy Spirit]
> Hopefully, all the Omahas that see him
> will have good feelings.
> That is what I am praying for,
> what I am asking you, Father.
> The white people have taken care of him
> and this day the Omaha people have welcomed him home.
> He is in the center of the Omaha people.
> He was to stand in the center of the Omaha people.
> That was probably his thought
> and you will make it possible.
> The tree that was living is a living being.
> They have said that for the Omaha.
> I pray that good things will come our way.
> I pray that you will hear these words.
> I pray with your name.
> My grandson here depends on you.
> I pray that you will listen to him.
> I hope that you will listen to us.
> I hope that you will see us and pity us.
> I pray for people on the council.
> I pray that you make life good for them.
> That is what I pray to ask you with these humble words.
> Plain humble prayer!
> Words that I pray to you, *Dadeho.*
> I pray that you see us and that you will pity us.
> Aho!

The following year, Doran Morris and the tribal council brought *Umon'hon'ti* back to the Omaha tribal powwow arena at Macy, Nebraska. They brought him back in the hope that his return to the tribal circle would bring all his relations what Omaha elder Clifford Wolfe called, a "blessing for a long time to come." Another elder, Lawrence Gilpin, spoke to the people and then prayed to *Umon'hon'ti* in Omaha. In English he said:

> This is a great day amongst our Omaha people. Those of you that are here, that made the effort to witness this homecoming of our Sacred Pole, *Umon'hon'ti*, I want to say thank you to you that you brought your little ones here, little children, to witness this. They will remember this day in days to come, in years to come. Maybe they will relate this to their little ones, those that are coming, and it's a great day for our Omaha people.
>
> We have our *Umon'hon'ti* back on the reservation, that it will be good for us. That it will bring unity and good things to come, good things to happen, that we would listen to one another when we talk to one another. That we will be good Indians, good Omahas. All these things we think about with *Umon'hon'ti* back on our poor reservation.
> It belongs to you, each one, each Omaha that is here. You have an undivided interest in this Sacred Pole. It's been gone for many years. Myself, I feel real thankful. I say thank you to the Omaha tribal council for making the effort to bring *Umon'hon'ti* back home on the Omaha reservation where it belongs. It belongs to no one else but the Omaha people. It is yours, and it has come home. In Omaha he prayed:
>
> *Aho! Umon'hon'ti!*
> We're humble people, the Omaha village
> that you have come home to.
> Today you have come home.
> There's a few words I want to say to *Wakon'da*.
> *Umon'hon'ti*,
> you have come back to the Omaha camp.
> I am very happy that you have come home.
> *Umon'hon'ti*,
> I am very happy that you have come home today
> to our poor, humble reservation.
> And towards *Wakon'da*, I'm going to say a few words.
> Today, we are just pitiful [deserving of love]
> and yet today we are celebrating.
> All the Omahas have come home together happy,
> feeling happy, good of heart.
> Our relatives have gathered.

They have entered the doorway, the entry,
and we are seated together.
From way back, our forefathers, there was a tree.
There was a tree that grew from the earth.
From way back they used him for our lives.
It's been over a hundred years, past a hundred years,
in a strange place with strange people.
Dadeho, Wakon'da Xube.
Today the head of the people, (the council)
have brought him home,
brought him home.
Dadeho, Wakon'da Xube.
Umon'hon'ti, they made him holy.
From way back in our camp he was the center,
lived in the center of the people.
And whatever they did, how they lived,
they did it with him, through *Wakon'da.*
Wakon'da made life in that tree from the earth.
Dadeho, Wakon'da Xube.
From God's power (*Wakon'da Xube*) he gave that tree.
Father, you made that tree, you gave it life,
You gave it life from the earth.
And that was through your goodness,
your power from the earth.
Dadeho, Wakon'da Xube.
You are the only one that has the power to do and give life.
It is yours.
Those, our elders, have brought him from way back,
and they have received nothing but good from him.
Whatever good that you have made, you have made for them.
Dadeho, Wakon'da Xube.
Our people carried you from way back,
and good things came from you.
And whatever you have made, you have made everything good,
Dadeho, Wakon'da Xube, Most Holy Spirit, you sit.
You do everything right.
You never make any mistakes.
[Lawrence, like Doran before him, begins to weep as he speaks.]
You are the only one that knows what our needs are.
You are the one that gave *Umon'hon'ti* life.
As we face the future
those that are coming, those that are coming
have pity on them.
Father, the most Holy Spirit,
You are the loving God.
You made it Sacred.

> Everything you made Sacred.
> Grandpa fire is Sacred.
> You made the fire Sacred.
> Nobody to look forward to, to depend on,
> have pity on me.
> Whatever their [the council's] wish is I tried to meet,
> I tried to fulfill
> in my humble words that I spoke with you,
> God's son Jesus.
> They made the fire Sacred,
> that we may get good from this from here on.
> Aho you singers, you drummers, that was my prayer

Lawrence concluded in English:

> All you people in the audience.
> It is my prayer that you be blessed by what you have seen today.
> Long, long time ago.
> *Umon'hon'ti* became a reality to the Omaha people,
> a symbol, something good from God.
> He was gone. Today he has come home.
> He's going to be with us. We have got to respect him.
> It's going to be good for us.
> I know that.
> Whenever you respect something,
> you do something good or say something or think good,
> it's always going to be good.
> You benefit from those thoughts.
> And it's going to be that way for our Omaha people.
> From this day on we're going to have a different feeling
> about our whole lives.
> We're going to be altogether different.
> We're going to respect one another,
> and we're going to smile at one another,
> and put that hatred off on the side.
> I want to say thank you to the singers out there
> on behalf of the Omaha people.
> On behalf of the Omaha tribal council,
> I want to say thank you.

The real Omaha in Tribal Life

Despite the good thoughts many Omahas expressed regarding the return of their Sacred Pole, others reacted to him with fear. Although I did not hear anyone cite specific traditions mentioned by Fletcher and La

Flesche, this fear recalled the "punishment by the supernatural" their informants said might follow "the revealing of these sacred traditions." They report that Joseph La Flesche took it on himself to "cheerfully accept for himself any penalty that might follow," and they go on to say that "by a singular co-incidence ... in a fortnight he lay dead in the very room in which had been revealed the Sacred Legend." Thus, they say, "the fear inspired by the Pole was strengthened in its passing away" (1911, 224).

During the Pole's last days on the reservation, they report, he was "dreaded as a thing that was powerful for harm but seemingly powerless to bring back the old-time prosperity to the people" (1911, 245). This fear seems also to have accompanied his return. No one doubted that he is a powerful living being who is intimately related to the well-being of Omahas, both individually and collectively, but I discovered a sharp difference of opinion about whether his influence would be beneficial or harmful. People of both persuasions agreed, though, that it would be inappropriate to house him on the reservation, at least until a secure and spiritually appropriate facility could be created. Some felt he should not return to the reservation at all.

Prior to the Sacred Pole's return in 1989, the council had negotiated an agreement with the University of Nebraska-Lincoln to give him curatorial care there for an indefinite period. As it turned out, he came to be housed in the same place as the physical remains of about a hundred Omahas from the early nineteenth-century village of *Ton'wontonga*, which had been excavated by the university prior to WW II. The Omahas who were involved in the Pole's return were astonished when they discovered what had happened. They expressed the view that *Umon'hon'ti* must have wanted to come home to deal with the plight of the people whose remains were being held by the university. Indeed, following his return to the tribe, the atmosphere of hostility and suspicion that had prevailed between Tribe and University changed to one of co-operation and mutual respect. The result of that new atmosphere was a sophisticated scientific study of the bones (Reinhard 1994) and their subsequent respectful reburial on reservation land. In the view of people like Doran Morris and Omaha tribal historian Dennis Hastings, *Umon'hon'ti* came back to relieve the suffering of these Omaha ancestors.

While those directly involved in the Sacred Pole's return focused on the good things that have happened to the tribe as a whole, others looked to individual misfortunes and attributed them to the Pole's power. When Lawrence Gilpin (a diabetic like a large number of adult

Omahas) suffered a stroke that left him with a slight speech disability, some people were quick to point out that he had been the first to touch the Pole in Nebraska and had been prominent in offering prayer upon his return. His misfortune, they said, was caused by the Pole.

A non-Indian summarized some of the fears she had heard as follows:

> I thought that one of the big reasons that people were opposing it was because the Pole had been gone for a hundred years and they were afraid, and sort of incarcerated, and he was never even carried on horseback, and he was carried in a plane, in the cargo thing of a plane, and in the back of a pick-up and that this was intended to be respectful but wasn't really respectful and appropriate and if it wasn't, that it could be very dangerous, which makes sense, I think.

Doran Morris recently reflected on the pressure he has been under from people who blame the Pole for misfortunes, ranging from a Sioux City air disaster to a series of recent deaths on the reservation:

> You know, a lot of our older people are really superstitious. They say if you do some things this way, something bad will happen to you or your family. I don't believe that. I think we ought to try to get rid of those things. It really hinders trying to go ahead, you know.
>
> Two, three weeks after I brought the Sacred Pole home they had a big plane crash here, killed hundred and some people. One guy, he went and told around the community that because Doran Morris brought the Sacred Pole home, they killed a lot of people up here ... I could hear a lot of talk about superstitious, about sacred things. A lot of people use that on each other today.
>
> There is something missing from the time the Pole left and the time I brought him home. The hatred in the community is a reason why a lot of people are against the Pole. And another big reason is that they don't know. Before the Pole left, the people were together back there. We addressed each other by relationship. The reason for that was that we had respect for one another. But the time the Pole left the reservation and it came back, we see those terrible things, problems amongst our people. The alcohol, the hatred of how they carry on politics. You can see that today. So you see the variance. When the Pole was here and when it wasn't here.
>
> I would like to say, ever since the Sacred Pole came home, there's been good things happening. Of course there's been bad things that happen

between, but overall, I think really good things happened to the Omaha tribe that never happened before. Not because I was the leader of the tribe, but because the Sacred Pole came home.

In 1990, the tribal council decided to bring *Umon'hon'ti* back again to the powwow. By this time a good deal of fear and opposition had developed. Lawrence Gilpin had suffered a stroke, but was well enough to preside over the Pole's entry into the powwow arena. As the time came to bring him into the arena with the Omaha Flag Song, people from a prominent family, the senior member of which had been educated in an Indian residential school in the East, turned away and pointedly left the arena. This placed the drum group in a difficult, even fearful, situation. Should anything bad happen to one of them, some people would blame them for having sung for the Pole. Should they do nothing, they risked causing further disrespect.

Lawrence Gilpin, in a remarkable display of courage and forthrightness, spoke directly to the fear that was an almost physical presence in the arena that day:

All you dancers. All you singers. Be ready to go.
They had a special deal the council is going to share with you and it is called the Sacred Pole. The Omaha tribe had this Sacred Pole in the center of where they lived, and it was a good omen. They went to this Pole on their way out to a hunt, on an expedition, or something that was good for them. It's a God-given thing. God give it to the Omahas for that purpose. And you believe in it that way it's going to be that way. It's gonna be good for you.

I hear somebody's afraid of it. They're not afraid of alcohol. They're not afraid of whiskey. They're not afraid of bad things. But this omen is a good thing. It'd be good for your everyday life. You should not be afraid of it. It'd be good for you. The more you believe in it, it be better for you. That's where they fall wrong.

Somebody's throwing gossip out there. That's no good. They should know what they're talking about. The old people didn't tell them. Maybe they weren't raised here, that's why. Amongst the Omahas. That is one reason that we make many mistakes. We make errors and that's where you are WRONG and I can say that with authority. That sacred wood is good for you. The old people believed in it. They had it in their camp wherever they camped. And they walked around it on the way out of that camp and it brought them good luck. And that is why we call it sacred. It was good medicine. The old people had this. They had it in their camp. And they thanked the creator for this. And they walked around it in camp where they could see it, where everybody could be amongst it. It was believe in it and it's gonna be that way.

An Omaha boy found this Sacred Pole. It was a tree. The tree lit up at night. It made light. And the the next night this boy went back and the same thing happened. That tree was lit, making light like electricity. That was way before electricity was thought of and it made light. And he went home and told his people, the Omahas, and they went over there and discovered their Sacred Pole. It wasn't a pole then. It was a tree that was lighting at night. That was something. They didn't know where that light came from. A God-given thing. So they took that tree and they made it sacred and they put it in front of the camp. It brought them good luck. They had good luck at their hunt. They were able to do those things they needed to do easily. That's why they called it the Sacred Pole, because it brought them good luck.

The head singer is here and he is waiting. Where is all the helpers? All you singers. Act like a good Omaha and come up here and help the head singer. There's a lot of worse things that you're not scared of. This is good medicine. Here you are, scared of it I understand.

The Sacred Pole is on its way to the arena and I was asked by the Omaha tribal chairman to say a prayer to God in front of the Pole that to do that might bring a better thing in life. That we might have a good life as Indian people. As Indian people we have a hard time. The whiteman he outnumbers us and we have to do as he says. Some of those things that we don't like we have to do. And here we are something real good and we're scared of it. We're worse than little kids. And I say this without hesitation.

As of my visit to the Omaha reservation for the 190th annual tribal powwow in August of 1994, Omahas continue to experience both fear and pride in the Sacred Pole. Lawrence Gilpin and venerable powwow announcer Clifford Wolfe had both passed away, as had the person who walked away from the arena in 1990. A number of deaths occurred in the early summer of 1994. Some people blamed the Pole, even though he has not been on the reservation since 1990. Others took the more positive measure of planning a series of four Native American Church healing ceremonies. A new chairman and a council with ties to factions opposed to the Pole's return had been elected. I wrote in my fieldnotes:

> There is no question that the council and other powers that be are inclined to have absolutely nothing to do with the Pole right now. This is fueled by rampant accusations that bringing the Pole back is the cause of "all these deaths at Macy."

Doran Morris and I had a long conversation over dinner the day before I left. He took a particularly strong position on the assertion that Sacred things will kill you if you don't handle them exactly as they were handled more than a century before:

> The main reason I went out and brought the Sacred Pole home; cause I know nobody's going to do it. Then if it was true what they're saying that the Sacred things will kill you if you don't handle or do things right, so I let it be me. I'll do it. So that's what happened. But they're saying that since the Pole came home, it's killing this one, it's killing that one. It's not true. I know that. That book that you're writing would make these guys aware. The younger people would come up with it and we'll try to get back to our ways. You might write in your book. We'll bring it home, and try to get back to the same ways we used to be, to dream about. Someday we will not be drinking that alcohol that ruins our people. That's my wish, for someday.

For now, the Sacred Pole remains in tribal control but in the safekeeping of the University of Nebraska at Lincoln. The Omahas have successfully reburied the remains of their ancestors formerly held by the University. As in the time when the Pole was first found, the tribe does not speak with one voice. Lawrence Gilpin's vision of "an undivided interest in this Sacred Pole" has yet to be realized. I share Doran's hope that a book about tribal tradition will help the tribe return to a common center.

Now, as in the time when a young man discovered "a tree that stands burning," Omahas are divided and seek some means of keeping the tribe together. Between that time and the 1870s, the Sacred Pole stood, as Eddie Cline said, "in the center of the Omaha people." When the Pole was in the care of a Honga Clan keeper, warnings about supernatural punishment for breaking the ritual order were tempered by prescribed means of restoring that order. The keeper's tears could take away the harm. Doran Morris was moved to weep when he first encountered the Pole. In his view, and in that of the others responsible for bringing him back, their actions have been respectful and provoke no cause for harm.

Discussion

Omaha oral tradition begins with the description of what appears to be a classic "revitalization movement" (Wallace 1956). A young man's visionary experience provided the symbol for a moral authority that would hold together a tribe on the move. The new "steady state" thus realized worked reasonably well until the buffalo disappeared in the 1870s and the Pole became "dreaded as a thing that was powerful for harm but seemingly powerless to bring back the old-time prosperity to the people" (Fletcher and La Flesche 1911, 245).

The Omahas who brought the Pole back in 1989 universally expressed the wish to find a center that would unify the tribe and bring a return of that "old-time prosperity." They called him *Umon'hon'ti*, "the real Omaha," a person who stands for all the people. They prayed for an "undivided interest" in his authority. They prayed for a revitalization of Omaha society. Even in those "old-time" days, however, Omahas achieved unity through the complementary opposition of clans, societies, and moieties. Competing factions existed then, as they do today. The nineteenth-century ethnography of James Dorsey (1884) is famous because of the many instances he cites of informants denying one another's testimony (Barnes 1984).

Authority within the tribe continues to be dispersed and the product of negotiation among competing interests. Different factions are contesting the meaning of their shared history in a way that looks very much like a tribal version of what I called the "medicine fight" in a band-level society (Ridington 1968). When misfortune comes to the family of someone associated with the Pole's return, opponents claim that it happened because of that person's disregard for the ritual order. They even claim that bringing the Pole back caused external events such as the Sioux City air disaster. In response, those under attack affirm their respect for tradition and their wish for tribal unity. They point to their accusers' lack of knowledge or bad habits. They hint at a superstitious and possibly malevolent use of power; "A lot of people use that on each other today." Neither side will, of course, admit to the other's claims. Each holds strongly to what it has made a public commitment to. Each reads recent tribal history as evidence for its claims.

Meanwhile, *Umon'hon'ti* himself continues to exist. He is in the thoughts of Omahas again for the first time in over a century. He continues to be a powerful cultural instrument, whether his return is viewed as harmful or as a blessing. Because he is a living being, as Omahas of all persuasions seem to agree, the controversy centers on whether it is best to keep him at a distance or to bring him close to the people, troubled and divided as they may be. The fear he commands is very real, but so is the faith in his power as a symbol of tribal unity.

Umon'hon'ti is a person whose life spans many human generations. The disputes of this generation will become part of his story. In years to come, Omahas may look back on the prayers of Eddie Cline and Lawrence Gilpin as part of their heritage. In years to come, *Umon'hon'ti* may continue to bless their quest for revitalization. I consider myself blessed for having been part of the story. I hope that my writing about Omaha tradition will help this and coming generations understand the historical depth that informs their situation. As Eddie Cline said in prayer:

> Whatever his thoughts, make them possible.
> Make his good thoughts possible.
> All my relations.

12

From Stone Tablets to Flying Saucers: Tradition and Invention in Hopi Prophecy

Armin W. Geertz

The systematic study of apocryphal expectations among the Hopi Indians of Arizona inevitably draws attention to their political ramifications. Confronted with questionable evidence, statements, and interpretations of and about Hopi prophecy, the obvious conclusion is that the fluid nature of the alleged revelations is primarily the result of political intrigue and social strategy. This was the main stance of my recent study on Hopi prophecy which documents it in a variety of ways (1992). In this paper I would like to carry out a more detailed comparison of three texts produced by the Hopi prophet Dan Qötshongva (known as Katchongva to his Euro-American audience) during key phases of his career. In the process I will attempt to explain what constitutes continuity and what constitutes invention in Qötshongva's prophetic texts. At the conclusion of this paper I suggest how we can explain the creative manipulation of apparent prophetic revelations.

Myths and Situational Personalities

Esther S. Goldfrank was the first scholar to cast light on the role of situation and personality in the production of mythical narrative. She did fieldwork among the Laguna, Cochiti, and Isleta, but produced in 1948 an important paper on the Hopi emergence myth. In her earlier work (1926), Goldfrank was evidently interested in the phenomenon of mythical variants, whereas in her early work on the Hopis, she was more interested in their socialization techniques (1945).

In her 1948 paper, Goldfrank sought to explain why Hopi myths simultaneously resist and incorporate change. Their stable patterning is often offset by the loss, incorporation, or manipulation of elements or motifs. Stability, she suggested, can be accounted for by the individual's and society's need for "canalization" whereas change can be accounted for by "a changing historical situation, as well as the narrator's personality and own experience" (1948, 241).

Goldfrank carefully described the personalities and situation of the four variants of the emergence myth recorded during a period of almost 50 years (1883-1932) at the village of Oraibi. The four narrators had played prominent roles before, during, and/or after the political and demographic division of Oraibi in 1906, and the results of Goldfrank's analysis show that the reformulation and reinterpretation of certain central themes was due to the differing political stances and social statuses of the narrators.

Goldfrank's explanations, however, are standard materialistic and behavioristic postulates based on a theory of irrigation and waterworks and consequent climatic or ecological factors (first raised in Wittfogel and Goldfrank 1943) and on a theory of the "fragmented nature" of Hopi society. I need not dwell on these outmoded theories, but it should be noted that already at this early stage in research on the Hopis, detailed descriptions of personality and situation revealed important interpretive factors in the study of the emergence myth with its prophetic elements.

At any rate, it is not very difficult to explain the changing fate of one particular myth in the hands of four speakers of different provenience over a period of 50 years. But when faced, as in this paper, with evidence of changes in one particular myth in the hands of the same speaker over a period of some 40 years, we are confronted with serious problems of interpretation. Indeed, in studying the versions of the emergence myth related by Dan Qötshongva, how do we account for the coherence of 1935 (Kotchongva 1936), the incoherence of 1956 (Bentley 1956), the almost totally new story of 1970 (Skidmore 1970), and the final return to the original story later that same year (Tarbet 1972)? The answers to these questions, I argue, are not to be found in the texts themselves rather in the emergent and cooperative nature of textualization, where rhetorical devices define historical realities. Our job must be, therefore, to pursue an interpretive description of the realities which the text is a product of.

Hopi Prophecy

Before I move on to Dan Qötshongva, a brief review of the emergence myth and its prophecies is necessary.

Hopi prophecy is intimately related to the emergence myth. In this narrative, Hopi mythographers postulate a series of worlds through which all humans have passed. These worlds are collectively experienced in cyclical terms whereby the paradisial beginnings are replaced by cataclysmic endings, which again lead humanity into the next cycle. At the beginning of this present "Fourth World," the Hopi tutelary deity Maasaw commanded them to follow his precepts until his return, which will signal the end of the world. There were two brothers who emerged among the races. The one was the Elder White Brother and the other was the Younger Hopi Brother. They agreed that the Elder Brother would move to the east and the Younger Brother would remain in the west. If the Younger Brother ever needed help, in other words, if he ever becomes plagued by enemies or internal strife, the Elder Brother will return to help or to punish as a prelude to Maasaw's return. To seal this pact, the brothers were given a stone tablet which would serve to legitimate their roles and identities at the end of the Fourth World. Details vary from clan to clan and individual to individual, but these two main events—the return of the White Brother with the stone tablet and the subsequent return of Maasaw—are central to the development and interpretation of Hopi prophecies.

The emergence myth is composed of a series of episodes structured around stories. The six main stories are: 1) the apocryphal conditions of the primordial Third World prior to the emergence; 2) the actual emergence to the Fourth World; 3) the post-emergence creations of the heavenly bodies, the distribution of languages and foodstuffs, and the establishment of death; 4) the meeting with Maasaw and/or the story of the two brothers and related prophecies; 5) the migrations of the clans; and 6) the settlement of Oraibi and the meeting between the Bear Clan and Maasaw. A frequency comparison of emergence myth variants indicates that despite slight variations in the order of events, the basic narrative structure remains, and the pivotal episodes are usually present. I have found that all important changes are explicitly and predictably due to matters of political and social status. Thus, for instance, details may vary concerning which group first met Maasaw, the order of the emergence of the clans, which clan was associated with the primordial witch, the exact prophetic words of Maasaw (which are ultimately related to the political persuasion of the narrator), and, of course, the details of each clan migration.

Hopi prophecy is a sub-category of clan tradition, which in Hopi is called *navoti*. The term itself indicates the narrative nature of clan tradition. It means literally "knowledge gained from hearing"—not from seeing or experience. *Navoti* covers not only the history of a clan, but it also provides an interpretive framework for life situations. *Hopinavoti*, i.e. Hopi clan tradition, expresses what I call "indigenous hermeneutics." *Navoti* qualifies as an indigenous analytical practice because it is expert and restricted. It provides frameworks for interpretations, but it also is part and parcel of the politics of knowledge in a society where knowledge is the basis of status and power. Thus, Hopi prophecy is intimately related to and part of clan identity and clan ideology, which defines individual identity within a network of political and social relationships.

Since the emergence narrative is identical for all clans, it must therefore be a common pan-clan narrative. The narrative consists of standard features which can be *predictably* characterized in terms of susceptibility to stability or change. I have shown that the continuity of the narrative is secured through ritual, social, and psychological mechanisms. The core narrative is emphasized in hundreds of ways in social praxis. In fact, it can be shown that every ceremonial and social drama either refers explicitly to this narrative or assumes it. The narrative provides powerful instruments for the creation and maintenance of meaning and significance. It especially provides continuity through mythological coherence, structural coherence in social and religious domains, and a coherent frame of reference for each individual. But more importantly for this paper, it also provides mechanisms for change.

Dan Qötshongva, Hopi Prophet

When the famous founding chief of Hotevilla, Yukiwma, died in 1929, there were three possible contenders to his office: Poliwuhiwma of the Spider Clan who was the nephew of Yukiwma's predecessor Lomahongyiwma (1894-1904), Yukiwma's son Qötshongva of the Sun Clan (who was born at the end of the nineteenth century), and Yukiwma's nephew Pongyayawma of the Kookop Clan.[1] The correct order of succession would have been to appoint Pongyayawma, and so he was appointed by Yukiwma, even though he was too young. According to Titiev, Poliwuhiwma became the acting chief because it was felt by many that the chieftainship should be linked to the possession of the Soyalangw Ceremony which at the time belonged to the Spider Clan (Titiev 1944, 211). Poliwuhiwma died before the year was out with the result that Qötshongva and Pongyayawma were appointed co-rulers during the period of 1930-1943 until Pongyayawma came of age. Pongyayawma was formally invested by Qötshongva in the presence of Commissioner John Collier (Bureau of Indian Affairs 1955, 285-86) and was chief during the period of 1943-1950. But due to a falling out with Qötshongva, he renounced the chieftainship, married a woman from Santo Domingo Pueblo, and moved to Albuquerque in 1950 (Clemmer 1978, 36), thereby leaving the power to Qötshongva who took over as chief from 1950 until his death in 1972. The threat of the chieftainship passing on to Qötshongva's lieutenant David Monongya was enough to move Pongyayawma to reassume the role of chief (even though his backing in the village was fragile) in 1972 until his death in 1989 (one year after Monongya's death).

These brief and dry facts do little justice to one of the most dramatic and colorful half centuries of Hopi history. This period corresponded to the rise and fall of the Traditionalist Movement, a movement curiously fluid in analytical terms: seen from within it was neither a movement nor did it tender anything new to the Hopis themselves. Its leaders simply attempted to usurp political power and to battle the Tribal Council with the help of outsiders. From without, the movement demonstrates all of the characteristics of millenarianism, but containing neither vision nor healing nor a new social community ideal. The Traditionalist Movement was a politicization of an already existing "reforming ethic" and a reaffirmation of traditional Hopi values which were exported to impressionable Europeans, Americans, and various religious and political support groups. The Traditionalist Movement succeeded in transforming, at least within the framework of political and social arenas defined by the movement itself (mainly outside the Hopi Indian Reservation), the local agricultural concerns of Hopi religion to universalistic and missionary ones.

Dan Qötshongva was the founder and leader of the movement, and his own career is an interesting example of the development from resistance to messianism. The Traditionalist Movement failed not because the end of the world failed to arrive, but because the Traditionalists failed to mobilize their own people and instead solely moved the hearts and imagination of White Euro-Americans.[2] And when Qötshongva died in 1972, he was marginalized in relation to the Hopis, but was a venerable and charismatic symbol for Euro-Americans.

The First Text: Exploring Intercultural Dialogue

Already at the beginning of the 1930s Qötshongva was very much concerned with prophecies about the end of the world and especially with the identity of the awaited Elder Brother. The first body of prophecies by Qötshongva was related to the Mormons in 1935 which was published a year later in the Mormon journal *The Improvement Era*. The Mormons were interested in the Indians and in their possible connection to the Book of Mormon. When Qötshongva heard about their magazine, which had published an issue on Indians in March 1933, he travelled to Salt Lake City for the specific purpose of relating the Hopi prophecies. He travelled with his spokesman Ralph Tawangyawma and interpreter Harry Nasewaytiwa, and related the prophecies to a group headed by President Levi Edgar Young.

What exactly were Qötshongva's motives? According to the editor, Qötshongva was "seeking his white deliverer and the deliverer of his people" (Kotchongva 1936, 82). Already at this time, we find the germinal idea of the soon to be established Traditionalist Movement that their mission is not concerned with converting new supporters but with the functional goal of precipitating the arrival of the White Brother:

> So I, Dan Kotchongva, Chief of Hotevilla Village, am not looking at the office at Washington for help right now, but we Hopis are looking for the return of our White Brother, who will come to us and bring forth a relief of the suffering of all the people. We have looked toward Washington, Chicago, and Santa Fe, New Mexico, as places for this Word to go out in search of our White Brother, but so far nothing has been done. That is why I am here today talking to you people and if this word goes out from here, maybe He will know of our search for Him and come to us. This is the time to which we have looked for generations. We were told that his time was when a road was made in the sky. The road of the airplane is well made. If we do not find Him through this effort we will keep on searching and shall not stop looking until He returns. (Kotchongva 1936, 119)

Qötshongva's statements reveal an emergent collated recension which became more evident and more refined in the discourses of the Traditionalist Movement by 1961.

Qötshongva's story is a standard but compact version of the emergence myth. His details are interestingly innovative already at this time. The two brothers (Hopi and White) are the sons of a fallen chief who had wrongly eaten the food of the people and had therefore resigned in favor of his two sons.

The two brothers part, as do the various races, in their search for the owner of the earth. In the process the White Elder Brother becomes wonderfully powerful, technically superior, and rich. In direct opposition to all other versions of the myth that give the honor of the discovery of Maasaw to the Bear Clan, Qötshongva claimed that the "Spirit Clan" found him first. He translates this name with "Maasaw Clan." Qötshongva claimed further, again inconsistent with all other known versions at that time, that all of the land from coast to coast was given to the Hopis in trust by Maasaw, and it was to be held in trust (not to be turned over to any other people) by the Maasaw Clan until Maasaw chose to return and reclaim his landholdings.

The myth ends with a description of Maasaw imparting his ceremony to the people and his prophecies concerning the sacred stone tablet and the coming of the White Brother who will be able to translate the symbols on the tablet. Natural calamities play a more dominant role in Qötshongva's version than in others, and they play a central role in a purgative destruction brought by the White Brother. With Qötshongva's myth, American technology entered into Hopi prophecy for the first time: the White Brother will return when "a road is made in the sky." Qötshongva's expectations were more soteriological than earlier prophecies, but he also envisioned a universal brotherhood, a common language, as well as intermarriage! And even though the land now became an issue, due to the enactment of the 1934 land bill (Geertz 1992, 196), Qötshongva actually envisioned a mutual sharing of the land by "the faithful Indians and the righteous Whites", which later turned out to be effective in recruiting outside support. Thus, the combination of political resistance, coupled with a fundamentalistic focus on morality, which became the mark of the later Traditionalist Movement, was already present in Qötshongva's statements. His emphasis on behavior and the possibility of averting catastrophe through proper behavior was actually a return to the traditional Hopi assumption that ecological and human events are directly influenced by human action.

Two Decades of Resistance

A few years later when Oliver LaFarge who wrote the "Constitutions and By-Laws of the Hopi Tribe, Arizona" tried to pressure the Hopis into accepting them, Qötshongva introduced a new prophecy making constitutional changes eschatologically dangerous (Bureau of Indian Affairs 1955, 58). Qötshongva became more active in his resistance to the U.S. Government especially during the second world war. In 1940 Don

Talayesva heard Qötshongva give a speech to a crowd of Indians and Whites during the Snake Ceremonial at Hotevilla in which he not only reaffirmed the basic prophecy, but also suggested that the White Brother might be Hitler (Simmons 1942, 379)! This idea is still evident among the Hopis today. Hitler's use of the venerable swastika symbol probably had something to do with this identification.

At any rate, Qötshongva gained notoriety together with Pongyayawma in 1941 when they tried to defend Hopi resistance to the draft system. They appeared at the Phoenix Federal Court in 1941 to explain the reasoning behind six Hopi youths' failure to register for selective service, for which they were waiting sentencing. The two chiefs, together with the young Thomas Banancya, were reported to have explained the Hopi prophecies to the court concerning engagement in the war. Their statements reveal that even though they recognized the legitimacy and the need for the American engagement, they felt bound by their traditions not to take sides. This argument did them little good however, since conscientious objector status was first conferred on the Hopis along narrowly defined lines in the 1960s. But the argument began a series of traditions about great wars which came to dominate later prophecies.[3]

Qötshongva and Pongyayawma held a press conference and displayed the sacred stone tablets in the court house. On page 10 of the May 23, 1941 afternoon edition of the *Arizona Republic*, a photograph was published picturing the co-rulers examining two stone tablets. The caption reads:

> The larger stone is sacred, and represents the Hopi land and its religion. Legends carved on it prophesied the present war of the nations and a great, equal peace which someday will be brought by a white man who can read the stone, the chief said. The smaller stone represents the home, but is of lesser importance, the chiefs explained, because without the land there is no place to put the home. (Anonymous 1941, 10)

The larger tablet belonged to the Bear Clan and the smaller to the Kookop. I have explained in detail elsewhere how it came about that Qötshongva had obtained the Bear Clan stone (Geertz 1992, 223-57) and will not go into it here. The article accompanying the photograph shows that Qötshongva used the tablets to emphasize his political position as well as to argue against the draft. Further details repeated his earlier prophetic ideas.

The Second Text: Meeting of Religious People

One of the most signal events in modern Hopi history was a meeting held in 1948 by a group of concerned leaders and elders who felt that the dropping of the atomic bombs fulfilled a crucial prophecy forewarning the end of the world. During this and similar meetings the traditions of various clans were collated into a corpus, and a number of young men knowledgeable in the White man's ways and able to speak fluent English were appointed as spokesmen and interpreters. During these meetings the participants were intensely involved in producing the ideology of the Traditionalist Movement. Its goals were to stop cultural disintegration and increase resistance against American policies.

A year later these ideological principles were articulated in a letter addressed to President Truman signed by the "hereditary Hopi Chieftains" of the "Hopi Indian Empire." The letter clearly demonstrated a carefully plotted and solid platform for the emerging Traditionalist Movement, and almost all of the co-signers later became leaders of the movement. An important point to note is that the letter lay claim to power, authority, and spokesmanship, and yet only two of the 26 co-signers were actually village chiefs; and, as noted, Qötshongva took over only after Pongyayawma left (who was one of the co-signers). On the other hand, a number of co-signers possessed priestly positions. In the letter they rejected the North Atlantic Alliance and a whole series of laws and resolutions. Besides cogent arguments against the imperialistic assumptions of the policies of the U.S. Government, the letter cast the Traditionalist stance in millenarian terms in which the inviolability of tradition was reaffirmed and served as a point of departure for their analysis of past, present, and future events. Hopi rights were God-given and will be proven so at the end of the world.

Even though the theme of resistance is present, the tone is global and universalistic in which the Hopis play a pivotal role in the world theatre:

> Today we, Hopi and white man, come face to face at the crossroads of our respective life. At last our paths have crossed and it was foretold it would be at the most critical time in the history of mankind. Everywhere people are confused. What we decide now and do hereafter will be the fate of our respective people... The time has now come for all of us as leaders of our people to reexamine ourselves, our past deeds, and our future plans. The judgment day will soon be upon us. Let us make haste and set our house in order before it is too late. (The Hopi Indian Empire, 28 March 1949; see Geertz 1992, 421)

Further prophetic statements were included in the letter, and a new idea was introduced claiming that a judgment would be initiated by the true White Brother in "the Hopi Indian Empire."

From that time on Qötshongva sent with the help of interpreters a "barrage of letters, statements, petitions, and declarations hurtling towards the Bureau of Indian Affairs" (Clemmer 1978, 36). This period also marked a veritable trafficking in prophecies that attracted many young Americans who searched out Qötshongva as a messianic figure.

Two important events occurred in the middle of the 1950s. Hearings were conducted by the BIA on the Reservation in 1955, and, in 1956 the "Meeting of Religious People" was held in Hotevilla by the Traditionalists. Both meetings gave ample opportunity to aire grievances against American policies and to discuss Hopi dissension and prophecy.

These two sources are significantly different in character even though both the Hearings and the Meeting were brought about by the energetic Qötshongva. The Hearings were a result of a meeting in Washington in May 1955 between Commissioner of Indian Affairs Glenn L. Emmons and a party of six led by Qötshongva. The 1956 Meeting was also orchestrated by Qötshongva, but this time the supporters and participants were outside religious organizations and activists who were attracted to the Traditionalists' "last stand" against the U.S. Government. Even though state and federal officials were invited, none showed up. The tone throughout the minutes of the meeting is both pious, strident, and posturing. Whereas the Hearings were truly representative of all persuasions in all the villages at the insistence of Glenn Emmons, the 1956 Meeting was mostly a stage for Hotevilla Traditionalists.

The statements of both meetings are far too numerous to reproduce, and I have documented them in my 1992 publication. Only trends and isolated examples will be mentioned here.

Reading the minutes of the Hearings, one cannot avoid noticing the obvious disagreement evident in statements from the opposing factions on the Reservation. The terminology and details of supposedly age-old prophecies were no exceptions. On the one hand, we read statements describing the coming White Man in messianic terms and, on the other, statements describing him as the great deceiver. Besides all of the traditional elements of Hopi prophecy, we find a whole array of statements that specifically address recent and contemporary problems confronting the Hopis: Navajo encroachments, the Indian Reorganization Act, wars, tricky legislation, the Tribal Council, stock reduction programs, the Oraibi split, land allotments, district programs, the Indian Claims Commission, and the leasing of mineral rights (Geertz 1992, 205-6).

New elements that came into prominence in Traditionalist statements concern the immanent Day of Purification. These statements emphasize the modern inventions of the White Man, but also the coming of a Third or Fourth World War. Qötshongva's statements make no reference to the emergence myth, but provide instead a highly detailed account of what Maasaw said to the people who had arrived at his home in Oraibi. These details, however, constitute a thinly disguised rationalization of his own power takeover and a legitimization of the Traditionalist Movement in general (see Geertz 1992, 395-96).

The following year, the Traditionalists and the interest groups who supported them were brought together at the "Meeting of Religious People," as it was called, in Hotevilla in 1956. The meeting and the people who attended it were placed in strongly millenaristic language, constituting a gathering of chosen ones selected from God's great variety of religions in North America. The Hopi stand was conceived as being the stand of every man on earth concerned with the cause and cure of humanity's global crisis (Bentley 1956). Thus the growing universalistic thrust of Hopi prophecy fit in well with the rhetoric of this group of concerned religious individuals and groups. As Dan Qötshongva stated in his opening speech: "Let us remember that we are gathered here not only for the Hopi people, but we are seriously thinking of the future and benefit of ALL other Indian people on this continent, and we include the white people who have come upon our land and settled with us" (1956, 2). Even though Qötshongva stated that all people will be involved, the Purification Day will nonetheless take place in Oraibi, as earlier traditions claim.

In the process of universalizing Hopi prophecy, the concerns of the end of the last century about a returning White Brother who will punish the bad Hopis and initiate the Purification Day have now been replaced with the return of Maasaw—now called the pan-Indian term "Great Spirit"—who will punish *all* bad people, especially the Whites! As Monongya said in his speech:

> When the Purification Day comes the white man will be allowed to live on this land again. Teachings tell us that a few of them will be saved. But perhaps all will be destroyed, we don't know. (Bentley 1956, 10)

Qötshongva's statements again pay little heed to the emergence myth and dwell on a detailed account of what Maasaw actually said to the first arrivals (Geertz 1992, 397-98). Furthermore perhaps in drawing on revivalist rhetoric, he placed great emphasis on the importance of groups and their leaders "keeping the faith" and adhering to their lifeways. He envisioned a faithful people awaiting the grand return of the Great Spirit. Qötshongva also developed the growing prophetic detail about the signs of the coming of the White Brother and the end of the world:

> One of the things that was told to us was that the white man will come and be a very intelligent man, bringing to us many things that he will invent. One of the inventions that our forefathers talked about was a machine or object that would move on the land with animals pulling it. Until the wagon came along we didn't know what this prophecy meant. Our forefathers spoke also of a machine which would afterwards move with nothing pulling it, and when we saw the automobile we knew what they were talking about. Then they told us that the land would be cut up and that there would be many roads, and today we see the pavement all over the land. Then later on there would be a road in the sky. How could anyone build a road in the sky? we wondered. But when we see airplanes going back and forth over us we know what they were talking about. We were told that there would be something that would be shiny and would run through our land and look like a path of water glittering. We found this to be referring to the roads which have been built on our land, because when we go down these roads we see they DO look like water ahead. These signs all tell us that we are nearing the end of our Life Patterns, that man will soon have to be judged. We call that Great Day the Purification Day, the white man calls it the Judgement Day. We look forward to it with great joy and the white man with horror and fear; and rightly so for both of us know that on that day each will be dealt with according to what he justly deserves.
> Another prophesy that has been passed down to us is that there will be three great wars which will take place on this earth. Someone will start the war and it will go a little way and it will come to an end; another person will start it again and then it will stop for a little while; then the third one will come and it will not stop until everything is purified on this earth and the wicked ones destroyed. (Geertz 1992, 398)

These prophecies formed the foundation of all later traditionalist versions, and the heights of prophetic fantasy were reached in Thomas Banancya's prophetic catalogue which first appeared in 1961 (Banyacya 12 January 1961; Geertz 1992, 408-10).

The transformation of Maasaw from a local tutelary deity to a universal supreme being is one of the clearest examples of the universalization of Hopi religion by the Traditionalists. Hamilton A. Tyler was the first to note Maasaw's transformation (see Tyler 1964, 36-40 and Geertz 1987, 41). He credited this transformation to Qötshongva and Simon Scott.

It seems as if Simon Scott was the more agile theologian of the two. And it seems, as well, that he was steeped in apocryphal imagery. He proclaimed at the hearings in 1955 that "this supreme being who is over all of us is here with us and listening to all of us in this meeting and will be with us until this meeting is adjourned" (Bureau of Indian Affairs 1955, 31). Later, he emphasized again that this supreme being, who created both Indian and White, had instructed both races to live peacefully (1955, 24). Through the use of biblical language and imagery, he identified the Hopi tutelary as the Supreme God who created and rules over all humanity. During the meeting of religious people in 1956, he went much further than transposing and identifying deities, and declared that the content of all religions—especially the eschatological content—is basically the same. Hopi religion was considered to be of the same nature as Christianity and Judaism and equally legitimate. Furthermore, Simon set the Traditionalists' political battle in universal religious terms so that it became a common battle for all religious people who consequently were portrayed as simply trying to obey the Supreme God.

During the next forty years, the Traditionalists continued to refer to Maasaw as the Great Spirit, even though there is no basis for this term in Hopi tradition. Even today, the term is still peculiar to Traditionalist terminology. I am also convinced that the Traditionalist concept of the "Great Spirit" was developed in direct relation to the religious and apocryphal language of non-Hopi interest groups and not so much as part of an indigenous need to reformulate the nature of Maasaw.

Keeping these observations on Maasaw in mind, we must look at another important facet of the universalization of Hopi religion, namely that it became a missionary endeavor. Hopi religion, as Traditionalists spoke of it, now began to look like a new religion, partly because of the dialogue with non-Hopis and partly because the importance of personal piety and participation in agricultural ceremonies was replaced by the importance of personal piety and participation in the apocryphal mission. This echoes Qötshongva's 1935 statements quoted above, and the type of missionizing they had in mind was also instrumental. The goal was not to convert Whites to the Hopi religion, but to make use of a growing communication network in order to capture the attention of the apocryphal White Brother thereby speeding him along on his predestined soteriological task. In other contexts, the missionizing took on a political nature. It is first during the later messianic stage of development that mission took on the full sense of the term, i.e., converting the world to the Hopi view of things.

The Flying Saucer Interim

In a letter sent to a pan-Indian meeting in 1958, Qötshongva indicated that the Traditionalists would present their grievances to the United Nations. In the letter, he claimed that it was prophesied that as the Day of Purification approaches, the Chief must knock on the door of the White House, and if the door is not opened, then he must knock on the door of the United Nations and tell about all the problems brought upon the Hopis by the White Man (Katchongva 1958). A six man delegation travelled to the U.N. the next year, but was not allowed to address the Assembly.

Evidently the turn of the decade bade Qötshongva ill. On the one hand he suffered from the loss of one of his closest political allies from Second Mesa, Andrew Hermequaftewa, and on the other hand he was under pressure from David Monongya and Thomas Banancya[4] to turn over the reins of power in the Traditionalist Movement. By 1960, Monongya and Banancya had become Qötshongva's interpreters and spokesmen—which earlier had been the prerogative of Ralph and Carolyne Tawangyawma, Ralph being one of the contenders to the chieftainship after Qötshongva. Shortly after the death of Hermequaftewa, Qötshongva made the following statement at a multi-cultural meeting held at Shongopovi on May 6-7, 1961:

> In a deeply moving, powerful declaration, Katchongva called upon the Sun as his witness, that he would not under any circumstances desert the Hopi way of life, and that from this moment forward he would give all of his energy to notify people throughout the land of the sacred teachings of the Hopi. In August, following his setting out of his crops and securing some food, he would convene another meeting, which would mark the first preparations for the Day of Purification. (Anonymous 1961, 12-13)

It seems that Qötshongva was frantically searching for the true White Brother while Monongya was trying to prevent him from ruining the reputation of the Traditionalist Movement. Anthropologist Shuichi Nagata described a situation which confirms this impression. Nagata attended a meeting held by the Traditionalists at Hotevilla in 1962 which also was attended by a Chinese Buddhist priest. Qötshongva was convinced that the priest was the mythical White Brother, and now that he had met him, "he was handing over the job of protecting the Hopi to Thomas and others, while Dan himself retired" (Nagata 1978, 78). During that episode, Nagata quoted Banancya as directly countermanding a request from Qötshongva to Nagata (1978, 81). This probably reflected that conflicts of interest were at stake at that time.

Dan Qötshongva was also convinced in 1962 that both the Russians and the Chinese were prophesied in Hopi tradition. So he tried to persuade Nagata to help him write a letter to the Russian and Chinese embassies. Banancya, however, persuaded Nagata not to send the letters, to which he acquiesced. But he kept them on file and published them in 1978. In the letters, Qötshongva was asking for nothing less than an apocryphal recollection. He was literally trying to get the Russians and the Chinese or Japanese to "re-cognize" their part in the primordial plot.

By 1963 Qötshongva had capitulated to Monongya. In an interview at Hotevilla on May 8, 1963, he said that Banancya and Monongya were his "ear and tongue:"

> ... they have my authority to listen and speak for me and they will convey all messages to me in turn. They have my authority to represent me and those who wish to talk [sic] with me can talk with them to inform or get information. It would be ill for anyone for whatever motive to try to deceive these two men. They have my authority to serve and represent me. (Anonymous 1963, 3)

Frank Waters described the struggle between Qötshongva and Monongya in his book *Pumpkin Seed Point* (Waters 1969, 38) which left the latter victorious. From then on we find no close association between them. By 1970, at least, the Tawangyawmas were once again Qötshongva's interpreters and spokesmen. Monongya and Banancya dominated the activities of the 1960s, orchestrating tremendous extrovertive activity on the part of the Traditionalists and attracting a large influx of adorants. By this time, Traditionalist activity was outrightly proselytical. After Qötshongva's death, the Movement itself continued going strong throughout the 1970's reaching its highest point around the middle of the decade by continually adjusting its image and language thereby remaining the focal point and symbol for Euro-American interest groups.

Evidently, one of the final blows to Qötshongva's position among the Traditionalists was his involvement with the "Flying Saucer Prophet" Paul Solem. During the period of approximately August 5th to August 21st, 1970, numerous night time sightings of unidentified flying objects were reported by hundreds of witnesses in Prescott, Arizona. A man from Idaho by the name of Paul Solem explained that the flying saucers were appearing because he called them there. They had first revealed themselves to him in 1948 and had followed him all over the country ever since where he would provide opportunities for sightings. Solem claimed to be an expert in Mormon doctrine and Hopi prophecy. He claimed that Mormon scripture teaches that the keys which the Latter-Day Saints Church hold will in the last days be turned over to the American Indians, and that was why he was in the area.

This event did not escape Qötshongva's attention. He had been waiting for something like this ever since the beginning of the 1960s and had already met Solem in 1969. The day after the front page story in the *Prescott Courier* on the August 7th sightings, the headlines of Monday the 10th read "Hopi Chief Arrives for Saucer Contact" accompanied by a photograph of Paul Solem, Dan Qötshongva, Ralph Tawangyawma and Carolyne Tawangyawma. They had come in order to witness the sighting which was to occur on the evening of August 10th:

> Chief Katchongva said he desires to make contact, ask for direction and to learn when the great migration of Indians in Hopi prophecy is to occur. According to the chief, flying saucers are not new to the Hopi. They play a big part in Indian history, he said, and are drawn on petrograph rocks near the Hopi mesas in Northern Arizona. (Anonymous 1970a, 1)

Cloudy conditions had evidently prevented the sighting, however, Solem was later quoted as saying, "The last day Chief Dan Katchongua of the Hopi Nation was here the ship came in real low, about 800 feet" (Anonymous 1970b, 1).

Qötshongva's saucer cult evidently meshed in well with his prophetic framework. By October 1970 he was characteristically pronouncing profoundly moralistic commands to his supporters:

> Do not drink strong drink. Stop all light mindedness. Live sober so that the Great Spirit may guide you through what is coming. Do not listen to rock and roll music, it will cast a spell on you. Young women dress so that your appeal is not to the body. Let our Indian people be an example to all people. (Rushton 1970, 12)

By the end of the year, an official pamphlet from the "Hopi Independent Nation, Hotevilla, Arizona USA" published "Chief Dan Katchongva's Message" (Skidmore 1970). The pamphlet was illustrated with a Second Mesa petroglyph and a flying saucer. Under the heading "Hopi Prophecy", Qötshongva opened with an abbreviated summary of the emergence and migration themes followed by specific references to the saucer cult. The pamphlet also incorporated the teachings of his rival

Monongya, even though neither Monongya nor Banancya are mentioned by name in the text. The text demonstrates three layers of lore: the traditionalist prophetic corpus of 1961 (Banancya's text), Paul Solem's eclectic mormonized ideas, and Qötshongva's own prophecies in connection with the flying saucers. In comparing this text with Yukiwma's emergence myth or Qötshongva's texts of 1935, 1955, 1956, or even the last text before his death, one is struck by the undeniable discontinuity. Qötshongva's last text of 1970 resembles more his father's tale and tones down the apocryphal detail of the Banancya text. On the other hand, the 1970 text emphasizes Qötshongva's divine nature—an idea equally foreign to indigenous thought, which will be analyzed in the following section.

The Third Text: Hopi Prophet and Messiah

In a talk recorded on January 29, 1970, Qötshongva related once again his account of the emergence myth and its prophecies. The account was published posthumously in several editions beginning in the year of his death in 1972 (Tarbet 1972; Katchongva 1973; Geertz 1992, 400-5). Even though the main actor is the Great Spirit, this myth is much closer to Qötshongva's 1935 myth and to the emergence myth in general than any of his versions in the intervening years.

In this version, he appropriated the many clan prophecies and collated them as if they were the prophecies of his own Sun Clan. He developed the story of the two brothers and the wayward father and claimed that the father was of the Bow Clan:

> The group leader was of the Bow Clan, a great chief with wisdom. But it was here that this great chief disappeared into the dark night. After putting his family to sleep he left in search of the Earth Center, where clever, ingenious people from all nations meet to plan the future. By some means he found the place, and was welcomed with respect. It was a beautiful place with all manner of good things. Good food was laid before him by most beautiful girls. It was all very tempting.
> Until today we did not know the significance of this action. It had to do with the future. By this action he caused a change to occur in the pattern of life as we near the end of the life cycle of this world, such that many of us would seek the materialistic world, trying to enjoy all the good things it has to offer before destroying ourselves. Those gifted with the knowledge of the sacred instructions will then live very cautiously, for they will remember and have faith in these instructions, and it will be on their shoulders that the fate of the world will rest. (Tarbet 1972, 8; Geertz 1992, 402)

In other words, the apocryphal cycle of the present world was begun by the wayward Bow Clan chief shortly after the emergence of humanity to this world. When his sons found out about this they initiated an agreement sealed by the two stone tablets, and the White Brother left for the east while the Hopi Brother stayed in the area until the end of time when they would meet again. At this crucial point in the text, Qötshongva mentions that the two brothers were of the Sun Clan, and in this single stroke, he elevated his clan and himself as saviors of humanity.

Having claimed to have received the instructions and prophecies directly from the Great Spirit in primordial times, Qötshongva stated: "Since I am Sun Clan, and the Sun is the father of all living things, I love my children. If they realize what I am talking about *they must help me save this world*" (Tarbet 1972, 20, my emphasis). He continued:

> The Hopi have been placed on this side of the Earth to take care of the land through their ceremonial duties, just as other races of people have been placed elsewhere around the Earth to take care of her in their own ways. Together we hold the world in balance, revolving properly. If the Hopi nation vanishes the motion of the Earth will become eccentric, the water will swallow the land, and the people will perish (1972, 20).

In his final statement, Qötshongva himself approaches divine status:

> I am forever looking and praying eastward to the rising sun for my true white brother to come and purify the Hopi. My father, Yukiuma, used to tell me that I would be the one to take over as leader at this time, because I belong to the Sun Clan, the father of all the people on the Earth. I was told that I must not give in, because I am the first. The Sun is the father of all living things from the first creation. And if I am done, the Sun Clan, then there will be no living thing left on the earth. So I have stood fast... I am the Sun, the father. With my warmth all things are created. You are my children, and I am very concerned about you. I hold you to protect you from harm, but my heart is sad to see you leaving my protecting arms and destroying yourselves. From the breast of your mother, the Earth, you receive your nourishment, but she is too dangerously ill to give you pure food. What will it be? Will you lift your father's heart? Will you cure your mother's ills? Or will you forsake us and leave us with sadness, to be weathered away? I don't want this world to be destroyed. I have spoken through the mouth of the Creator. May the Great Spirit guide you on the right path. (Tarbet 1972, 32-33)

The gradual development of Hopi prophecy from local, apocryphal clan traditions to universalism, ecological mysticism, and a final messianism is much the story of Qötshongva's life. But by 1970 the Traditionalist Movement had adjusted course, changed leadership, widened the corpus of prophecies to appeal to an ecology-conscious audience, and especially gave no precise date for the end of the world. The movement as well as the general Hopi populace (which had very little to do with each other) still believed in the immanent Last Day, but in each their own way and for each their own purpose. Qötshongva's personal fate was not essential to either of these.

Some Conclusions

The idea of tradition and invention as constituting a dichotomous relationship is problematical. Having written about this problem elsewhere in more detail (Geertz 1992, 145-181, 1993a, 1993b, Geertz and Jensen 1991, 11-27), I will simply repeat Roger M. Keesing's insight in his study of the politics of Melanesian traditionalism that we err in thinking that inventions that we can witness are any different than "genuine" culture (Keesing 1982, 300-1). Continuity and change go hand in hand with the continual invention and reproduction of cultural meaning.

In this I draw inspiration from the phenomenological sociology of Alfred Schutz and those who have carried his ideas forward, especially Peter Berger and Thomas Luckmann as well as Clifford Geertz. Berger and Luckmann's sedimentation theory presents a plausible explanation of why humans invent traditions and yet seriously hold that they stem from time immemorial. Sedimentation theory posits that human experiences congeal in recollection as sediment. This sediment becomes social when objectivated in a sign system, that is, when the reiterated objectification of shared experiences becomes possible. They argued that its transformation into a generally available object of knowledge allows it to be incorporated into a larger body of tradition "by way of moral instruction, inspirational poetry, religious allegory and whatnot" (Berger and Luckmann 1966, 86). The argument runs further that this aggregate of collective sedimentation can be acquired monothetically, that is, as cohesive wholes, "without reconstructing their original process of formation" and therefore inventing other origins does not necessarily upset the institutional order (1966, 87).

An important factor in this process is the control and legitimization procedures of the definition, transmission, and maintenance of social meaning. These control and legitimization procedures are often the source and/or arena of social conflict and social movements, such as the

Hopi Traditionalist Movement. Like Berger and Luckmann, I have attempted to analyze the socially constructed universe of the Hopis by looking in passing at the social organization and the subsequent cultural logic that "permits the definers to do their defining" (1966, 134). And we have seen in the process how the powerful personality of Dan Qötshongva helped shape the constructed universe of traditionalist prophecies until he was forced to relinquish control of the process to his aggressive younger colleagues. He continually adjusted his tale in relation to changing historical situations and social problems. But as he moved off on his own apocryphal tangent, his rivals changed arenas with visions larger than Qötshongva's own personal apotheosis. And, yet, the movement never succeeded in emancipating itself from powerful personalities, and thus has passed on with the death of David Monongya.

Notes

1. For information on Qötshongva and the succession see Titiev 1944, 211; Waters 1963/71, 383-384; Clemmer 1978, 36; Nagata 1978; Whiteley 1988, 230-231; and Geertz 1992.
2. See Clemmer's praise of Qötshongva, whom he had met during the 1960s (Clemmer 1978, 36), and Frank Waters' admiration of him (1969, 38).
3. The youths were sentenced to three years' hard labor and were taken to a prison camp at Tucson. Waters wrote in more detail about their experiences at the camp, especially concerning their belief that Maasaw was with them there (Waters 1963/71, 390-391).
4. See my article on Thomas Banancya in Geertz 1995.

13

Empirical Anthropology Postmodernism, and the Invention of Tradition

F. Allan Hanson

Many anthropologists perceive postmodernism to be a serious threat to the empirical, scientific status of the discipline. People have voiced concern that the postmodernists are taking over the *American Anthropologist*, and several prominent anthropologists have recently circulated a letter exploring the possibility of stemming the tide by forming a new professional organization devoted to "empirical anthropology."

One stream of investigation—by no means the only one—where elements of postmodernism permeate anthropological research and publication goes under the name of the "invention of tradition." Roughly, this large group of studies is united by the notion that "tradition" and "culture" are not fixed and static things that get passed through the generations in unchanging form. Instead, they constantly undergo reworking, redefinition and reformulation such that the image of the past can often be understood in terms of the political and other agendas of the present. My aim in this essay is to review the debate surrounding anthropological approaches to the invention of tradition with the ultimate intention of demonstrating that postmodernism, so far as it is represented in studies of this genre, poses no threat to empirical social science.

Objectivists and Constructivists

To analyze tradition as invented is not necessarily to employ postmodernist assumptions and approaches at all. Some scholars, whom Jocelyn Linnekin terms "objectivists" (1992, 254), distinguish between authentic and inauthentic traditions. In their vocabulary, invention refers to the latter, spurious traditions, not to the genuine ones. A well-known example of this approach is Hugh Trevor-Roper's (1983) debunking of Scottish kilts and clan tartans as invented traditions. Other examples, closer to anthropology, are most of the essays in *The Invented Indian* (Clifton 1990). The objectivist approach holds that there are such things as genuine traditions or cultures, which can be identified by careful scholarship, and which are subject to politically-motivated distortion or displacement by inauthentic, invented traditions. There is nothing postmodernist in this.

Linnekin contrasts the objectivists with "constructionists" (1992, 254). The large majority of anthropologists who have studied the invention of tradition, including myself, embrace this approach. For us, tradition and culture are constantly in the process of renegotiation and redefinition, such that invention is a normal and inevitable part of the perpetuation and use of all culture and tradition. Therefore the fact that any and every tradition regularly undergoes the process of invention and reinvention in no way compromises its authenticity. In contrast with the absence of postmodernism in the objectivist approach, the constructionist perspective on culture invention definitely has postmodernist tendencies in its "decentering" of tradition and culture. There is no Archimedean point where the core of any culture is and always has been located. Most anthropologists who work in this field deconstruct this essentialist view with the argument that culture is always in a state of flux and play, lacking any fixed center at all.

Certainly anthropologists favor the constructionist view of invention because their studies have convinced them that a dynamic view of culture is more useful than a static, essentialist one for understanding the processes of culture growth, adaptation and change, particularly in politically charged situations. There is, in addition, a more practical reason for preferring the constructionist perspective on culture invention. Typically anthropologists adopt a supportive and respectful attitude toward the people they study, particularly those whom they know first-hand, through fieldwork. Because they work so frequently in third and fourth world societies, the people anthropologists study have often been subjected to colonial domination. Although political engagement may or may not occupy a prominent place in their published reports, most anthropologists feel sympathy—and, many, outrage—for the exploitation the people they study have suffered and solidarity with their efforts to achieve self-determination. To report that the traditions those people profess are spurious, that their cultural beliefs, values, and behavioral expectations are inauthentic, would be to go diametrically against the grain of these convictions, attitudes and feelings. Therefore anthropologists who take an interest in the process of culture invention are drawn for practical, political, or ethical reasons as well as for theoretical ones to the postmodernist or constructionist attitude that traditions are no less genuine for having been invented.

While good reasons exist for preferring the constructivist over the objectivist view of the invention of tradition, at a higher level serious criticisms have been raised against the whole practice of analyzing tradition as invented. They also take both practical/political and theoretical forms. My intention below is to pass these criticisms in review and to argue that, in the last analysis, their objective of revealing fatal flaws in the invention of tradition approach does not succeed.

The New Zealand Maori

The issues raised by the notion of culture invention can be developed most clearly against the background of a concrete example of the process. The following is a synopsis of a previous analysis of culture invention among the New Zealand Maori (Hanson 1989). The Maori case is particularly instructive because it is possible to identify at least two distinct inventions of Maori tradition, and comparing them makes it easier to identify each one as an invention. Moreover, anthropologists themselves have been among the influential authors of both inventions. This enables us to recognize that anthropology not only analyzes culture invention but may also play an active role in the process. One final turn of the screw is that several of the anthropologists involved are themselves Maori.

Both versions of Maori culture give prominence to two famous traditions. One is the idea that the Maori ancestors originally settled New Zealand in a "Great Fleet" of seven canoes that sailed from the mythic homeland of Hawaiki in about 1350 AD. The other is that an esoteric cult devoted to a supreme creator god named Io existed in New Zealand prior to European contact. Archaeological, genealogical and textual research has questioned the historical accuracy of both of these traditions. Nevertheless they have been, as I say, important in both of the versions or inventions of Maori culture, albeit for very different reasons.

The first version flourished around the turn of the present century. Its main goal was to present the Maoris as an indigenous people with sufficient character and intelligence to be able to acquire British culture and thus assimilate fully with the white settlers in the building of the new nation of New Zealand. As described by (often amateur) anthropologists such as Percy Smith, Edward Tregear and Elsdon Best, the Io cult demonstrated that the Maori mind could grasp concepts as abstract as monotheism, and was thus fertile ground for Christianity and other civilizing Western ideas and principles. The Great Fleet tradition proved that Maoris come from a race endowed with the courage, technology, and navigational skills requisite to accomplish arduous ocean voyages. Indeed, reconstructing their wanderings long before the Great Fleet, these scholars proposed that the Maoris, like the British themselves, are descended from Aryans who, at some time lost in the mists of antiquity, left their homeland in central Asia. One group travelled westward to arrive in Europe; another set out toward the east. Finally, with the Great Fleet and European voyages of discovery,

> the two vast horns of the Great Migration have touched again; and men whose fathers were brothers on the other side of those gulfs of distance and of time meet each other, when the Aryan of the West greets the Aryan of the Eastern Seas. (Tregear 1885, 105)

The other version has dominated the last thirty years or so under the name of "Maoritanga," or "Maoriness." This is a liberation movement that struggles to end discrimination, recover confiscated lands, and achieve equality for Maoris in all facets of New Zealand society. Somewhat in common with the earlier invention, Maoritanga advances the traditions of the Great Fleet and the Io cult as evidence that Maoris descend from ancestors just as courageous and just as intelligent as the Pakehas (whites). However, the earlier invention aimed for Maori assimilation into a national culture that would be fundamentally British, and thus it stressed the similarities between Maoris and Pakehas. In contrast, Maoritanga seeks a bicultural New Zealand that would draw upon both Maori and Pakeha sources. Therefore it stresses the differences between the two cultures, especially those which imply an advantage on the Maori side such as respect for elders and the dead, affinity with the land, and a capacity to go beyond cold rationality and materialism to an intuitively spiritual mode of relating and knowing. The vast majority of professional anthropologists in New Zealand support the Maoritanga movement, and many of them have contributed to the image or invention of Maori culture promulgated by the movement. That group includes activist-anthropologists who are themselves Maori, such as Pat Hohepa, Sidney Moko Mead, and Ranginui Walker.

Practical/Political Objections to the Invention of Tradition

The scholarly approach to culture and tradition as invented has aroused a certain ire both within academia and in society at large. We may now turn to a closer investigation of these issues, in an effort to understand the source of the discontent and to develop responses to it.

Given our tendency to support native liberation movements, it is not surprising that anthropologists should be numbered among those for whom it is politically correct to deconstruct Western, colonialist versions of tradition, but politically incorrect to deconstruct indigenous ones (Linnekin 1992, 258). For example, my own work on Maori culture treats the turn-of-the-century version more critically than Maoritanga, and as a supporter of Maoritanga I have always felt less comfortable applying the term "invention" to it. Nevertheless, I was sufficiently persuaded by the theoretical position that all culture is invented, and is rendered in no way inauthentic for that fact, that in my original article I did not hesitate to apply the term "invention" to both versions of Maori culture. (As will be discussed in some detail later, I also took pains to argue that my own analysis, and the tradition of anthropological discourse to which it belongs, are also inventions in the same sense of the term [Hanson 1989, 899]).

As it happened, my essay got picked up by the popular press and several New Zealand newspapers carried the story, one of them under the headline "U.S. Expert Says Maori Culture Invented" (Wilford 1990; Freeth 1990a, 1990b). Although the article was a reasonably accurate summary of my essay, nothing could undo the impression fostered by that headline: that Maori culture is a fake. The response was immediate. An anthropologist wrote to me from New Zealand with the news that "a copy of the *Herald* article [a New Zealand newspaper account of my essay] was posted on a bulletin board of a school in a largely Maori community and that the general sentiment expressed was that people 'never wanted to see another American anthropologist.'" And the press quoted Maori anthropologist Ranginui Walker as saying "The American Indians don't like anthropologists sitting in the tepees any more—and neither do we" (Nissen 1990).

The matter disappeared from the newspapers in a week or so. But the damage the essay was perceived to have done to Maoritanga was discussed in a panel (one commentator described it as "a tribunal of sorts" [Lamb 1990, 667]) convened by the Anthropology Department at the University of Auckland (Webster 1993, 231), and the New Zealand Association of Social Anthropologists even voted to censure the *American Anthropologist* for having published it (ibid., 233).

Why should my essay have provoked such outrage? Many people, I suppose, simply misunderstood what I was saying and took me to be claiming that the cultural traditions associated with Maoritanga are false. In my first reflection on the brouhaha stimulated by the essay I suggested that misunderstanding of this sort might stem from my and others' use of the term "invention" (Hanson 1991, 450). When combined with "tradition" that word undeniably conveys the initial impression that the tradition in question is made up, fabricated, and therefore inauthentic. This sets the reader up for something of a surprise because it opens an analytic and rhetorical space in which the anthropologist can develop elaborate arguments to demonstrate that in fact it is in the nature of all tradition to be invented and therefore invented tradition may well become authentic. There is an element of postmodernism in this move, for the tactic of leading the reader to expect one thing and then developing a more subtle and complex line of reasoning leading to the opposite conclusion partakes of the irony, decentering and "play" commonly associated with postmodernist analyses. But the danger, of course, is that the inattentive reader, or someone who learns about it through newspapers or hearsay, may not follow the argument and, never getting beyond the initial impression, end up with a radical misunderstanding of it. Perhaps that danger would be diminished if we replace "invention" with less inflammatory terms that do not carry so much connotation of being made up, such as "reformulation."

This move would not, however, solve the problem completely. The most persistent and vociferous critics of my essay were academics who, presumably, eventually got around to actually reading the paper with understanding. They could well have taken the essay to be insensitive to Maoris and other New Zealanders who devote their efforts to the Maoritonga movement and define their aspirations in terms of it. For these people, the cultural elements of Maoritanga provide a sense of identity and a basis for political commitment and action. The tradition from which that identity is formed gains meaning from the belief that this was indeed the way of the Maori ancestors, handed down through the generations as a cherished object (*taonga*). Comes now the anthropologist to tell them that the traditions they value so highly have been invented by themselves and their contemporaries for their own political ends, but that, never mind, they are no less authentic for all that. This news threatens the sanctity and legitimacy of the traditions that constitute the movement's cultural charter. People will more readily stake their identities and aspirations on eternal verities than on contingent inventions. To tell them that what they thought were the former are really the latter seems insensitive.

More than that, it was undoubtedly viewed as intrusive. Edward Bruner distinguished several senses of "authenticity," one of them referring to "who has the authority and the power to authenticate" (1994, 400). My argument that Maori culture is authentic even if "invented" was doubtless perceived as a move by a foreign anthropologist to appropriate the authority of Maori people to define and authenticate their own heritage. This would seem to be the sentiment behind the criticism of Graham Smith, one of the Maori participants in the University of Auckland Anthropology Department colloquium regarding my original essay, that my discourse was "hegemonic and presumptuous" (Lamb 1990, 667). From this perspective, it might easily be characterized as yet another example of Western imperialism (see Trask 1991).

Thus we arrive at the practical/political dilemma posed by the invention-of-tradition approach. Most anthropologists support indigenous peoples in their quest for self-determination. In addition to its compatibility with their political ideals, this is conducive to maintaining good relations with the people they study (a goal in its own right), and it also protects prospects for future work in that community. On the other hand, many anthropologists are also interested in how traditions come into being, what contemporary purposes they serve, and how they gain authenticity. But when they raise those questions they risk alienating people in the community who reject such analyses as unwelcome intrusions that challenge their authority and propriety over their own culture (see Gable, Handler, and Lawson 1992, 791).

So what can we do to resolve or circumvent the dilemma? One possibility, of course, is to bull ahead with our studies, insisting that it is not our fault if people don't understand what we say, and hold fast to our commitment to the quest for knowledge. Insofar as we continue to cast our analyses in terms of "inventions" or talk about "deconstructing" cultural traditions, the cost of this strategy is that the postmodernist approach to tradition is almost certain to insult the people we study. This would render the anthropologist's so-called support for nativistic movements suspect, irrelevant and unwelcome.

The opposite course would be to throw our lot totally behind nativistic movements, affirming that what they claim to be the tradition handed down in changeless form from their ancestors is precisely that. At first blush this would appear to be the strategy that would most endear us to the people we study. The matter is not so simple as that, however, because competing native factions often argue over just what is the authentic tradition, leaving the anthropologist in the position of having to choose between two or more versions, all with their indigenous adherents (Thomas 1992; Linnekin 1992, 258, 260). Furthermore, this would entail abandoning any postmodernist orientation for an objectivist or essentialist one that acknowledges the existence of history in unchanging form. Many anthropologists would probably shed no tears at not qualifying for the label "postmodernist." It is difficult, however, to imagine how anthropologists could certify the versions of tradition promulgated by nativistic movements as ancient and pristine without simultaneously shedding their standards of documentary, archaeological, and other forms of evidence, abandoning the requirements of their own tradition of scholarship in favor of political correctness.

A third strategy is refrain from studying and writing about these matters altogether. In this way one avoids offending those we study while at the same time not overtly compromising one's own scholarly principles. This appears, initially, to be the most prudent course. It seems to avoid the imperialistic maneuver of co-opting other people's authority to define and authenticate their own cultures, and it does not threaten good relations and possibilities for future fieldwork. However, this position does not stand up under closer scrutiny. While discourse about the "invention of tradition" may represent the most obvious threat to a community's authority to authenticate its own heritage and culture, in fact virtually anything a foreign anthropologist might say about them has the same effect. This is because the notion of authenticity as the power to authenticate does not refer to the sort of thing that is being said, but to who says it. For an outside anthropologist to characterize a community as patrilineal, or hierarchical, or based on reciprocal exchange, is, in principle at least, no less an appropriation of their power to define their own culture than to say that their traditions are invented. If anthropology is about depicting other cultures, this throws the entire enterprise into jeopardy. If we were seriously to adopt this strategy we would either have to refrain from saying anything about another culture without having it approved in advance by the members of the community, or redefine the discipline and give up doing research in any society but our own.

Another possibility, mentioned already, is to continue analyzing tradition as we have been but to forego easily-misunderstood words such as "invention" and "deconstruction" in favor of others that are less likely to attract attention and give quick offence. On one way of thinking about it, this might seem to be a rather cowardly and even duplicitous strategy of assuring the people we study of our support for their aspirations while simultaneously pursuing a camouflaged scholarship that has the potential to undermine or co-opt those very aspirations, and hoping all the while that nobody will notice. I have something very different in mind, however. To say that our work is embedded in the cultural tradition of Western scholarship is to say that we operate according to its rules and values. One of its paramount values is the idea that knowledge is preferable to ignorance. If we adopt the position, set out above, that sensitivity demands we not express our view that what people take to be ancient and permanent tradition is actually a reworking of cultural material in the context of current conditions, we do a double violence. On the one hand, a decision to remain silent does violence to our own convictions about the desirability of contributing to knowledge. On the other, to refrain out of sensitivity from telling anyone who wants to listen about our ideas regarding tradition—theirs, ours, anyone's—is to sell them short as thinking human beings. As Roger Keesing put it:

> specialists on the Pacific do not best serve the interests of a less hegemonic scholarship or best support the political struggles of decolonizing and internally colonized Pacific peoples by suspending their critical judgment or maintaining silence—whether out of liberal guilt or political commitment—regarding mythic pasts evoked in cultural nationalistic rhetoric. Our constructions of real pasts are not sacrosanct, but they are important elements in a continuing dialogue and dialectic. (1989, 37)

We actually show the imperial hand, I suggest, when we condescendingly decide that what we can confide in our students and colleagues is too threatening for them, the "natives," to handle. Surely if we have learned anything at all in the last several decades, it includes the realization that we must reject that attitude!

One of the few gratifying moments in the whole affair regarding the reception of my essay in New Zealand was a trans-oceanic telephone conversation with three Maori activists, which was aired live on New Zealand radio. The conversation began with some tension, as they demanded I explain how I could claim that Maori culture is invented. As I laid out my ideas regarding the nature of culture invention and its relation to authenticity, assuring them of my conviction that all culture, including my own, is invented, their annoyance and suspicion dissipated and we ended a constructive conversation on a cordial note. Maoris, Hawaiians, Tukanoans are thoughtful human beings. Like anyone else, some of them have strong opinions, others have open minds, and still others have both. They can cope with ideas—even threatening ideas—as well as anyone, and we should not hide our ideas from them.

But this is emphatically not the entire story. I am not calling for a monologue wherein we present our ideas to the Others and their role is to appreciate them. This is a two-way street. As Jocelyn Linnekin has argued, "it may... be possible for foreign scholars to enter into a local dialogue—and to contextualize points of disagreement—without positing a single vision of the past as exclusively authoritative" (1992, 259). Anthropologists are well situated to foster and contextualize just such a dialogue. It is our line of work to analyze cultural differences, among them the epistemological differences that underlie different modes of reasoning and believing. Our telling of our ideas concerning the reformulation of culture (note well: not "invention;" it is no good to mislead at the outset) should include information about the rules of evidence and reasoning that inform those ideas. The dialogue should equally bring out the corresponding rules, from other epistemological traditions, that underlie the convictions and conclusions of the other participants in the discussion. The goal is not to convince the others of our rightness, nor to abandon our own opinions in favor of theirs. Indeed, what is postmodernist about this sort of dialogue is that there is no expectation of a center where transcendental truth lies, no single locus where all should ideally settle. There will probably not be consensus; there may well be bafflement, discomfort and anger (Linnekin 1992, 260). But there might emerge some measure of understanding of how the other operates, and why. Then we would learn something from each other, and one or more of the participants—be it "us," or "them," or both—might even be moved by the conversation to shift their own positions.

Of course, it is wildly unrealistic to think that such advanced seminars in cross-cultural epistemology would occur very often. Many (probably most) native nationalists, government officials, ordinary people living uneventful lives, and even anthropologists, have other fish to fry and will, for their own reasons, find this project irrelevant, possibly even detrimental. But this should not dissuade those who are intrigued by the nature and development of cultural traditions from studying them, writing about them forthrightly (and sensitively, in terms least likely to mislead or annoy), and engaging in dialogue about them with anyone who is interested.

Theoretical/Methodological Objections to the Invention of Tradition

In my original essay I argued that, just as the history of any human culture is a decentered play of sign-substitutions, so too is the history of any academic discipline, such as anthropology. Therefore, if the versions of being Maori sponsored by turn-of-the-century colonialists or contemporary adherents of Maoritanga are two formulations (or "inventions") in the on-going series of sign-substitutions that is the history of Maori culture, it is equally the case that the scholarly approach concerned to analyze tradition as "invented" is itself one formulation (or "invention") in the on-going series of sign-substitutions that is the history of social science (Hanson 1989, 899). This view has, of course, a great deal in common with that articulated long ago by Thomas Kuhn (1962) for science in general.

Construed like this, the anthropological approach to the "invention of tradition" is a fairly radical postmodernism for it squares the decentered play of sign-substitutions. That is, both the subject matter and the mode of analysis are moments in their respective histories of foundationless flux. Such ubiquitous rejection of anchors, which might be termed "hyperrelativist," has spurred serious misgivings among many scholars. Even Jocelyn Linnekin, a leading proponent of the postmodernist or constructionist approach to the "invention" of tradition, has worried that if everything gets deconstructed, one runs the risk of losing all methodological constraints. One interpretation is as good another, anything goes, and analytic anarchy threatens the scholarly enterprise (1992, 261). Grounds for such anxieties definitely exist, for at least one anthropologist discards scientific thought as an "archaic mode of consciousness" and welcomes postmodernist ethnography as an "esoteric conjunction of reality and fantasy" that eschews such inappropriate notions as facts, generalization, and verification (Tyler 1986, 123, 134, 130). Small wonder that many observe the progress of postmodernism with sentiments akin to horror, and a long for a return to the more substantial stuff of an "empirical anthropology."

While I cannot speak for everything that styles itself postmodernist, I do maintain that the "invention of tradition" approach is no less empirical or methodologically regulated than, say, ecological anthropology or cultural materialism. To redeem that point, let us consider the specific criticisms that have been raised against this approach.

Emic vs Etic Subject Matter

Analyses of tradition as invented or reformulated concentrate on cultural meanings, beliefs, and symbols that constitute a people's representation of their culture. Steven Webster charges that such discourse about the play of sign-substitutions captures only the appearance or shadow of culture, while the real thing is to be found in the concrete history of oppression and struggle for liberation as worked out in the material (economic and political) realities of life (Webster 1993, 237-38). This critique is not specific to a postmodernist approach to the reformulation of tradition. It may be equally leveled against virtually all anthropological studies of religion, mythology, and symbolism, many of which were undertaken long before anyone had ever heard of postmodernism. Nevertheless, given that most studies of the formulation and reformulation of tradition do highlight ideological issues of meaning and value, they belong to the category against which this critique is directed.

In these days of the declining influence of Marxism, the claim that the material part of culture and history is more important than the ideological is less a matter of methodological rigor than of scholarly taste. Studies of both have been conducted for a very long time, and have generated important insights. However, from a methodological point of view one might argue that the material conditions of life offer a more fruitful ground for systematic, scientific study because their data are hard and can be collected by direct observation while studies of ideological issues rely on the insubstantial stuff of people's thoughts and beliefs. Thus Marvin Harris has urged anthropologists to concern themselves with "etic" things—measurable facts that may be observed directly by the anthropologist—rather than fretting over "emic" matters that lurk inside people's heads. The anthropologist has no direct access to these data and so must infer them, he claims, and there is no way of verifying that the inference is correct (Harris 1976).

If, indeed, the interior of heads were the only location of ideological data, this would be a trenchant critique against the "invention of tradition" and any other attempt to analyze meanings and symbols because no one has direct access to the sequestered contents of other minds. But this is a most infelicitous and unnecessary view of the matter. As Clifford Geertz has argued, cultural meanings are public: they are found in the things that people openly say and do (Geertz 1973). Even mental events are not necessarily hidden from public view. From the perspective developed by Gilbert Ryle, many of them are overt acts as observable by others as delivering a lecture or participating in an interview. There is no fundamental difference, for example, between someone saying "I believe in a truine deity" out loud and silently entertaining the same belief in one's private thoughts. It is definitely not the case that the latter holds a privileged position and somehow causes or produces the former. Both are activities of mind or, as Ryle styles them, "intelligent performances." The only distinction between them is that the one is done overtly, in public view, and the other is done covertly (Ryle 1949). The consequences of these views are immense for anthropological understanding, for from them it follows that, contrary to the claims made by Harris, ideas, values and meanings are as empirical and can be studied as objectively as birth rates, election tallies, and calorie or body counts (Hanson 1975, 1982).

Consider, for example, the Maori tradition of the Great Fleet. The questions about it that are relevant to a constructivist analysis are whether such a story actually exists in Maori lore, what events the story describes, whether a significant number of people believe the story to be true, and if that story signifies—to both turn-of-the-century Pakeha anthropologists and to contemporary advocates of Maoritanga—a certain nobility and courage on the part of the Maori ancestors. These are all empirical questions. One finds the answers to them by reading books, talking to people, observing them as they tell the story and discuss it at tribal gatherings. There is, of course, no guarantee that one will inevitably get the answers to these questions right, but then there is also no guarantee that one's calculations about the annual number of calories produced by a sweet potato field and expended in cultivating it will unfailingly be correct. Errors in data collection and analysis can occur in both cases, and in both cases techniques exist for identifying and working to correct them. Thus the study of ideological aspects of culture is no less empirical than the study of those apparently (but only apparently) "harder" realities of economics and politics.

Understanding

Even if it be granted that ideas, beliefs and meanings are empirical, there remains the question of how they can be understood. I have indicated above that the postmodernist approach to the "invention of tradition" assumes that both the cultures under study and the social scientific paradigms for studying them constantly undergo a decentered process of sign-substitution, of formulation and reformulation. In this hyper-relativist situation, what is the basis for understanding and what legitimates the validity of the understanding we achieve?

Imagine fixing the location of a ship sailing on the open ocean. One way is with reference to some point of land ("two hundred miles northeast of Tristan da Cunha"); another is to specify coordinates of longitude and latitude. But in this imaginary world there is no land, only ocean, and no transcendental grid of longitude and latitude has been imposed on it. In that event, the only ways to specify the present location of a ship are with reference to some past position of that ship, or with reference to the present or past position of one or more other ships. This is very much our situation: there is no culture-free position from which any cultural tradition can be described. Any description of a cultural tradition is itself always already embedded in the same or some other cultural tradition, situated on the same or some other ship.

One school of thought holds that the perspective from another ship is illegitimate, that any effort to understand by someone who is not a member of the culture under study must be rejected as misunderstanding. This argument was raised in the 1990 University of Auckland colloquium assessing my analysis of the "inventions" of Maori culture. Webster reports that, for some of the speakers, their "commitment to an ahistorical sense of cultural uniqueness was, equally a commitment to an intuitive basis of understanding, a position which also excluded Hanson" (1993, 232).

If the argument was that I had gotten my facts and interpretations of Maori culture wrong, that could be addressed by pointing out where and how I had gone astray. That apparently did not happen and at stake seems to have been the more theoretically fundamental claim that I was not situated to achieve the requisite intuitive level of understanding. Thus Webster reports that those embracing this position "took up a much more emphatically cultural relativist position than Hanson" (ibid., 232). The sort of intuitive understanding they had in mind seems to be available only to Maoris, a stance with the general implication that no outsider can ever hope to achieve understanding of another culture.

Obviously such a radical demand that understanding be internal is corrosive to the entire anthropological enterprise, which is committed before anything else to understanding different cultures. The notion that "you've got to be one to know one" also leads to self-defeating solipsism. What goes for culture presumably also goes for sub-cultures, so that, for example, a Maori of the Tuwharetoa tribe lacks the requisite intuition to understand the culture of the Maori Tuhoe tribe. And certainly age and gender are also relevant. There is no obvious point where the reduction to absurdity can stop, and ultimately one arrives at the position that one can understand only oneself—and even then perhaps only oneself at the present moment.

This intuitive, exclusive notion of understanding represents an extreme form of cultural relativism, but it is not postmodernist. As we have pictured it, postmodernism is "hyperrelativist" in that it cuts both the culture under study and the scholarly tradition that is studying it loose from any anchored position. Each one is following the trajectory of its own history of sign-substitutions, of formulation and reformulation. The knowledge that emerges from their encounter is therefore doubly contingent: a relation between two modes of discourse, both of which are decentered. The extreme relativism of the intuitionists is entirely different. It generally takes a logocentric position that culture has a fixed essence. As far as the analyst is concerned, contrary to seeing his or her position as variable or contingent, only one perspective is valid: the perspective from within the culture one seeks to understand. Therefore the extreme relativism of the intuitionists and the hyper-relativism of the postmodernists are poles apart.

Rejecting the intuitionists' insistence that internal understanding alone is valid, we still need to ask what validates understanding that comes from the outside, when passengers on one ship try to gain information about another. Postmodernist analysts of the "invention of tradition" insist that being invented does not compromise the authenticity of tradition. Critiquing my analysis of Maori culture, Webster asks what authorizes the anthropologist to say that a given tradition is "authentic," and that the people under study accept it as such (1993, 230)? I take this to be a question about how the claims of a postmodernist anthropologist about the nature of other cultures and the beliefs of other people can be verified.

Let me respond by means of an example. In 1977 my family and I attended a program of Maori dances in the large carved meeting house Tama-Te-Kapua, located at Ohinemutu, Rotorua. At the conclusion of the dances, a Maori youth asked if anyone in the audience had questions. One woman asked about the age of the house we were in, and the youth replied that it was between 600 and 700 years old. I was quite surprised by this, because the information I had read about that house indicates that it was built in 1870 (Phillipps 1946, 8). The question arises: is the statement that the age of Tama-Te-Kapua is 600 to 700 years authentic Maori tradition? Or even more starkly: is it true that the house is 600 to 700 years old?

The hallmark of the postmodernist approach as it is conceived here is that there exists no absolute or universal ground upon which questions of truth, authenticity, knowledge and so on may be ultimately arbitrated. These matters are internal to the several cultural traditions or modes of discourse, not external and superordinate to them. Therefore questions about truth and authenticity are always contextualized: true or authentic for whom, or in what mode of discourse? This means that, depending on the rules and criteria of the relevant mode of discourse, it might indeed be true that the house at Rotorua is between 600 and 700 years old.

But what it does not mean is that we stand ready to certify any cockamamie statement as true just because somebody—even some member of the society under study—says it. Consider the logical possibilities of the Maori youth's statement regarding the age of Tama-Te-Kapua. One is that he either believed the house is much more recent, or had no idea of its actual antiquity, and made up the age of between 600 and 700 years on the spot without believing it himself. In that event his statement would have been a lie. It is true neither in his mode of discourse nor in any other mode, and thus is no part of any tradition that is authentic for anyone.

On the other hand, he might have sincerely believed that the house is 600 to 700 years old, and thus not have been lying when he said it. It is possible, however, that he is the only person who holds that belief. In that event I would argue that there is no cultural tradition to which that belief belongs because cultural traditions are social phenomena. Regardless of the degree of his personal conviction, his idiosyncratic belief is devoid of social significance and thus of no interest to anthropological analysis.

Alternatively, he might be one of a group of people who believe the house to be 600 to 700 years old, and that belief might qualify as true according to the relevant standards governing discourse in that community. Such standards can be indentified in Maori culture. Maoris commonly state that carved houses represent the ancestors for whom they are named, Maori lore contains stories about how carvings actually are the human individuals they represent (Mead 1984b, 65, 68-69), and contemporary interpretations of the meaning of Maori art stress the presence of the personality and power of the ancestors and artists in art objects (Mead 1984a, 22-23; Manuera Benjamin Riwai Couch, in Mead 1984, 12). Putting these propositions together, it is entirely possible that some Maoris believe that carved houses literally are the ancestors whose names they bear. Tama-te-Kapua the ancestor was captain of the

Arawa canoe, that reputedly arrived in New Zealand with the Great Fleet in about 1350, some 650 years ago. If the Maori youth was articulating a belief held by his community that the house Tama-Te-Kapua is the ancestor by that name, by the criteria just outlined his statement that the house is 600 to 700 years old would be true in that mode of discourse, and part of authentic tradition (see Dickson-Gilmore 1992, 499; Jackson 1995, 18-20).

Assume that we have thoroughly studied the situation (in fact I have not, so the example must remain hypothetical) and on that basis we opt for the third possibility: that in the relevant Maori mode of discourse it is true and authentic tradition that the house is 600 to 700 years old. The critique that led us to introduce this example had to do with how such a conclusion can be validated or verified. My answer is that it is according to the same procedures that are used to evaluate any scientific conclusion. The data upon which our conclusion is based have to do with whether the youth himself believes his statement about the age of the house, how many other people believe it, and what assumptions about art and the ancestors ground such a belief. These are all empirical matters, ascertainable by methods such as library research, surveys, interviews, and participant observation. They are available for other anthropologists to investigate, and our conclusion may be confirmed, modified, or disconfirmed (always subject, of course, to still further studies) depending on the results of those other studies. Hence I maintain that there is nothing unscientific, nonempirical, or unconfirmable about the postmodernist study of cultural traditions and their reformulations.

Methodological Anarchy?

Probably the most persistent criticism raised against a postmodernist approach to the "invention of tradition" is that it observes no methodological constraint. No explanation, so the charge goes, is given for the passage from one formulation of tradition to the next in the decentered play of sign-substitutions. All bets are off, all rules suspended. Hence Jonathan Friedman fails to find much rhyme or reason in the sequence of figurations of culture in my Maori analysis, claiming "there are neither motivations, nor a strategy of appropriation-transformation, nor a process of identification that might make sense out of this apparently neutral process that simultaneously harbors the connotation of falsity" (Friedman 1992, 852; see also Barber 1990). So too with Webster, who perceives postmodernist analyses such as mine to reflect a "fragmentary or atomistic view of the world" and to be preoccupied with "the apparently random 'play of sign-substitutions'" (1993, 237).

Frankly I am mystified by the criticism that postmodernist anthropologists identify no motivation for the reformulation of tradition, or the shift from one formulation to another, because it is simply wrong. The assumption that there is no center, no fixed essence for the sequence of sign-substitutions that constitutes the history of cultural tradition, does not imply that the process is willy-nilly. Each successive figuration is systematically related to the preceding ones in a connected process, each reformulation is motivated by political or other objectives, and this is explicitly and repeatedly spelled out in the literature.

For example, the two formulations of Maori culture that I have identified are closely linked, sharing as they do ideas about the Great Fleet, the cult of Io, and any number of other elements. And the process of cultural reformulation is highly charged or motivated by aspirations of political liberation, nation-building, and identity formation. This includes the development of a specifically French-Canadian identity as part of the movement for an independent Quebec, the formation of a uniquely Hawaiian identity and cultural tradition in the cause of Hawaiian political liberation (Handler and Linnekin 1984) and, in New Zealand, the goal of building an assimilated, monocultural, British society for the turn-of-the-century formulation and the objective of a bicultural society congenial to Maori interests and a distinctive Maori identity in the contemporary formulation that is Maoritanga (Hanson 1989, 893, 894). To cut culture loose from essentialist moorings is only to abandon the assumption (did we ever really believe it anyway?) that there is a central, fixed point around which the evolution of tradition eternally revolves and to which it invariably returns. It is emphatically not to sacrifice notions about order or meaning in history.

Conclusion

Friedman argues that, no less than for the versions of history and tradition espoused by the people we study, we should examine our own motivations for analyzing them as we do (1992, 855). Having insisted that anthropology is also a cultural tradition, and that the "invention of tradition" approach is one of its sign-substitutions, I could not agree more. So far as that approach is concerned, I think the motivations are simultaneously political and scholarly. Anthropologists observe that the peoples they study are often engaged in a struggle to define a distinctive cultural heritage with which they may identify, as a step toward unifying. and empowering themselves in order to improve their economic, social and political position. The anthropologists also notice that some or many of the claims which the people make about their past, and which they use to define their cultural heritage, are inaccurate according to the historical record and standards of evidence as these have been developed in the context of Western scholarship. Because those anthropologists think that the development of any culture is something other than a sequence of dissimulation and fake traditions, and because they support native liberation movements, they have no inclination to debunk indigenous claims about tradition. Their motivation in this situation is the difficult and intellectually stimulating challenge of staking out a position from which they may remain loyal to both indigenous discourse and the scientific standards of Western scholarship. The solution, for many of them, is the constructivist or postmodernist approach to the "invention of tradition."

That approach may well annoy native activists who wish to mono-polize discourse about their culture and traditions, anthropologists who are convinced that the only valid ethnographic work is total commitment to the political struggle of the people we study, and perhaps other constituencies as well. But then, the work of any anthropologist—foreign or home-grown—who does not share their precise agenda would also annoy them. The best we can do in an environment as highly politicized as the contemporary world is to proceed with as much sensitivity as possible, to remain true to our own principles and interests, and to engage in open and forthright dialogue with anyone who is interested.

The "invention of tradition" approach also provokes some scholars (let us call them "positivists") on theoretical and methodological grounds. This ultimately stems, I think, from deep misgivings about what we have called the hyperrelativism of postmodernism. It is true that this cuts everything loose from solid moorings. While the process is anything but random, cultural traditions do pass from one formulation or sign-substitution to another with no fixed center or essence. Among those cultural traditions is the tradition of anthropological research and analysis itself. Thus observers are no more anchored than the observed; everyone and everything is carried along in a coherent but foundationless flux. It is not difficult to imagine how this image could provoke visions of methodological anarchy in someone who yearns for facts to be irrevocably solid and truth to be eternally certain.

For postmodernist hyperrelativism, notions like "truth" and "fact" are embedded within cultural modes of discourse rather than superordinate to them. Therefore what is true in one mode may be false in another (e.g.

the age of Tama-te-Kapua). Positivists, who entertain more absolute, transcendental concepts of truth and facts, perceive an ultimate futility in this. What is the point, they ask, of trying to ascertain facts and develop true analyses of them when some paradigm shift or sign-substitution will eventually come along and redefine everything, including the nature of facts and truth?

My response is that the exercise appears futile only when one clings to the assumption that invariant facts and absolute truth really do exist somewhere. If one completely lets go of that assumption, then all that is left are variable, fluctuating modes of discourse with their more or less different notions of fact and truth. From that point of view the notions of truth and fact in the several modes of discourse are not second-best, subordinate to something on a higher level; they are all there is. One result of this perspective might be to increase tolerance for other ways of thinking and valuing, as we no longer entertain the notion that our own assumptions and values are absolute, or, at least, closer to it. For another, this point of view does not necessitate erosion of commitment to our own assumptions and values. Apart from a hopefully-expanded tolerance, the absence of absolutes and transcendental standards leaves us in very much in the same position as we were before. We can be as critical as we ever were of certain of our culture's standards and their implications, basing those criticisms on competing standards from within our culture or standards that we have encountered in other cultures. And where we are inclined to react positively, our appreciation for the value and beauty of facts, our passion for truth, our commitment to morality and humanity, as all of these things are organized in the modes of discourse we affirm, need in no way slacken

It seems that ultimately the choice between affirming that facts, truth and morality are superordinate to cultural modes of discourse and affirming that they are subordinate to them seems to have more in common with a Kierkegaardian leap of faith than with the outcome of a rational train of thought. That is, some people can entertain hyper-relativist principles with minimal turmoil, while for others they threaten something of fundamental importance, and the issues at stake are not easily resolved by debate. For those in the latter camp, the idea of a post-modernist approach to anthropology, or to anything else, is much more menacing than to the others.

References

AAA. 1990. "Principles of Professional Responsibility." Washington, D.C.: American Anthropological Association.

Adler, Alfred. 1987. "Tradition orale et historicité chez les Moundang du Tchad." Pp. 49-67 in *Poikilia. Etudes offertes à Jean-Pierre Vernant*. Paris: Editions de l'EHESS.

Allen, Paula G. 1986. *The sacred hoop*. Boston: Beacon Press.

Alsop, Joseph. 1982. *The rare art traditions. The history of art collecting and its linked phenomena*. London: Thames and Hudson, Ltd.

Angelino, Henry, and Shedd Charles L. 1955. "A Note on Berdache." *American Anthropologist* 57:121-126.

Anonymous. 1941."Hopi Claim Religion Is Bar To Service," *Arizona Republic*, 23 May 1941.

———. 1961. Minutes of a Meeting at Shungopavy, May 6-7, 1961. An Unsigned Ms Typescript from Files to Thomas Banancya. 13 pp. Tucson: Special Collections, The University of Arizona.

———. 1963. Interview with Chief Dan Katchongva of Hotevilla, Independent Hopi Nation, Arizona. David Monongye as Interpreter. Evening of May 8, 1963 at the Home of David Monongye. An Unsigned MS Typescript. 4 pp. Tucson: Special Collections, The University of Arizona.

———. 1970a. "Hopi Chief Arrives for Saucer Contact." *Prescott Courrier* 88 (186), Monday, 10 August 1970.

———. 1970b. "UFO Sightings to End—Solem." *Prescott Courrier* 88 (193), Tuesday, 18 August 1970.

———. 1992. "On the Warpath." *The Economist*, 5 September 1992, p. 118.

Arctic Trading Company. 1985. *Catalogue*. Churchill.

———. 1990. *Catalogue*. Churchill.

Arendt, Hannah. 1972. *La crise de la culture*. Paris: Gallimard.
Aron, Raymond. 1961. *Dimensions de la conscience historique*. Paris: Plon.
Ashton, Robert, Jr. 1976. "Nampeyo and Lesou." *American Indian Art Magazine* 1 (3):24-33.
Astington, Janet W., Paul Harris, and David R. Olson, eds. 1988. *Developing theories of mind*. Cambridge: Cambridge University Press.
Atran, Scott. 1990. *Cognitive foundations of natural history: Towards an anthropology of science*. Cambridge: Cambridge University Press.
Avis, Jeremy, and Paul L. Harris. 1991. "Belief-Desire Reasoning among Baka Children: Evidence for a Universal Conception of Mind." *Child Development* 62:460-467.
Babadzan, Alain. 1988. "Kastom and Nation-Building in the South Pacific." Pp. 199-228 in *Ethnicities and Nations*, ed. Remo Guidieri, Francesco Pellizzi, and Stanley J. Tambiah. Houston: Rothko Chapel.
Banyacya, Thomas. 1961. Letter to M. Muller-Fricken (White Star), January 12, 1961. Hotevilla, Independent Hopi Nation. Tucson: Special Collections, The University of Arizona.
Barbeau, Marius. 1950. *Totem poles*. 2 vols. Ottawa, National Museum of Canada, Bulletin 119.
Barber, Keith. 1990. "More on the Politics of Interpretation." *New Zealand Association of Social Anthropologists Newsletter* 2 (June).
Barett, Justin, and Frank C. Keil. 1996. "Conceptualizing a Non-Natural Entity: Anthropomorphism in God Concepts." *Cognitive Psychology* 31 [forthcoming].
Barnes, R. H. 1984. *Two Crows denies it: A history of controversy in Omaha sociology*. Lincoln: University of Nebraska Press.
Barnett, Homer G. 1953. *Innovation: The basis for cultural change*. New York: McGraw-Hill.
Barsook, Beverly et al. 1974. *Seven families in Pueblo pottery*. Albuquerque, N. Mex.: University of New Mexico Press.
Barthes, Roland. 1972. *Mythologies*, trans. Annette Lavers. London: Paladin.
Bates, Craig D., and Martha J. Lee. 1990. *Tradition and innovation. A basket history of the Indians of the Yosemite-Mono Lake area*. Yosemite: Yosemite Association.
Baudrillard, Jean. 1988. *America*, trans. Chris Turner. London: Verso.
Beidelman, Tom O. 1971. "Nuer Priests and Prophets: Charisma, Authority, and Power" in *The translation of culture*, ed. Tom O. Beidelman. London: Tavistock.
Bentley, Wilder, ed. 1956. *Hopi "Meeting of religious people."* Hotevilla: Hopi Indian Nation.
Berger, Peter L., and Thomas Luckmann. 1966. *The social construction of reality: A treatise in the sociology of knowledge*. Garden City: Doubleday.
Berkhofer, Robert F. Jr. 1978. *The white man's Indian: Images of the American Indian from Columbus to the present*. New York: Vintage.
Berlo, Janet C., ed. 1992. *The early years of Native American art history*. Seattle: University of Washington Press.

Berman, Judith. 1991. "The Seals' Sleeping Cave: The Interpretation of Boas' Kwakw'ala Texts." Ph.D. diss., University of Pennsylvania.

Bieder, Robert E. 1986. *Science encounters the Indian, 1820-1880: The early years of American ethnology.* Norman and London: University of Oklahoma Press.

Bloch, Maurice. 1989. "Literacy and Enlightenment." Pp. 15-37 in *Literacy and Society,* ed. K. Schousboe and M. Trolle Larsen. Copenhagen: Akademisk Forlag.

———. 1993. "Time, Narratives and the Multiplicity of Representations of the Past." *Bulletin of the Institute of Ethnology,* Academia Sinica 75:29-45.

Boas, Franz. 1908. "Decorative Designs of Alaska Needlecases: A Study in the History of Conventional Designs, Based on Materials in the U.S. National Museum." *Proceedings of the U.S. National Museum* 34:321-344.

Bowers, Alfred W. 1950. *Mandan social organization.* Chicago: University of Chicago Press.

Boyer, Pascal. 1990. *Tradition as truth and communication.* Cambridge: Cambridge University Press.

———. 1992. "Cognitive Aspects of Religious Symbolism." Pp. 1-47 in *Cognitive aspects of religious symbolism,* ed. Pascal Boyer. Cambridge: Cambridge University Press.

———. 1994. *The Naturalness of religious ideas: A cognitive theory of religion.* Los Angeles/Berkeley: University of California Press.

Brotherston, Gordon. 1990. "The Time Remembered in the Winter Counts and the Walam Olum." Pp.307-337 in *Circumpacifica. Festschrift für Thomas S. Barthel,* ed. Bruno Illius and Matthias Laubscher. Frankfurt /Main, Germany: Peter Lang.

Brownstone, Arni. 1993. *War paint: Blackfoot and Sarcee painted buffalo robes in the Royal Ontario Museum.* Toronto: Royal Ontario Museum.

Bruner, Edward M. 1994. "Abraham Lincoln as Authentic Reproduction: A Critique of Postmodernism." *American Anthropologist* 96:397-415.

Bullock, Merry. 1985. "Animism in Childhood Thinking: A New Look at an Old Question." *Developmental Psychology* 21:217-225.

Bureau of Indian Affairs, Phoenix Office, Hopi Agency. 1955. *Hopi Hearings. 15-30 July 1955.* Keams Canyon: Hopi Agency.

Callender, Charles, and Lee Kochems. 1983. "The North American Berdache." *Current Anthropology* 24 (4):456-470.

Canada House. 1985. *Mohawk Micmac Maliseet... and other Indian souvenir art from Victorian Canada.* London.

Cannadine, David. 1983. "The Context, Performance and Meaning of Ritual: The British Monarchy and the 'Invention of Tradition' c. 1820-1977." Pp. 101-164 in *The invention of tradition,* ed. Eric Hobsbawm and Terence Ranger. Cambridge: Cambridge University Press.

Caribou Clothes. 1993. (*Catalogue*). Mountain View.

Carroll, John B., ed. 1956. *Language, thought, and reality: Selected writings of Benjamin Lee Whorf.* Cambridge, Mass.: MIT Press.

Cassidy, Frank, and Norman Dale. 1989. *After native land claims?* Halifax,

Nova Scotia: Institute for Research on Public Policy.

Cassirer, Ernst. 1951. *The Philosophy of Enlightenment*. Boston: Beacon Press.

Ceci, Lynn. 1990. "Squanto and the Pilgrims: On Planting Corn 'in the Manner of the Indians'." Pp. 71-90 in *The invented Indian: Cultural fictions and government policies*, ed. James A. Clifton. New Brunswick, NJ: Transaction.

Clemmer, Richard O. 1978. *Continuities of Hopi cultural change*. Ramona: Acoma Books.

Clifford, James. 1988. *The predicament of culture*. Cambridge: Harvard University Press.

Clifton, James A. 1990a. "Introduction: Memoir, Exegesis." Pp. 1-27 in *The invented Indian: Cultural fictions and government policies*, ed. James A. Clifton. New Brunswick, NJ: Transaction.

———. 1990b. "The Indian Story: A Cultural Fiction." Pp. 28-49 in *The invented Indian: Cultural fictions and government policies*, ed. James A. Clifton. New Brunswick, NJ: Transaction.

———. 1994a. "From Shaman to Medicine Man: Transformations of Shamanic Roles and Styles in the Upper Great Lakes Region." Pp. 187-209 in *Ancient traditions: Shamanism in Siberia and America*, ed. Gary Seaman and Jane S. Day. Boulder, CO: University of Colorado Press.

———. 1994b. "Pioneer Advocates of Methodism Among the Lake Superior Chippewa." Pp. 115-143 in *The message in the missionary: Local interpretations of religious ideology and missionary personality*, ed. Elizabeth Brusco and Laura F. Klein. Williamsburg, VA: Studies in Third World Societies.

———. 1997. "Tribe, Nation, Estate, Racial, Ethnic, or Special Interest Group? Michigan's Indians." In *Ethnic Michigan: Ex Uno Plures*, ed. Arthur Helweg. Ann Arbor, MI: University of Michigan Press [forthcoming].

Clifton James A., ed. 1990. *The invented Indian: Cultural fictions and government policies*. New Brunswick, NJ: Transaction.

———. ed. 1993 *Being and becoming Indian: Biographical studies of North American frontiers*. 2d ed. Prospect Heights, IL: Waveland Press.

Cole, Douglas, and Ira Chaikin. 1990. *An iron hand upon the people: The law against the potlatch on the Northwest Coast*. Vancouver: Douglas and McIntyre.

Conrad, Lawrence A. 1989. "The Southeastern Ceremonial Complex on the Northern Middle Mississippian Frontier: Late Prehistoric Politico-Religious Systems in the Central Illinois River Valley." Pp. 93-113 in *The southeastern ceremonial complex: artifacts and analysis*, ed. Patricia Galloway. Lincoln: University of Nebraska Press.

Couture, Joe. 1983. "Traditional Aboriginal Spirituality and Religious Practice in Prison." Pp. 199-203 in *Aboriginal peoples and Canadian criminal justice*, ed. R. Silverman and M. Nielsen. Toronto: Butterworths.

Cranmer-Webster, Gloria. 1992. "From Colonization to Repatriation." Pp. 25-37 in *Indigena: Contemporary native perspectives*, ed. Gerald McMaster and Ann Martin. Ottawa: Canadian Museum of Civilization.

D'Emilio Sandra, and Suzan Campbell. 1991. *The art and artists of the Santa Fe Railway*. Salt Lake City: Peregrine Smith.

Daly, Richard, and Antonia Mills. 1993. "Ethics and Objectivity: AAA Principles of Responsibility Discredit Testimony." *Anthropology Newsletter* 34 (November):1, 6.

Deloria, Vine, Jr. 1992. "Afterword." Pp. 429-443 in *America in 1492. The world of the Indian peoples before the arrival of Columbus*, ed. Alvin M. Josephy, Jr. New York: Alfred A. Knopf.

Dempsey, Hugh A. 1978. *Tailfeathers. Indian artist.* Art Series n° 2. Calgary: Glenbow-Alberta Institute.

Detienne, Marcel. 1981. *L'invention de la mythologie*. Paris: Gallimard.

Detienne, Marcel, ed. 1994. *Transcrire les mythologies*. Paris: Albin Michel.

Dewdney, Selwyn. 1975. *The sacred scrolls of the southern Ojibway*. Toronto: University of Toronto Press.

Dickson-Gilmore, E. J. 1992. "Finding the Ways of the Ancestors: Cultural Change and the Invention of Tradition in the Development of Separate Legal Systems." *Canadian Journal of Criminology* 34:479-502.

Dominguez, Virginia. 1986. "The Marketing of Heritage." *American Ethnologist* 13:546-555.

Dorsey, James Owen. 1884. *Omaha sociology*. Washington, D.C.: Third Annual Report of the Bureau of Ethnology.

Dunn, Dorothy. 1968. *American Indian painting of the Southwest and Plains areas*. Albuquerque, N. Mex.: The University of New Mexico Press.

Durkheim, Emile. 1915. *The elementary forms of the religious life*, trans. J.W. Swain. London: Allen and Unwin.

Edwards, Elizabeth, ed. 1992. *Anthropology and photography 1860-1920*. New Haven, CT: Yale University Press with the Royal Anthropological Institute.

Eggan, Fred. 1967. "From History to Myth: A Hopi Example." Pp. 33-53 in *Studies in Southwestern Ethnolinguistics*, ed. Dell H. Hymes and William E. Bittle. The Hague and Paris: Mouton & Co.

Eisenstadt, S. N. 1973. "Post-Traditional Societies and the Continuity and Reconstruction of Tradition. " *Daedalus* 1 (Winter):1-28.

Ellis, C. Douglas. 1989. *"Now then, still another story—" Literature of the western James Bay Cree: Content and structure*. The Belcourt 1988 Lecture. Winnipeg: Voices of Rupert's Land.

Epstein, Arnold, L. 1978. *Ethos and identity*. London: Tavistock Publications.

Evans-Pritchard, Edward E. 1940. *The religion of the Nuer*. Oxford: Clarendon Press.

Ewers, John C. 1939. *Plains Indian painting: A description of an aboriginal American art*. Stanford, CA: Stanford University Press; London: Oxford University Press.

———. 1964. *The emergence of Plains Indians as the symbol of the North American Indian*. Washington, D.C. Pub. 4636, Smithsonian Report for 1964.

Fabian, Johannes. 1983. *Time and the other. How anthropology makes its object*. New York: Columbia University Press.

Feest, Christian F. 1974. "Another French Account of Virginia Indians by John Lederer." *The Virginia Magazine of History and Biography* 83 (2):155-159.

———. 1978. "Virginia Algonquians." Pp. 253-270 in *Handbook of North*

American Indians, vol 15, *Northeast*, ed. Bruce G. Trigger. Washington, D.C.: Smithsonian Institution Press.

———. 1992a. "The Pervasive World of Arts." Pp. 405-428 in *America in 1492*, ed. Alfred. L. Josephy, Jr. New York: Alfred Knopf.

———. 1992b. *Native arts of North America*. 2d ed., rev. London: Thames and Hudson.

———. 1993. *Über/Lebenskunst nordamerikanischer Indianer*. Wien: Museum für Völkerkunde.

———. 1995. "'Repatriation': A European View on the Question of Restitution of Native American artifacts." *European Review of Native American Studies* 9 (2):33-42.

Feest, Christian F., ed. 1987. *Indians and Europe*. Aachen: Edition Herodot.

Feit, Harvey. 1982. "The Future of Hunters within Nations-States: Anthropology and the James Bay Cree." Pp. 373-411 in *Politics and history in band societies*, ed. E. Leacock and R.B. Lee. Cambridge: Cambridge University Press.

Ferguson, Russel et al. 1990. *Out there. Marginalization and contemporary cultures*. Cambridge and London: MIT Press.

Finley, Moses I. 1971. *The Ancestral constitution*. Cambridge: Cambridge University Press.

Fisher, Robin. 1977. *Contact and conflict: Indian-European relations in British Columbia, 1774-1890*. Vancouver: University of British Columbia Press.

Flannery, Regina. 1939. *An analysis of coastal Algonquian culture*. Washington, D.C.: Catholic University of America, Anthropological Series 7.

Fletcher, Alice C., and Francis La Flesche. 1911. *The Omaha tribe*. Washington, D.C.: Twenty-seventh Annual Report of the Bureau of American Ethnology.

Freeth, Martin. 1990a. "Modern Maori Image 'Invented'." *New Zealand Herald*, February 24, 1990, sec. 1 p. 20.

———. 1990b. "US Expert Says Maori Culture Invented." *The Dominion*, February 24, 1990, p. 1.

Friedman, Jonathan. 1992. "The Past in the Future: History and the Politics of Identity." *American Anthropologist* 94 (4):837-859.

Fuller, Nancy J., and Susanne Fabricius. 1992. "Native American Museums and Cultural Centers: Historical Overview and Current Issues." *Zeitschrift für Ethnologie* 117:223-237.

Gable, Eric, Richard Handler, and Anna Lawson. 1992. "On the Uses of Relativism: Fact, Conjecture, and Black and White Histories at Colonial Williamsburg." *American Ethnologist* 19:791-805.

Gardner, Don S. 1983. "Performativity and Ritual: The Mianmin Case." *Man* 18:346-360.

Garros, Véronique. 1992. "Dans l'ex-URSS: de la difficulté d'écrire l'histoire." *Annales ESC* 4-5:989-1002.

Geertz, Armin W. 1984. "A Reed Pierced the Sky: Hopi Indian Cosmography on Third Mesa, Arizona." *Numen* 31 (2):216-241.

———. 1987. "Prophets and Fools: The Rhetoric of Hopi Indian Eschatology." *European Review of Native American Studies* 1 (1):33-45.

———. 1991. "Native American Art and the Problem of the Other: An

Introduction to the Issues." *European Review of Native American Studies* 5 (2):1-5.

———. 1992. *The Invention of prophecy: Continuity and meaning in Hopi Indian religion*. Knebel: Brunbakke Publications.

———. 1993a. "Theories on Tradition and Change in Hopi Studies." *Anthropos* 88:489-500.

———. 1993b. "Theories of Tradition and Change in Sociology, Anthropology, History, and the History of Religions." Pp. 323-347 in *Religious transformations and socio-political change in Eastern Europe and Latin America*, ed. Luther Martin. Berlin: Mouton de Gruyter.

———. 1995. "Worlds in Collusion: On Social Strategies and Misrepresentations as Forces of Syncretism in Euro-American and Native American Affairs." Pp. 84-103 in *Syncretism and the commerce of symbols*, ed. Göran Aijmer. Gothenburg: The Institute for Advanced Studies in Social Anthropology.

Geertz Armin, and Michael Lomatuway'ma. 1987. *Children of cottonwood: Piety and ceremonialism in Hopi Indian puppetry*. Lincoln and London: University of Nebraska Press.

Geertz Armin, and Jeppe Sinding Jensen, eds. 1991. *Religion, tradition, and renewal*. Aarhus: University of Aarhus Press.

Geertz, Clifford. 1973. "Thick Description: Toward an Interpretive Theory of Culture." Pp. 3-30 in *The interpretation of cultures*, ed. Clifford Geertz. New York: Basic Books.

Gelman, Rochel. 1990. "First Principles Organize Attention to and Learning about Relevant Data: Number and the Animate-Inanimate Distinction as Examples." *Cognitive Science* 14:79-106.

Gelman, Rochel, Elizabeth Spelke, and E. Meck. 1983. "What Preschoolers Know about Animate and Inanimate Objects." In *The Acquisition of symbolic skills*, ed. D. Rogers and J. A. Sloboda. London: Plenum.

Gelman, Susan. 1988. "The Development of Induction within Natural Kind and Artefact Categories." *Cognitive Psychology* 20:65-95.

Gelman, Susan, and Ellen Markman. 1986. "Categories and Induction in Young Children." *Cognition* 23:183-209.

———. 1987. "Young Children's Inductions from Natural Kinds: The Role of Categories and Appearances." *Child Development* 58:32-41.

Gill, Sam. 1990. "Mother Earth: An American Myth." Pp. 129-144 in *The invented Indian: Cultural fictions and government policies*, ed. James A. Clifton. New Brunswick, NJ: Transaction.

Glassner, Jean-Jacques. 1993. *Chroniques mésopotamiennes*, trans. and ed. J.-J. Glassner. Paris. Les Belles Lettres.

Godelier, Maurice. 1984. *L'idéel et le matériel: pensée, économies, sociétés*. Paris: Fayard.

Goldberg, Jonathan. 1992. *Sodometries*. Stanford: Stanford University Press.

Goldfrank, Esther S. 1926. "Isleta Variants: A Study in Flexibility." *Journal of American Folklore* 39:70-78.

———. 1945. "Socialization, Personality, and the Structure of Pueblo Society (with particular reference to Hopi and Zuni)." *American Anthropologist* 47:516-539.

———. 1948. "The Impact of Situation and Personality on Four Hopi Emergence Myths." *Southwestern Journal of Anthropology* 4:241-262.

Goody, Jack. 1977. *The domestication of the savage mind*. Cambridge: Cambridge University Press.

Graburn, Nelson H. H. 1976. *Ethnic and tourist arts. Cultural expressions from the Fourth World*. Berkeley and Los Angeles: University of California Press.

Edwin S., Margaret B Blackman, and Vincent Rickard. 1981. *Northwest Coast Indian graphics. An introduction to silk screen prints*. Seattle: University of Washington Press.

Hallowell, A. Irving. 1960. "Ojibwa Ontology, Behavior, and World View." Pp. 49-82 in *Primitive views of the world*, ed. Stanley Diamond. New York and London: Columbia University Press.

———. 1973. "Temporal Orientation in Western Civilization and in a Pre-Literate Society." *American Anthropologist* 39:647-670.

Handler, Richard, and Jocelyn Linnekin. 1984. "Tradition, Genuine or Spurious." *Journal of the American Folklore* 97:273-290.

Hanson, F. Allan. 1975. *Meaning in culture*. London: Routledge and Kegan Paul.

———. 1982. "Method in Semiotic Anthropology; Or, How the Maori Latrine Means." Pp. 74-89 in *Studies in symbolism and cultural communication*, ed. F. Allan Hanson. Lawrence: University of Kansas Publications in Anthropology 14.

———. 1989. "The Making of the Maori: Culture Invention and Its Logic." *American Anthropologist* 91:890-902.

———. 1991a. "Reply to Langdon, Levine, and Linnekin." *American Anthropologist* 93:449-450.

———. 1991b. "When the Natives Talk Back: Thinking about Narrative in Anthropology." Paper presented at the Hall Narrative Seminar, University of Kansas.

Harbour Springs Historical Commission. 1982. *Ottawa quillwork on birchbark*. Harbour Springs.

Harkin, Michael. 1985-87. Fieldnotes Made at Waglisla, British Columbia. In possession of the author.

———. 1993. "Power and Progress: The Evangelic Dialogue among the Heiltsuk." *Ethnohistory* 40:1-33.

———. 1996. "Carnival and Authority: Heiltsuk Cultural Models of Power." *Ethos* 24:281-313.

Harris, Marvin. 1976. "History and Significance of the Emic/Etic Distinction." *Annual Review of Anthropology* 5:329-350.

Hartog, François. 1989. "L'evidenza della storia. " *Nuove Effemeridi* 3: 67-71.

———. 1991. "Ecritures, généalogies, archives, histoire en Grèce ancienne." Pp. 177-188 in *Mélanges Pierre Lévêque*. Tome V. Besançon.

Hieb, Louis Albert. 1979. "Hopi World View." Pp. 577-580 in *Handbook of North American Indians*, vol. 9, *Southwest*, ed. Alfonso Ortiz. Washington, D.C.: Smithsonian Institution.

Hill, Jonathan. 1992. "Contested Pasts and the Practice of Anthropology." *American Anthropologist* 90:809-815.

Hill, Willard, W. 1935. "The Status of the Hermaphrodite and Transvestite in Navajo Culture." *American Anthropologist* 40:273-279.

Hilton, Susanne. 1990. "Haihais, Bella Bella, and Oowekeeno." Pp. 312-322 in *Handbook of North American Indians*, vol. 7, *Northwest Coast*, ed. Wayne Suttles. Washington, D.C.: Smithsonian Institution Press.

Hirschfeld, Lawrence A. 1986. "Kinship and Cognition: Genealogy and the Meaning of Kinship Terms." *Current Anthropology* 27:235-246.

———. 1988. "On Acquiring Social Categories: Cognitive Development and Anthropological Wisdom." *Man* 23:611-638.

Hirschfeld, Lawrence A., and Susan Gelman. 1994. *Mapping the mind. Domain-specificity in cognition and culture.* Cambridge: Cambridge University Press.

Hobsbawm, Eric, and Terence Ranger, eds. 1983. *The invention of tradition.* Cambridge: Cambridge University Press.

Hocart, Arthur Maurice. 1979. "Are Savages Custom-Bound." Pp. 205-207 in *The life-giving myth and other essays*. London: Metheuen & Co Ltd.

Hochbruck, Wolfgang. 1991. *I have spoken: Die Darstellung und ideologische Funktion indianischer Mündlichkeit in der nordamerikanischen Literatur.* Tübingen: Gunter Narr Verlag.

Holm, Bill. 1965. *Northwest Coast Indian art. An analysis of form.* Seattle: University of Washington Press.

———. 1977. "Tradition and Continuity in Kwakiutl Winter Dance." *Arctic Anthropology* 14:5-24.

Hopi Empire, (The). 1949. Letter to the President, Hotevilla: The Hopi Empire. Tucson, March 28, 1949: Special Collections, The University of Arizona.

Hough, Walter. 1917. "A Revival of the Ancient Hopi Pottery Art. " *American Anthropologist* 19:322-323.

Houle, Robert et al. 1982. *New work by a new generation.* Regina: Norman Mackenzie Art Gallery.

Howard, James H. 1979. *The British Museum winter count.* London: British Museum, Occasional Paper 4.

Izard, Michel. 1992a. "Réaction au thème 1: 'Les régimes d'historicité'." Paper presented at the Symposium "Anthropologie contemporaine et anthropologie historique." Ecole des hautes études en sciences sociales, Marseille, September 1992. (*Bulletin de préparation* 4:4-11. Paris, Ministère de la recherche et de la technologie).

———. 1992b. *L'odyssée du pouvoir. Un royaume africain: Etat, société, destin individuel.* Paris, Editions de l'EHESS.

Jackson, Jean E. 1995. "Culture, Genuine and Spurious: The Politics of Indianness in the Vaupés, Colombia." *American Ethnologist* 22:3-27.

Jacobs, Sue-Ellen, and Wesley Thomas. 1994. "Native American Two-Spirits." *Anthropology Newsletter* 35 (November):7.

James H L. 1988. *Rugs and posts: The story of Navajo weaving and Indian trading.* West Chester: Schiffer Publishing Ltd.

Jaspers, Karl. 1976. *The origin and goal of history*. Westport, Conn.: Greenwood Press.

Jauss, Hans R. 1982. *Toward an aesthetic of reception*, trans. Tomothy Bahti. Minneapolis: University of Minnesota Press.

Johannsen, Christina B., and John P. Ferguson, eds. 1983. *Iroquois arts. A directory of a people and their work.* Warnerville: Association for the Advancement of Native North American Arts and Crafts.

Katchongva, Dan. 1958. Message Delivered to Albuquerque Indian Meeting, 1958. Hotevilla, Hopi Indian Nation, March 21, 1958. Tucson: Special Collections, The University of Arizona.

———. 1973. "Hopi. A Message for All People." Rooseveltown: *Akwesasne Notes* 1973.

Keesing, Roger M. 1982. "Kastom in Melanesia: An Overview." In *Reinventing traditional culture: The politics of kastom in Island Melanesia*, ed. Roger M. Keesing and Robert Tonkinson. Special issue, *Mankind* 13 (4): 297-301.

———. 1989. "Creating the Past: Custom and Identity in the Contemporary Pacific." *The Contemporary Pacific* 1:19-42.

Kehoe, Alice. 1990. "Primal Gaia: Primitivists and Medicine Men." Pp. 193-210 in *The invented Indian: Cultural fictions and government policies,* ed. James A. Clifton. New Brunswick, NJ: Transaction.

Keil, Frank C. 1986. "The Acquisition of Natural Kind and Artefact Terms." In *Conceptual change*, ed. A. Marrar and W. Demopoulos. Norwood, N.J: Ablex.

———. 1989. *Concepts, kinds and conceptual development*. Cambridge, Mass.: MIT Press.

King, Jonathan. 1986. "Tradition in Native American Art." Pp. 65-92 in *The arts of the North American Indian: Native traditions in evolution*, ed. Edwin L. Wade. New York: Hudson Hill Press.

Koselleck, Reinhart. 1979. *Le règne de la critique*. Paris: Editions de Minuit.

———. 1985. *Futures past: On the semantics of historical time*, trans. Keith Tribe. Cambridge, Mass.: MIT Press.

Kotchongva, Dan. 1936. "Where is the White Brother of the Hopi Indian." *The Improvement Era* 39 (2): 82-84, 116-119.

Krickeberg, Walter. 1954. "Ältere Ethnographica aus Nordamerika im Berliner Museum für Völkerkunde." *Baessler-Archiv*, N.F. 2.

Kuhn, Thomas. 1962. *The structure of scientific revolutions*. Chicago: University of Chicago Press.

Kuper, Adam. 1994. "Culture, Identity and the Project of a Cosmopolitan Anthropology." *Man* 29 (3): 537-554.

Kuper Adam, and Jessica Kuper, eds. 1989. *The social science encyclopedia*. London: Routledge.

Kutsche, Paul. 1963. "The Tsali Legend: Culture Heroes and Historiography." *Ethnohistory* 10 (4):329-357.

La Fédération des Coopératives du Nouveau-Québec. 1988. *Fine Arts and Crafts from Nouveau Québec. Montreal.* (Prepared by Mary Craig).

Lamb, Jonathan. 1990. "The New Zealand Sublime." *Meanjin* 49:663-675.

Leach, Edmund R. 1954. *Political systems of Highland Burma*. Boston, Mass.: Beacon Press.
Lee, Molly. 1991. "Appropriating the Primitive: Turn-of-the-Century Collection and Display of Native Alaskan Art." *Arctic Anthropology*: 28 (1):6-15.
Lefort, Claude. 1978. *Les formes de l'histoire. Essais d'anthropologie politique*. Paris: Gallimard.
Leland, Charles G. 1884. *The Algonquin legends of New England*. London: Sampson Low, Marston, Searle and Rivington.
Lenclud, Gérard. 1994. "Qu'est-ce que la tradition?" Pp. 25-44 in *Transcrire les mythologies*, ed. Marcel Detienne. Paris: Albin Michel.
Lester, Joan M. 1993. *History on birchbark: The art of Tomah Joseph, Passamaquoddy*. Bar Harbor, Maine: Robert Abbe Museum.
Lévi-Strauss, Claude. 1983. "Histoire et ethnologie." *Annales ESC* 38(6):1217-1231.
———. 1992. "Un autre regard." *L'Homme* 126-128:220-221.
Levinson, Stephen. 1983. *Pragmatics. Cambridge textbooks in linguistics*. Cambridge: Cambridge University Press.
Lincoln, Bruce. 1994. *Authority: Construction and corrosion*. Chicago: University of Chicago Press.
Lindstrom, Lamont. 1982. "Leftamap Kastom: The Political History of Tradition on Tanna, Vanuatu." *Mankind* 13:316-329.
Linnekin, Jocelyn. 1983. "Defining Tradition: Variations on the Hawaiian Identity." *American Ethnologist* 10: 241-252.
———. 1991. "Cultural Invention and the Dilemma of Authenticity." *American Anthropologist* 93:444-449.
———. 1992. "On the Theory and Politics of Cultural Construction in the Pacific." *Oceania* 62:249-263.
Lippard, Lucy R 1990. *Mixed blessing. New art in a multicultural America*. New York: Pantheon Books.
———. 1991. "Shimá: The Paintings of Emmi Whitehorse." In *Neeznáá: Emmi Whitehorse. Ten years*. Santa Fe, N. Mex.: The Wheelwright Museum of the American Indian.
Lockard, Denise. 1986. "The Lesbian Community." Pp. 83-95 in *The many faces of homosexuality: Anthropological approaches of homosexual behaviour*, ed. Evelyn Blackwood. New York and London: Harrington Park Press.
Lowie, Robert H. 1917. "Oral Tradition and History." *The Journal of American Folklore* XXX (116):161-167.
MacCannell, Dean. 1992. *Empty meeting grounds. The tourist papers*. London: Routledge.
Macnair, Peter L., and Alan L Hoover. 1984. *The magic leaves. A history of Haida argillite carving*. Victoria: British Columbia Provincial Museum.
Malotki, Ekkehart. 1983. *Hopi time. A linguistic analysis of the temporal concepts in the Hopi language*. Trends in Linguistics, Studies and Monographs 20. Berlin: Mouton.
Marcus, George E., and Michael M. J. Fisher. 1986. *Anthropology as cultural critique*. Chicago and London: University of Chicago Press.

Massey, Christine, and Rochel Gelman. 1988. "Preschoolers' Ability to Decide Whether Pictured Unfamiliar Objects Can Move Themselves." *Developmental Psychology* 24:307-317.

Mauzé, Marie. 1992. *Les Fils de Wakai: Une histoire des Lekwiltoq*. Paris: Editions Recherche sur les Civilisations.

———. 1993. "Exhibiting One's Culture. Two Case Studies: The Kwagiulth Museum and the U'Mista Cultural Centre." *Abhandlungen und Berichte des Staatlichen Museums für Völkerkunde Dresden* 47:25-36.

———. 1995 "Les Kwakwaka'wakw de la Colombie britannique. D'une société secrète à l'autre." Pp. 335-344 in *Peuples des Grands Nords. Traditions et transitions*, textes recueillis par A.-V. Charrin, J.-M. Lacroix et M. Therrien. Paris: Presses de la Sorbonne, Institut des Langues orientales.

McClurken, James. 1990. "Boundaries of the Reservation: Social, Political, and Geographical Considerations for Defining the Limits of the Keweenaw Bay Chippewa Reservation." In *Advocacy and claims research*, ed. Frank Tough and Arthur J. Ray. Special Issue, *Native Studies Review* 6: 65-79.

McCoy, Ronald. 1986. *Painted words. R. Lee White and Plains Indian pictography*. Phoenix, Ariz.: The Heard Museum.

McDonald, James. 1990. "Poles, Potlatching, and Public Affairs: The Use of Aboriginal Culture in Development." *Culture* 10 (2):103-120.

McEachern, Allan. 1991. *Reasons for Judgement: Delgamuukw v. B.C.* Smithers, British Columbia: Supreme Court of British Columbia.

McKervill, Hugh. 1964. *Darby of Bella Bella*. Toronto: The Ryerson Press.

Mead, Sidney Moko 1984a. "Nga Timunga me nga Paringa o te Mana Maori: The Ebb and Flow of Mana Maori and the Changing Context of Maori Art." Pp. 20-36 in *Te Maori: Maori art from New Zealand collections*, edited by Sidney Moko Mead. New York: Abrams.

———. 1984b. "Ka Tupu te Toi Whakairo ki Aotearoa: becoming Maori art." Pp. 63-75 in *Te Maori: Maori Art from New Zealand Collections*, ed. Sidney Moko Mead. New York: Abrams.

Mead, Sidney Moko, ed. 1984. *Te Maori: Maori art from New Zealand collections*. New York: Abrams.

Merrill, R. H. 1945. "The Calendar Stick of Tshi-zun-hau-kau." *Bulletin of the Cranbrook Institute of Science* 24:1-11.

Merrill, William L., E. J. Ladd, and T. J. Ferguson. 1993. "The Return of the Ahayu:da." *Current Anthropology* 34:523-568.

Miller, Bruce, ed. 1992. *Anthropology and history in the courts*. Special Issue, *B.C. Studies* 95 (Autumn).

Miller, Jay. 1988. *Shamanic odyssey: The Lushootseed Salish journey to the land of the dead*. Menlo Park, CA: Ballena Press.

Mills, Antonia. 1994. *Eagle down is our law*. Vancouver: University of British Columbia Press.

Momigliano, Arnaldo. 1966. "Time in Ancient Historiography." *History and Theory* 6: 1-23.

Mooney, James. 1898. "Calendar History of the Kiowa Indians." *Seventh Annual Report of the Bureau of American Ethnology*, 1:129-444.

Morris, Rosalind C. 1994. *New worlds from fragments: Film, ethnography, and the representation of Northwest Coast cultures.* Boulder, CO: Westview.
Müller, Klaus E. 1993. "Prähistorisches Geschichtsbewußtsein. Versuch einer ethnologischen Strukturbestimmung." Preprint from *Historische Sinnbildung.* Universität Bielefeld: Zentrum für interdisziplinäre Forschung.
Nagata, Shuichi. 1978. "Dan Kochhongva's Message: Myth, Ideology and Political Action among the Contemporary Hopi." *The Yearbook of Symbolic Anthropology* 1: 73-87.
Neel, David. 1994. "Bella Bella: The Rebirth of the Northwest Coast Canoe. " *Native Peoples* 7 (2):10-18.
——. 1995. *The great canoes: Reviving a Northwest Coast tradition.* Vancouver/Toronto: Douglas & McIntyre.
NFBC (National Film Board Canada). 1975. *Bella Bella,* 16 mm, 27 mn, dir. Barbara Green.
Nicks, Trudy. 1982. *The Creative tradition. Indian handicrafts and tourist art.* Edmonton: Provincial Museum of Alberta.
Nietzsche, Friedrich. 1990. *Considérations inactuelles I et II.* Paris: Gallimard.
Nipperdey, Thomas. 1992. *Réflexions sur l'histoire allemande.* Paris: Gallimard.
Nissen, Wendy. 1990. "Academics to Stand Up For Maoritanga." *New Zealand Herald,* March 1, 1990, sec. 1 p. 20.
Orlando, Weibel J. 1991. *Indian Country L.A.* Urbana and Chicago: University of Illinois Press.
Ortner, Sherry. 1973. "On Key Symbols." *American Anthropologist* 75:1338-1346.
Pasmeny, Erica. 1992. "Aboriginal Offenders: Victims of Policing and Society." *Saskatchewan Law Review* 56(2):403-425.
Pearce, Roy H. 1988. *Savagism and civilization.* Berkeley: University of California Press.
Perner, Joseph. 1991. *Understanding the representational mind.* Cambridge, Mass.: MIT Press.
Phillipps, W. J. 1946. "Carved Houses of Te Arawa." Wellington: *Dominion Museum Records in Ethnology* 1(1).
Phillips, Ruth B. 1991. "Glimpses of Eden: Iconographic Themes in Huron Pictorial Tourist Art." *European Review of Native American Studies* 5 (2):19-28.
Popper, Karl. 1957. *The poverty of historicism.* London: Routledge and Kegan.
Pouillon, Jean. 1975. *Fétiches sans fétichisme.* Paris: François Maspero.
——. 1980. "Anthropological Traditions: Their Uses and Misuses." Pp. 36-51 in *Anthropology: Ancestors and heirs,* ed. Stanley Diamond. The Hague-Paris, New York: Mouton
——. 1991. "Tradition." Pp. 710-712 in *Dictionnaire de l'ethnologie et de l'anthropologie,* ed. Pierre Bonte and Michel Izard. Paris: Presses universitaires de France.
Price, John A. 1990. "Ethical Advocacy Versus Propaganda: Canada's Indian Support Groups." Pp. 255-270 in *The invented Indian: Cultural fictions and*

governments policies, ed. James A. Clifton. New Brunswick, N.J: Transaction.
Price, Richard. 1983. *First-time: The historical vision of an Afro-American people*. Baltimore: The Johns Hopkins University Press.
Ray, Dorothy Jean. 1977. *Eskimo art: Tradition and innovation in North Alaska*. Seattle: University of Washington Press.
Reinhard, Karl. 1994. *Preliminary report of skeletal remains from Ton'wontonga*. Lincoln: Department of Anthropology, University of Nebraska at Lincoln.
Richards, Dean, and Robert S. Siegler. 1986. "Children's Understanding of the Attributes of Life." *Journal of Experimental Child Psychology* 42: 1-22.
Richter, Daniel K. 1993. "Whose Indian History?" *William and Mary Quarterly*, 3rd ser., 50:379-393.
Ridington, Robin. 1968. "The Medicine Fight: An Instrument of Political Process among the Beaver Indians. " *American Anthropologist* 70 (6):1152-1160.
Robles, Jennifer. 1992. "Tribes and Tribulations. " *The Advocate* 17 (November):41-43.
Rodee, Marian E. 1977. *Southwestern weaving*. Albuquerque: University of New Mexico Press.
Rohner, Ronald, and Evelyn P. Rohner. 1970. *The Kwakiutl: Indians of British Columbia*. New York: Holt, Rinehart, and Winston.
Rosaldo, Renato. 1980. *Ilongot Headhunting: 1883-1974*. Stanford: Stanford University Press.
Roscoe, Will. 1987. "Bibliography of Berdache and Alternative Gender Roles among North American Indians." *Journal of Homosexuality* 14 (3-4): 81-171.
———. 1994. "How to Become a Berdache: Toward a Unified Analysis of Gender Diversity." Pp. 329-372 in *Third sex, third gender: Beyond sexual dimorphism in culture and history*, ed. Gilbert Herdt. New York: Zone Books.
Roscoe, Will, ed. 1988. *Living the spirit: A gay American Indian anthology*. New York: St. Martin's Press.
Rossi-Landi, Ferriccio. 1975. *Linguistics and economics*. The Hague: Mouton.
Rubin, William, ed. 1984. *Primitivism in 20th century art*. 2 vols. New York: Museum of Modern Art.
Rushton, Mary. 1970. "Do Flying Saucers Indicate Truth of Hopi Prophecy?" *Independent* 81 (253), Tuesday, October 27, 1970.
Ryle, Gilbert. 1949. *The concept of mind*. London: Hutchinson.
Sahlins, Marshall. 1985. *Islands of history*. Chicago: The University of Chicago Press.
Schechner, Richard. 1977. *Essays in performance theory: 1970-1976*. New York: Drama Book Specialists.
———. 1993. *The future of ritual*. London: Routledge.
Schneider, Janet et al. 1984. *Common heritage: Contemporary Iroquois artists*. New York: The Queens Museum.
Scott, Colin H. 1993. "Custom, Tradition, and the Politics of Culture: Aboriginal Self-Governement in Canada." Pp. 311-333 in *Anthropology, public policy*

and native peoples in Canada, ed. Noel Dyck and James B. Waldram. Montreal and Kingston: McGill-Queens's University Press.

Sears, John F Sacred Places. 1989. *American tourist attractions in the nineteenth century*. New York: Oxford University Press.

Seguin, Margaret. 1985. *Interpretive contexts for traditional and current Coast Tsimshian feasts*. National Museum of Man, Ethnology Division, Mercury Series, Paper no. 98. Ottawa: National Museums of Canada.

Seiler, Hansjakob. 1970. *Cahuilla texts with an introduction*. Language Science Monographs 6. Bloomington, Ind.: Indiana University Press.

Seymour-Smith, Charlotte. 1986. *Dictionary of anthropology*. Boston, Mass.: G.K. Hall.

Sheehan, Carol. 1981. *Pipes that won't smoke; coal that won't burn*. Calgary: Glenbow Museum.

Simard, Jean-Jacques. 1990. "White Ghosts, Red Shadows: The Reduction of North-American Natives." Pp. 333-369 in *The invented Indian: Cultural fictions and government policies*, ed. James A. Clifton. New Brunswick, N.J: Transaction.

Simmons, David R. 1976. *The great New Zealand myth: A study of the discovery and origin traditions of the Maori*. Wellington: Reed.

Simmons, Leo W., ed. 1942. *Sun Chief: The autobiography of a Hopi Indian*. New Haven and London: Yale University Press.

Sioui, Georges. 1992. *For an Amerindian autohistory: An essay on the foundations of a social ethic*. Montreal and Kingston: McGill-Queen's University Press.

Skidmore, Nonnie S. 1970. *Chief Dan Katchongva's message. Hopi prophecy*. Hotevilla: Hopi Independent Nation.

Skinner, Alanson, and John V. Satterlee. 1915. "Folklore of the Menomini Indians." *Anthropological Papers of the American Museum of Natural History* 13:217-546.

Smith, Ben. 1993. "Return of the Great Canoes." *Native Peoples* 6 (2):10-20.

Smith, Watson. 1952. *Kiva mural decorations at Awatovi and Kawaika-a*. Papers of the Peabody Museum of American Archaeology and Ethnology 27. Cambridge, Mass.:The Museum.

Sobrero, Alberto M. 1992. *Antropologia della Citta'*. Roma: La Nuova Italia Scientifica.

Sorrenson, M. P. K. 1979. *Maori origins and migrations: The genesis of some Pakeha myths and legends*. Auckland: Auckland University Press.

Speck, Frank G. 1919. *The functions of wampum among the Eastern Algonkian*. American Anthropological Association, Memoir 6. Lancaster, PA.

Spelke, Elisabeth S. 1990. "Principles of Object Perception."*Cognitive Science* 14:29-56.

Stephenson, Sue H. 1977. *Basketry of the Appalachian mountains*. New York: Van Nostrand.

Stocking, George, ed. 1985. *Objects and others. Essays on museums and material culture*. Madison: The University of Wisconsin Press.

Tanner, Clara Lee. 1973. *Southwest Indian painting*. 2d ed. Tucson, Ariz.: The University of Arizona Press.

Tarbet, Thomas V., Jr., ed. 1972. *From the beginning of life to the day of purification: Teachings, history and prophecies of the Hopi people as told by the late Dan Katchongva, Sun Clan (c. 1865-1972)*, trans. Danaqyumptewa. Los Angeles: Committee for Traditional Indian Land and Life.

Tentori, Tullio. 1990. *Antropologia delle Societa' Complesse*. Roma: Armando.

Thomas, Nicholas. 1992 "The Inversion of Tradition." *American Ethnologist* 19:213-232.

Titiev, Mischa. 1944. *Old Oraibi: A study of the Hopi Indians of Third Mesa*. Papers of the Peabody Museum of American Archaeology and Ethnology XXI(1). Cambridge, Mass.: The Museum.

Tonkin, Elizabeth. 1992. *Narrating our pasts: The social construction of oral history*. Cambridge Studies in Oral and Literate Culture 22. Cambridge: Cambridge University Press.

Trask, Haunani-Kay. 1991. "Natives and Anthropologists: The Colonial Struggle." *The Contemporary Pacific* 3 (Spring):159-167.

Treeline Trappings. A Division of NWT Native Arts and Crafts. 1986. (*Catalogue*). Yellowknife.

Tregear, Edward. 1885. *The Aryan Maori*. Wellington: Government Printer.

Trevor-Roper, Hugh. 1983. "The Invention of Tradition: The Highland Tradition of Scotland." Pp. 15-41 in *The invention of tradition*, ed. Eric Hobsbawm and Terrence Ranger. Cambridge: Cambridge University Press.

Turner, Terrence. 1993. "Anthropology and Multiculturalism." *Cultural Anthropology* 8:411-429.

Tyler, Hamilton A. 1964. *Pueblo gods and myths*. Norman: University of Oklahoma Press.

Tyler, Stephen A. 1986. "Post-Modern Ethnography: From Document of the Occult to Occult Document." Pp. 122-140 in *Writing culture*, ed. James Clifford and George Marcus. Berkeley: University of California Press.

U'mista Cultural Society. 1975. *Potlatch: A Strict Law Bids Us Dance,*16 mm, 55 mn., dir. Chuck Olin Associates.

Underhill, Ruth. 1938. "A Papago Calendar Record." *University of New Mexico, Anthropological Series* 2 (5):3-66.

Valéry, Paul. 1930. *Morceaux choisis*. Paris: Gallimard.

Vandermeersch, Léon. 1989. "Vérité historique et langage de l'histoire en Chine." Pp. 65-75 in *La vérité est-elle scientifique?*, ed. André Lichnerovicz and Gilbert Gadoffre. Paris: Editions universitaires.

Vatter, Ernst. 1927. "Historienmalerei und heraldische Bilderschrift der nordamerikanischen Präriestämme: Beiträge zu einer ethnographischen und stilistischen Analyse." *IPEK* 1927:46-81.

Veyne, Paul. 1971. *Comment on écrit l'histoire*. Paris: Le Seuil.

Vizenor, Gerald. 1990. *Crossbloods: Bone, courts, bingo, and other reports*. Minneapolis: University of Minnesota Press.

―――. 1994. *Manifest manners: Postindian warriors of survivance*. Hanover, NH: Wesleyan University Press.

Wagner, Roy. 1981. *The invention of culture*. 2d ed. rev. and expanded. Chicago and London: The University of Chicago Press.

Waldram, James B. 1993. "Aboriginal Spirituality: Symbolic Healing in Canadian Prisons." *Culture, Medicine and Psychiatry* 17:345-362.

———. 1994. "Aboriginal Spirituality in Corrections: A Canadian Case Study in Religion and Therapy. " *American Indian Quarterly* 18(2):197-214.

Walker [Jeyifous], Sheila. 1986. "Atimodemo: Semantic Conceptual Development among the Yoruba." PhD diss., Cornell University.

———. 1992. "Developmental Changes in the Representation of Word-Meaning: Cross-Cultural Findings." *British Journal of Developmental Psychology* 10:285-299.

Wallace, Anthony. 1956. "Revitalization Movements: Some Theoretical Considerations for Their Comparative Study." *American Anthropologist* 58 (2):264-281.

Waters, Frank. 1963. *Book of the Hopi*. New York: Viking Press/ Ballantine Books.

———. 1969. *Pumpkin seed point*. Chicago: The Swallow Press Inc.

Weber, Max. 1981. *Soziologische Grundbegriffe*. [1920-1921] 5th ed., rev. Tübingen: Mohr.

Webster, Steven. 1993. "Postmodernist Theory and the Sublimation of Maori Culture." *Oceania* 63:222-239.

Weil, Eric. 1991. *Essais et conférences*. Paris: Librairie philosophique J. Vrin.

Wellmann, Henry M. 1990. *The Child's theory of mind*. Cambridge, Mass.: MIT Press.

Wenzel, George. 1991. *Animal rights, human rights: Ecology, economy ideology in the Canadian Arctic*. Toronto: University of Toronto Press.

West Earth. 1983. *Catalogue*. Seattle.

White, Hayden. 1973. *Metahistory: The historical imagination of nineteenth-century Europe*. Baltimore, MD: Johns Hopkins University Press.

Whitehead, Harriet. 1981. "The Bow and the Burden Strap: A New Look at Institutionalized Homosexuality in Native North America." Pp. 80-115 in *Sexual meanings. The cultural construction of gender and sexuality*, ed. Sherry B. Ortner and Harriet Whitehead. Cambridge and London: Cambridge University Press.

Whitehead, Ruth Holmes. 1982. *Micmac quillwork*. Halifax: The Nova Scotia Museum.

Whiteley, Peter M. 1988. *Deliberate acts: Changing Hopi culture through the Oraibi split*. Tucson: The University of Arizona Press.

Whiten, Andrew, ed. 1991. *Natural theories of mind: The evolution, development and simulation of everyday mindreading*. Oxford: Blackwell.

Wilcox, U. Vincent. 1976. "The Manufacture and Use of Wampum in the Northeast. " *The Bead Journal* 3(1):10-19.

Wildhage, Wilhelm. 1988. *Die Winterzählungen der Oglala*. Wyk: Verlag für Amerikanistik.

Wilford, John Noble. 1990. "Anthropology Seen As Father of Maori Lore." *New York Times,* February 20, 1990, sec. B., p. 5.

Willey, Gordon R., and Philip Phillips. 1953. "Method and Theory in American Archaeology." *American Anthropologist* 55:615-633.

Williams, Walter. 1986a. *The Spirit and the flesh*. Boston: Beacon Press.

———. 1986b. "Persistence and Change in the Berdache Tradition among Contemporary Lakota Indians." Pp. 191-200 in *The many faces of homosexuality: Anthropological approaches to homosexual behaviour,* ed. Evelyn Blackwood. New York: Harrington Park Press.

Wittfogel, Karl A., and Esther S. Goldfrank. 1943. "Some Aspects of Pueblo Mythology and Society." *Journal of American Folklore* 56:17-30.

Wyatt, Victoria. 1989. *Passage. An Alaskan portrait by Winter & Pond*. Seattle: University of Washington Press.

Wyman, Leland C. 1983. *Southwest Indian dry painting*. Santa Fe and Albuquerque, N. Mex.: School of American Research and University of New Mexico Press.

Yukon Native Products. 1986. *Catalogue*. Whitehorse.

Contributors

PASCAL BOYER studied philosophy and anthropology in Paris and Cambridge, and was a Fellow of King's College Cambridge before joining the Centre national de la recherche scientique at Lyons, France. He has done fieldwork on oral litterature of the Fang of Cameroon, and is now working on the cognitive aspects of cultural transmission. His research combines experimental cognitive research with traditional anthropological description, and is concerned mainly with early conceptual development. The effects of such cognitive structures on cultural categories, particularly on religious traditions, have been examined in various papers and books, including *Tradition as Truth and Communication* (1990) and the *The Naturalness of Religious Ideas* (1994).

MASSIMILIANO CAROCCI is currently studying for a Master's degree in Cultural Studies at the University of East London. He graduated from the University of Roma in Cultural Anthropology with a thesis on female societies among Northern Plains Indians. His main interest is the impact of historical and social factors on the cultural construction of gender. For two years, he has done fieldwork in major American cities on modern berdachism among urban American Indians. He is also currently working on a documentary on the same topic.

JAMES A. CLIFTON earned his Ph.D. in anthropology in 1960, at the University of Oregon, under the tutelage of Theodore Stern and Homer

G. Barnett. Until his retirement from the University of Wisconsin-Green Bay in 1990, he was Frankenthal professor of anthropology and history at that institution. He is presently scholar-in-residence with the Department of Anthropology, Western Michigan University, in Kalamazoo. He is the author and editor of several books and monographies. Recent publications include: *The Potawatomi: A Great Lakes Odyssey* (1987); *Being and Becoming Indian: Biographic Studies of North American Frontiers* (1989); *The Invented Indian: Cultural Fictions and Government Policy* (1990); and *365 Ratified Indian Treaties: A Computerized Database* (1990).

CHRISTIAN F. FEEST received his Ph.D. in anthropology from the University of Vienna in 1969 with a dissertation on 17th-century Virginia Algonquian historical ethnography and ethnohistory. From 1963 to 1993 he was employed at the Museum für Völkerkunde in Vienna, mostly as curator of the North and Middle American and of the photographic collections. After teaching anthropology at the University of Vienna since 1975, he became professor of anthropology at the University of Frankfurt in 1993. His research and numerous writings focus on the anthropology of art, and of visual representation, the ethnohistory of eastern North America (including contemporary issues), and the history of ethnographic collecting. He is editor of the *European Review of Native American Studies (ERNAS)*.

ARMIN W. GEERTZ, Dr. Phil., is professor in the history of religions at the Department of the Study of Religion, University of Aarhus, Denmark. His main area of research is the religions of Native North Americans especially the Hopi Indians among whom he had conducted fieldwork. He is associate editor of a number of international journals and is presently General Secretary of the International Association for the History of Religions. His major publications include *Hopi Indian Altar Iconography* (1986); *Children of the Cottonwood. Piety and Ceremonialism in Hopi Indian Puppetry* (1987, assisted by Michael Lomatuway'ma); *A Concordance of Hopi Indian Texts* (1989); *Du er slave, ej menneske! Vestafrikansk religion i Amerika* (1989); *Mystik - Den indre vej? En religionhistorisk udfordring* (1990, edited with Per Bilde; *Religion, Tradition, and Renewal* (1991, edited with Jeppe Sinding Jensen); and *The Invention of Prophecy: Continuity and Meaning in Hopi Indian Religion* (1992/94). He is currently working on a critical selection of essays on the study of Hopi Indian religion.

F. ALLAN HANSON is professor of anthropology at the University of Kansas. He was educated at Princeton University and the University of Chicago (Ph.D. 1966), and has conducted anthropological research in French Polynesia, New Zealand, and contemporary American society. Among his books are *Rapa, une île polynésienne hier et aujourd'hui* (1973); *Meaning in Culture* (1975); *Counterpoint in Maori Culture* (1983), with Louise Hanson; and *Testing Testing: Social Consequences of the Examined Life* (1993). He is currently studying the social consequences of technological developments in contemporary society, including prenatal testing and human genome research.

MICHAEL HARKIN is assistant professor of anthropology at the University of Wyoming. He received his Ph.D. from the University of Chicago in 1988. He has worked with several British Columbia First Nations. His recent publications include articles in *Ethnohistory*, *Ethos*, and *American Ethnologist*. His book, *The Heiltsuks: Dialogues of Culture and History on the Northwest Coast* is forthcoming from the University of Nebraska Press. He edited, with Sergei Kan, a special issue of *Ethnohistory* entitled "North American Indian Women's Responses to Christianity" (1996).

JONATHAN C. H. KING is curator of North American Collections in the Department of Ethnography, British Museum, at the Museum of Mankind. Current projects include the installation of a North American Gallery at the British Museum, opening in 1998; a catalogue of the collection made by Captain George Vancouver in Pacific North America, 1791-5; and an exhibition of contemporary Yup'ik and Inuit clothing. Recent articles were published in the *American Indian Art Magazine*, the *Journal of the History of Collections*, and in *Masks. The Art of Expression* (1994), edited by John Mack.

GÉRARD LENCLUD is directeur de recherche at the Centre national de la recherche scientifique (CNRS), Paris, and a member of the Laboratoire d'anthropologie sociale. He has done extensive fieldwork in Corsica, mainly in the field of politics and the implementation of violence. He has been the editor of *Etudes rurales* (1982-1988). He is the author of numerous articles published in *L'Homme*, *Gradhiva*, *Terrain*, *Ethnologie française*, and in other journals. He is a member of a research group on the anthropology of historical knowledge and is currently writing a book of essays on the epistemology of anthropology.

MARIE MAUZÉ is chargée de recherche at the CNRS, Paris, and a member of the Laboratoire d'anthropologie sociale. She has conducted fieldwork in British Columbia with the Kwakwaka'wakw (Kwakiutl) since 1980. She has published several articles in *L'Homme, Gradhiva, Journal des Américanistes, The European Review of Native American Studies*, etc. She is the author of *Les fils de Wakai. Une Histoire des Lekwiltoq* (1992). Her current interests are in the field of the anthropology of art (especially Northwest Coast art in European collections).

JEAN POUILLON has been the editor of *L'Homme, Revue française d'anthropologie* since 1961 when the journal was founded by Claude Lévi-Strauss. He is also a member of the editorial board of *Les Temps modernes*. He has mainly published in *L'Homme, Les Temps modernes, La Nouvelle Revue de psychanalyse, Le Temps de la réflexion, Le Genre humain,* and in other journals. He is the author of *Temps et Roman* (1946, republished in 1993); *Fétiche sans fétichisme* (1975); and *Le cru et le su* (1993). He has conducted research in Chad and Ethiopia.

ROBIN RIDINGTON received his Ph.D. in anthropology from Harvard University in 1968. He has done fieldwork with the Dunne-za (Beaver Indians) of British Columbia and the Omaha Tribe of Nebraska. His publications include *Trail to Heaven: Knowledge and Narrative in a Northern Native Community* (1988) and *Little Bit Know Something: Stories in a Language of Anthropology* (1990). His book about the Sacred Pole of the Omaha tribe, *Blessing for a Long Time*, will be published in 1997. His current interests include anthropological poetics and First Nations literature. He is Professor Emeritus at the University of British Columbia.

JAMES B. WALDRAM has a Ph.D. in medical anthropology (Connecticut 1983). He is professor in the Department of Native Studies, University of Saskatchewan, Saskatoon, Saskatchewan, Canada. He is currently researching the therapeutic nature of aboriginal spirituality within Canadian prisons. Recent publications include articles in *Culture, Medicine and Psychiatry* and in the *American Indian Quarterly*. He is the editor of *Anthropology, Public Policy and Native Peoples in Canada* (1993) with Noel Dyck; and *Aboriginal Health in Canada: Historical, Cultural and Epidemiological Perspectives* (1995) with D. Ann Herring and T. Kue Young.

Index

Aboriginal inmates: cultural competence and, 138-141; cultural and spirituality programs and, 134-140; definition of culture and, 133, 136, 140, 141-142
Aboriginal peoples: bi-cultural, 132-133; incarceration rates and, 132; traditional, 132
activists, 8, 99, 111n1, 184, 203
Allen, Paula Gunn, 126
Algonquian, 13, 67, 71, 93, 154-158; political and economic status, 149-151; rites, 154-155. *See also* Green Corn Ceremony; medicine man
Alsop, Joseph, 66
American Anthropologist, 195, 200
American Indian Arts and Crafts Act, 77
anganon (narrative), 57
anthropologists, role of. *See* authority; tradition
Arendt, Hannah, 48
Aron, Raymond, 47
art(s): acculturation in, 68, 83; high art, 86; modern art, 78-79; native label and, 12, 91, 92; painting, 75-78; revival and, 78; ritual arts, 67, tourism and, 74-75, 81-83, 89; tourist arts. *See* souvenir industries; uses of the past in, 65-79; Western appreciation of, 68-69. *See also* collecting, forms of; Navajo
artists (Native), 74-79, 84, 86
Assiniboine, 58-59
authenticity, 8, 12, 97-98, 100, 104, 110, 201, 202, 204. *See also* tradition, invention of
authority, 5, 57, 74, 97-98, 172-173, 202; anthropologist and, 10-11, 100, 147, 157, 158, 174; charismatic authority, 32-33
autohistory, 61
Avis, Jeremy, 28
Bades, 119. *See also* berdache
bagascia. *See* berdache
baldracca. *See* berdache
Banancya, Thomas, 182, 189, 191
bardah. *See* berdache
bardaj. *See* berdache
bardascio. *See* berdache

Barett, Justin, 28
Barnett, Homer G., 156
Barthes, Roland, 100, 111n2
Beidelman, Tom, 32, 33
Bella Bella, 103
berdache, 13, 113-128; cultural productions and, 124; definition of word, 114-115, 119; modern (two spirits), 116, 118, 119, 123; rituals and, 126-127; spirituality and, 117, 123-124. *See also* gay and lesbian Indians
berdachism, alternative gender roles and, 13, 113, 114, 115, 120-121. *See also* pan-Indianism
Berger, Peter, and sedimentation theory, 193
Best, Eldson, 198
birchbark scrolls, 72
birchbark sgraffito, 75
Blackbird (Chief), 162
Blackfoot, 134
Bloch, Maurice, 57
Boas, Franz, 68, 104
Boyer, Bob, 77-78
Boyer, Pascal, 6, 155
Brother, Elder White, 177, 180, 181, 184, 185, 186, 187, 188, 192. *See also*, myth, emergence
Brother, Younger Hopi, 177
Brown, Frank, 108, 110
Bruner, Edward, 201
Cahuilla, 72
calendar sticks, 71
Cannadine, David, 97, 108
canoe: festival, 109-110; journey, 108-109; symbol of, 12, 107-110
causal-representational account. *See* evidential accounts
Cherokee. *See* souvenir industries
Chomsky, Noam, 17
Clifford, James, 9
Clifton, Billy (Chief), 101, 109
Clifton, James, 13, 14, 99, 100
Cline, Eddie, 163, 172, 179

collecting, native and western forms of, 65-67. *See also* art
Collier, John, 179
conservatism, 5
counter-intuitive assumptions. *See* intituitive assumptions
Cranmer, Dan (Chief), 102
Cranmer-Webster, Gloria, 102, 111n4
Cree, 13, 134, 139
Curtis, Edward S., 2
Danay, Ric Glazer, 71
Deloria, Vine, 73
Dene, 13, 134, 139
divide (great), 44-47, 52, 62
domain-specificity, religious representations in, 24-25, 26, 29-30
Dorsey, James, 173
Dunn, Dorothy, 78
emic/etic, 45, 206-207
Emmons, Glenn L., 184
Enlightenment, 49, 50, 51
ethnohistory, 45, 59, 61
Evans-Pritchard, Edward E., 32, 53
event(s): mental, 206; notion of, 50, 61; recording of. *See* history
evidential accounts, 34-38
feast. *See* potlatch
Fewkes, Jesse Walker, 75
films (ethnographic). *See* stereotypes
Finley, Moses, 53, 58
Fletcher, Alice, 160-162, 167-168
Friedman, Jonathan, 7, 211
gay Indian identity, 113-114, 120-122, 125-126, 127-128. *See also* identity
gay/lesbian (urban) Indians, 117, 119. *See also* berdache
Geertz, Armin, 6, 13
Geertz, Clifford, 193, 206
Gilpin, Lawrence, 159, 165, 170-171, 172, 174
Glassner, Jean-Jacques, 56
God, concept of, 30-31
Goldfrank, Esther S., 175-176

Index

Goody, Jack, 57, 71
Graburn, Nelson H.H., 83
Great Fleet (tradition), 197-198, 207, 212
Great Spirit, 185, 186, 187, 191, 192. *See also* Maasaw
Green Corn ceremony, analysis of, 155-157; description of, 151-153
Griaule, Marcel, 53
Halévy, Daniel, 53
Hallowell, A. Irving, 64n13
Hanson, F. Allan, 157, 158n4
Harris, Marvin, 206
Harris, Paul L., 28
Hartog, François, 51
Hastings, Dennis, 168
Heiltsuq, 12, 103-110
Hermequaftewa, 188
heterohistory, 61
Hill, Jonathan, 8
Hirschfeld, Lawrence A., 34
historical consciousness, 46, 50, 51, 52-54, 58, 60, 62
historicity, 43, 45, 47, 52, 61, 62, 63n5
historiography, 46, 56, 63n5
history: concept of, 44, 49-50, 70, 72-74; events recording and, 56-57, 58-62, 65, 71-72; *Geschichte,* 50; history v. memory, 44, 53; history v. myth, 44, 45, 59, 60, 70; societies with/without, 43, 44, 70, 73. *See also* divide (great); tradition
Hobsbawm, Eric, 5, 7, 97, 157
Hocart, Arthur M., 18, 19
Hohepa, Pat, 199
Holm, Bill, 88, 111n7
Honga clan, 163
Hoover, Allan, 83
Hopi, 70, 175; chieftainship, 179, 183, 188; language, 70; painting 76; pottery, 74-75; Snake ceremonial, 182
Hopi clans: Bear, 177, 181, 182; Bow, 191, 192; Kookop, 178, 182; Maasaw, 181; Spider, 178, 179; Spirit, 181; Sun, 178, 191, 192
Hopi Indian Empire, 183
Hopi prophecy, 13, 175-194; invention in, 184-185, 189-191; political resistance and, 182, 183-184; texts and, 180-181, 188, 489, 190, 191-192; traditionalist versions of, 184, 186, 191. *See also* myth, emergence; Mormon doctrine; saucer cult
Hopi religion, universalization of, 186, 187
Hopi Traditionalist Movement, 179-194
Houle, Robert, 78
identity, 8, 12, 13, 14, 141-142, 147, 149, 155-156, 161, 178. *See also* Hopi prophecy; Maoritanga; pan-Indianism; tradition
Ilongot, 60, 62
Indian Act (Canada), 102
Indian Arts and Crafts Board, 92
Indian Reorganization Act, 184
Indian symbols, appropriation of, 82
Indian time, 70-72
Indianness. *See* identity
intuitive assumptions, 28-32
intituive ontologies, 25-28, 34, 33
intuitive psychology, 26-28
invented Indian, 99, 199
invention. *See* tradition
Io cult, 197, 212
Iroquois, 71
Izard, Michel, 60
Joseph, Thomas, 75
Kabotie, Fred, 75-76
kastom, 24
Katchongva. *See* Qötshongva
Keesing, Roger, 193, 203
Keil, Frank, 28
kinikinick, 152
Kiowa, 71
Koselleck, Reinhart, 50

Kotchongva. *See* Qötshongva,
Kuhn, Thomas, 205
Kwagiulth Museum, 4
Kwakwaka'wakw (Kwakiutl), 2, 102-105
LaFarge, Oliver, 181
LaFlesche, Francis, 160-162, 167-168
Lakota, 71
Lee, Molly, 84
Lekwiltoq (Kwakwaka'wakw), 2-4
Leland, Charles, 75
Lenclud, Gérard, 1, 4, 7
Lévi-Strauss, Claude, 20, 43
Linnekin, Jocelyn, 8, 196, 204, 205
Locke, John, 49
Lomahongyiwma, 178
London Great Exhibition, 82
Lowie, Robert, 58, 59, 63n6
Luckmann, Thomas. *See* Berger
Maasaw (Hopi deity), 177, 178, 181, 185, 186, 187. *See also* Great Spirit
Macnair, Peter, 83
Malotki, Ekkehart, 70
Maori (New Zealand) traditions. *See* Great Fleet, Io cult
Maoriness. *See* Maoritanga
Maoritanga, 198, 199-200, 205, 207, 212
Mead, Sidney Moko, 199
medicine man, 13, 148-149, 154
medicine wheel, 142
Menominee (Menomini), 72, 100
messianism, 184, 192-193
Michelet, Jules, 53
millenarism, 179, 183, 185
Momigliano, Arnaldo, 52, 64n10
Monongya, David, 179, 189, 191, 194
Mormon doctrine, 180, 190, 191
Morris, Doran, 163, 165, 168, 169-170, 172
Mother Earth, 99
myth, disappearing savage of, 99-100

myth, emergence, 175-178, 180, 185, 191, 192
myth, history and. *See* history
Nagata, Shuichi, 188-189
Nampeyo (potter), 74-75, 78
native art. *See* art
native claims, 111n1
Navajo: painting, 78; rug weaving, 84; sand painting, 67, 77
navoti, 178
New Age religion, 145, 151
New Zealand Association of Social Anthropologists, 200
Northwest Coast. *See* canoe; potlatch; poles; winter ceremonies
Nuer, 32-33
Nuxalk (Bella Coola), 103
Ojibwa, 72, 139
Omaha Tribe, 8, 159; social and political organization of, 160-163; revitalization of, 173-174. *See also* Sacred Pole
Oowekeeno, 103
Pakeha (white), 198; anthroplogists, 207
pan-Indian fundamentalism, 142;
pan-Indianism, 12, 14, 113-114, 122, 133, 135-138,144
Papago, 71
Passamaquoddy, 75
past: as history. *See* history; as present, 6, 50, 159; as tradition, 1, 45, 48. *See also* tradition; uses of, 9, 70, 65-79, 213
Plains tribes, cultural models, as. *See* pan-Indianism
pole, crest (Northwest Coast), symbol of, 12
Poliwuhiwma, 178-179
Ponca
Pongyayawma, 178-179, 182, 183
postmodernism, 200, 205-206, 212. *See also* tradition, invention of
potlatch, 11, 12, 101; revival of, 102-103, 105, 107

Index

potlatch law, 4, 101-102
Pouillon, Jean, 6
powwow, 84, 114, 128n2, 136, 137, 138, 165, 170
Price Richard, 61
primitive, notion of, 12, 99; art, 68. *See also* stereotypes
prison Aboriginal Programs. *See* Aboriginal inmates, spirituality programs and,
Pueblo, 67
Qötshongva, Dan, 13, 175-194
Ranger, Terence, 97, 157
Ranguini, Walker, 199
reburial, 69, 128
relativism (cultural), 73, 208-209; hyperrelativism, 208-209, 213. *See also* postmodernism
repatriation, 4, 69
Richter, Daniel, 73
Ridington, Robin, 14, 15
Rosaldo, Renato, 60, 62
Ryle, Gilbert, 207
sacred circle, 13
sacred pipe, 13, 139, 142
Sacred Pole (Omaha): feelings and emotions towards, 167-172; prayers to 163-167; symbol of, 1, 8-9, 14, 159, 161, 162
salvage ethnology, 3
Samaraka, 61
saucer cult, 188-191. *See also* Hopi prophecy
Saulteaux, 135
Schechner, Richard, 107
Scott, Duncan Campbell, 100, 102
Scott, Simon, 186-187
sedimentation theory, 193-194
Seguin, Margaret, 101, 108
Seneca, 76
Sheehan, Carol, 83
Sioui, Georges, 61, 73
Skenandore, Olivia, 77
Smith, Ernest, 76
Smith, Graham, 201
Smith, Percy, 198

Solem, Paul, 189-190
souvenir industries (native-style) 83-95; North, 82, 93-95; Norh Carolina Cherokee, 82, 95, 89-92; Northeast, 82, 85, 92-93; Northwest Coast, 82, 84, 85-89
Squanto, 99
stone tablets, 177, 181, 182, 192
stereotypes, 11, 70, 81, 82, 91
Stoney, 135
Sun Dances, 11; berdaches and, 126-127
sweatlodge, 136, 138, 141, 142
sweetgrass, 13, 136, 141, 142
Tailfeathers, Gerald, 77
Talayesva, Don, 182
Tama-Te-Kapua, 29-211
Tanner, Clara Lee, 76
tantara (narrative), 57
taonga, 200
Tawangyawma, R. and C., 188, 190
Temporary Emergency Relief Administration, 76
Titiev, Mischa, 178
tourist arts. *See* art; souvenir industries
tradition, 5, 10-11, 19 age of, 5, 19; definition of, 4, 5, 6, 17, 18, 24-25, 48, 49, 97, 145-146; history and, 44, 45, 47, 51, 55-56, 62; transmission of, 6, 24, 38-40; as totem, 18. *See also* authenticity; authority; identity; history
tradition, invention of, 4, 7, 9, 99-110, 156-157, 175, 193-194, 195, 200; anthropologists and, 201-202, 206-207 ; approaches (positivist and constructionist) to, 97, 99, 195-197, 199, 201-205, 207-209, 210, 211, 213-214; reformulation or, 200, 204, 208. *See also* activists, authenticity
traditionalism, 11, 193
Traditionalist Movement. *See* Hopi Traditionalist Movement

traditionality, 5
transvestism. *See* berdachism
Tregear, Edward, 198
Trevor-Roper, Hugh, 196
tribal arts. See art
truth, 5, 24, 34, 213-214
Tsimshian
two-spirits (or two-spirited person). *See* berdache, modern
Tyler, Hamilton A., 186
U'Mista Cultural Centre, 102
Umon'honti. See Sacred Pole
Veyne, Paul, 14, 63n5, 64n11, n15
Vizenor, Gerald, 142
Waldram, James, 13
Walker-Jeyifous, Sheila, 27
wampum belts, 71
Waters, Frank, 189

Weber, Max, 32, 74
Webster, Steven, 206, 208, 209, 211
Weil, Eric, 47, 48, 49
White Brother
White Man (coming of)
White, Hayden, 73
White, Randy Lee, 77, 78
Whitehorse, Emmi, 78
Whorf, Benjamin Lee, 70
Willie, Ernie, 105, 111n6
winter ceremonials (Northwest Coast), revival of, 103-107
winter counts, 71, 77
Wolfe, Clifford, 165, 171
Yellow Smoke, 162
Yoruba, 27
Yukiwma, 178